STOP photoshop type effects
visual encyclopedia

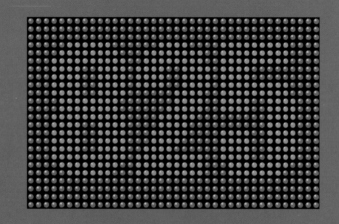

photoshop
type effects visual encyclopedia

ROGER PRING

New Riders

For Sarah, Katy, and Sally

First published in the United States in 2002 by New Riders Publishing
201 West 103rd Street, Indianapolis, IN 46290-1097

This book was conceived, designed, and produced by THE ILEX PRESS LIMITED
THE BARN, COLLEGE FARM, 1 WEST END, WHITTLESFORD, CAMBRIDGE, CB2 4LX

Sales and Editorial Office
THE OLD CANDLEMAKERS, WEST STREET, LEWES, EAST SUSSEX, BN7 2NZ

Publisher SOPHIE COLLINS
Art Director ALASTAIR CAMPBELL
Editorial Director STEVE LUCK
Design Manager TONY SEDDON
Project Editor GEORGA GODWIN
Designers HUGH SCHERMULY, NICK BUZZARD
Editors ASGARD PUBLISHING SERVICES

ISBN 0-7357-1190-9

Library of Congress Catalog Number: 2001093807

Originated and printed by Hong Kong Graphics, China

For further information on this title refer to: www.pstypefx.com

A Message from New Riders

As the reader of this book, you are our most important critic and commentator. We value your opinion and want to know what we're doing right, what we could do better, in what areas you'd like to see us publish, and any other words of wisdom you're willing to pass our way.

As Executive Editor at New Riders, I welcome your comments. You can fax, email, or write me directly to let me know what you did or didn't like about this book as well as what we can do to make our books better. When you write, please be sure to include this book's title, ISBN, and author, as well as your name and phone or fax number. I will carefully review your comments and share them with the authors and editors who worked on the book.

Please note that I cannot help you with technical problems related to the topic of this book, and that due to the high volume of email I receive, I might not be able to reply to every message. Thanks.

email: steve.weiss@newriders.com

mail: Steve Weiss
      Executive Editor
      New Riders Publishing
      201 West 103rd Street
      Indianapolis, IN 46290-1097

Visit Our Web Site: www.newriders.com

On our Web site, you'll find information about our other books, the authors we partner with, book updates and file downloads, promotions, discussion boards for online interaction with other users and with technology experts, and a calendar of trade shows and other professional events with which we'll be involved. We hope to see you around.

Email Us from Our Web Site

Go to www.newriders.com and click on the Contact Us link if you:

- Have comments or questions about this book.
- Want to report errors that you have found in this book.
- Have a book proposal or are interested in writing for New Riders.
- Would like us to send you one of our author kits.
- Are an expert in a computer topic or technology and are interested in being a reviewer or technical editor.
- Want to find a distributor for our titles in your area.
- Are an educator/instructor who wants to preview New Riders books for classroom use. In the body/comments area, include your name, school, department, address, phone number, office days/hours, text currently in use, and enrollment in your department, along with your request for either desk/examination copies or additional information.

FOREWORD

Good typography should convey information with dignity and economy, but sometimes type needs to deliver the goods with more emphasis and seductive power. This book aims to fix chrome-plated fins, turbocharger, and whitewall tires to the familiar alphabet. Most of these techniques were developed using the basic Adobe Photoshop package, though you will also find some suggestions that involve a selection of third-party filters and plug-ins. Though the dominant aim has been to create recipes for useful, even everyday, type effects, there are also many curious side roads to follow.

Those who have dabbled with the various earlier versions of this software will know that there is in reality no such thing as a Photoshop recipe book. The endless combinations of filter effects, layer blend modes, and channel manipulations stretch out into the far distance. The techniques shown in this book offer a starting point for the enthusiastic operator—swap the layers around, reverse the color values, cut and paste, press a few "wrong" buttons, and though some will need to be discreetly trashed, you'll soon have a range of effects no-one ever saw before. So, Edit > Preferences > General, set the History States to 100 if your machine will stand it, hit OK, go to File > New . . .

ROGER PRING

CONTENTS

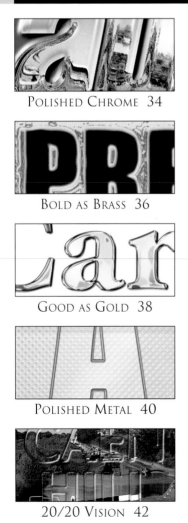
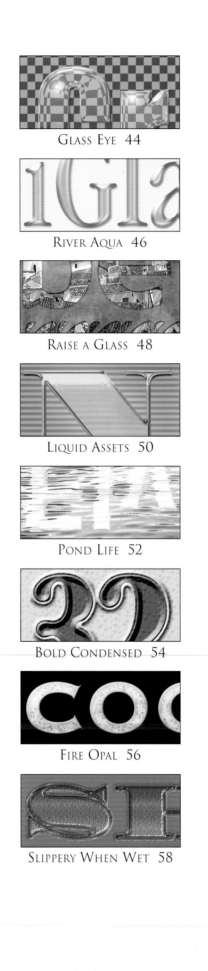

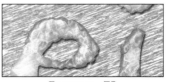
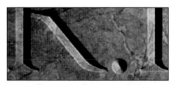

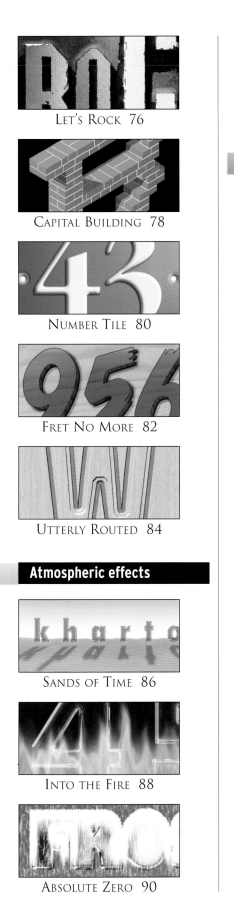
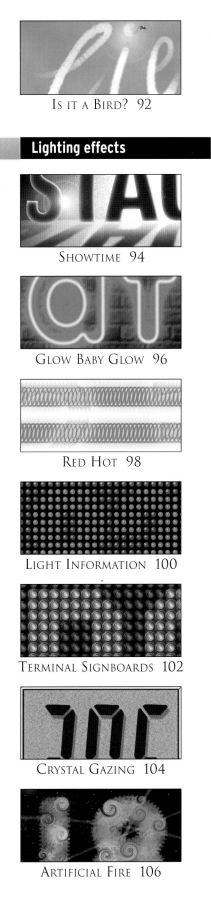

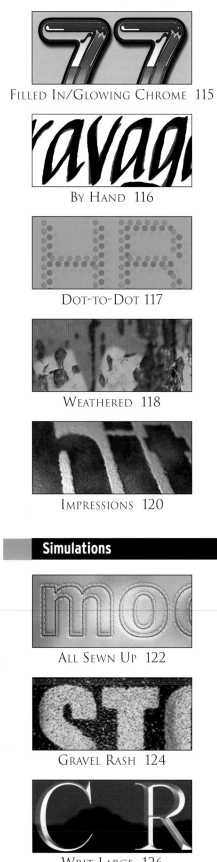
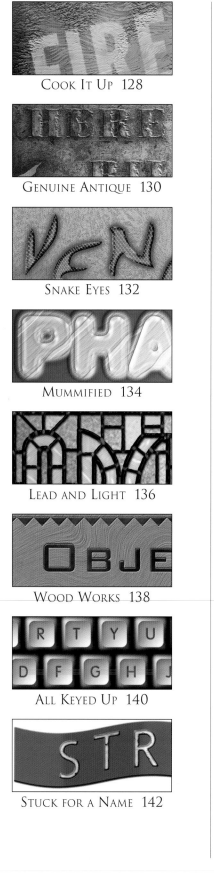

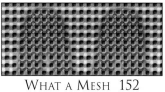

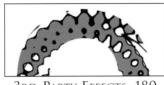
ALTERED IMAGES

In an effort to cover all the bases in record time (and to demonstrate a thoroughly even-handed approach throughout this book), we show screen images in various flavors of Photoshop 7. You'll find examples showing signs of Windows 98 and XP: on the Macintosh front there are screen grabs from OS 9 and OS X. But whatever platform you stand on, all the examples follow the same track, and where Photoshop 7 branches off in a new direction compared with its predecessor, we've tried to point out the difference. Please excuse us if your screen doesn't exactly resemble ours. If you find a better way of producing type effects, please let us know. If you find this book useful, contact us–there's a huge folder called "maybes" which would look very good in Photoshop 8.

ABOUT THIS BOOK

This book is divided into two main sections. It begins with an overview of the type-handling qualities of Photoshop. The improvements in this area make the program much more useful as a design tool; even long-time Photoshop operators are likely to find novelties here. The section concludes with a look at type effects in normal use, together with a collection of real-world type examples. The main Encyclopedia section has 72 different effects, organized into groups according to their nearest real-world equivalent. So, looking for a way to simulate skywriting, for example, go to the "Atmospheric Effects" heading, or scan "Solid Effects" for lookalike wood or stone. Alternatively, just dip in. Many pages have alternative effects described more briefly. The section ends with a flourish of uncategorizable items grouped as "Mood Effects." And don't neglect the Appendix—there's a comprehensive (and very time-saving) show of all the built-in Photoshop filters and type actions. You'll also find the regular actions applied to type, examples of the effects produced by ready-made third-party actions, as well a survey of the most useful third-party filters and plug-ins. Speed enthusiasts can brush up their keyboard skills at the back of the book with all the Photoshop shortcuts laid out for both Macintosh and Windows platforms.

THE FUNDAMENTALS

SETTING THE STAGE

AN ANCIENT definition states that "a gentleman is a person who knows how to play the piano accordion, but doesn't." To update: "a lady (or gentleman) is a person who knew how to get editable type into early versions of Photoshop, but didn't." It could be done, but it was an ugly and tortuous procedure. The answer was to generate and edit type in another, more forgiving, application and to import the result, fully formed, into Photoshop. Much quality family time was lost whenever the imported text needed correcting.

With Photoshop 6.0 the landscape has been transformed. There is now a familiar-looking type cursor in the active window, and a small flock of accompanying palettes offering genuine typographic control. With few provisos, what you type is what you get, and if you favor 1,296-point type horizontally scaled to 1,000%, faux-bolded, set vertically with negative leading, and warped into a fish shape, then all you have to do is enter the text, hit the well-named Commit button, and your creativity will be instantly rewarded. Moreover, if you misspoke yourself while typing the words, just re-insert the cursor to make the correction.

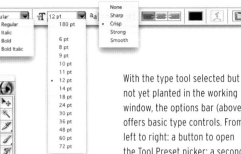

Create a new document and click on the type tool in the toolbox (left).

With the type tool selected but not yet planted in the working window, the options bar (above) offers basic type controls. From left to right: a button to open the Tool Preset picker; a second button toggling between horizontal and vertical text entry (dimmed if no type has yet been set); font name (showing here a selection of installed faces); style (dimmed if the selected font has no variations); size–from less than 1 to 1,296 points; degree of anti-aliasing; choice of three paragraph alignment styles; type color selection; the warp type button (dimmed if no type has yet been set); and the palettes button, which reveals the Character and Paragraph palettes (more usefully stored as here in the palette dock at far right).

When you click in the image window, the options bar (above) changes slightly: the button toggling between horizontal and vertical text entry and the warp type button become active and two new buttons appear. The cross and tick respectively Cancel or Commit the type edits. The Cancel button will discard any text entry and the T symbol will disappear from the layer icon. The Commit button must be clicked (or Enter pressed) when the text is complete, although selecting some controls, such as Layer Styles or Blend Modes will also commit the type. Until then, the only useful tools that can be accessed are the type controls and the zoom and navigation functions, though by holding down the Cmd/Ctrl key you can move text around the screen.

A line near the foot of the type cursor (left) indicates the baseline, so click where you want the first character to sit. In Photoshop terms, this form of composition is "point type." You can highlight letters and words by clicking and dragging in the familiar way. Click the Commit button when you're done.

To create paragraph type, click and drag the type tool to create a bounding box (left). Its shape and size can be changed immediately if necessary via the resulting box handles.

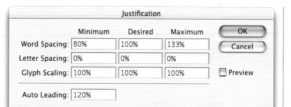

A Man's women folk, whatever their outward show of respect for his merit and authority, always regard him secretly as an ass, and with something akin to pity.

H. L. Mencken's acid observation fits neatly in the bounding box (left). After committing the type, the box can be transformed with all the commands in *Edit > Transform* except, unfortunately, *Skew* and *Distort*.

The type tool always creates a new layer. In a new document, it will replace layer 1 and rename it according to the character(s) typed in the window (left). The T symbol will remain as the thumbnail until the type is rasterized.

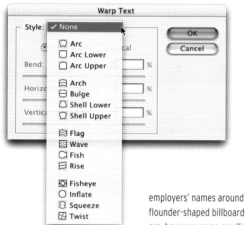

Everything you ever wished for, and more, is in the Warp dialog (above). Fishmongers' sign writers, for example, will value the opportunity to bend their employers' names around flounder-shaped billboards. There are, however, some small pearls on this swinish menu: a light application of Arc, Flag, or Wave might enliven tired lettering; but overall this window is probably best left shut.

Justification

	Minimum	Desired	Maximum
Word Spacing:	80%	100%	133%
Letter Spacing:	0%	0%	0%
Glyph Scaling:	100%	100%	100%

Auto Leading: 120%

OK Cancel ☐ Preview

The default settings shown above closely resemble those of regular page layout applications. Glyph Scaling allows for lines of characters to be compressed or expanded to achieve better breaks. This feature is off by default.

Hyphenation

☑ Hyphenation

Words Longer Than:	7	letters
After First:	3	letters
Before Last:	3	letters
Hyphen Limit:	2	hyphens
Hyphenation Zone:	3 pica	

☑ Hyphenate Capitalized Words

OK Cancel ☑ Preview

If you have to hyphenate automatically, this is the place to do it (above). The alternative Cmd/Ctrl-hyphen (soft-hyphen) technique is not available in Photoshop; that keystroke combination just makes the image window smaller.

A NOTE ON DEFAULT SETTINGS

All the techniques in the body of the book start with settings at their default values. You can reset all, or individual, tools to these values by clicking on the icon at the left end of the options bar. Except where stated, the foreground color is set to black, the background to white (hit key D to set these colors, and X to change them over). All documents are in RGB mode except where stated. The transparency settings, which determine the appearance of one layer above another, have been set (in *Edit > Preferences > Transparency & Gamut*) to Grid Size Medium and Grid Colors Light for clarity when assembling the effect. A white or colored layer has been inserted where necessary to highlight an effect on the layer above, but does not ordinarily form part of the technique.

A NOTE ON THE CHOICE OF WORDS IN THE EFFECTS

The Character Palette (above) allows control of leading, letter spacing, horizontal and vertical scaling, quality of antialiasing and also allows you to select one of 17 languages for spelling. Icons repeat some of the character style controls in the pop-up menu.

The Paragraph palette (above) has four more alignment styles, as well as controls for indents and interparagraph spacing. Justification and hyphenation settings are set in separate dialogs reached through the pop-up menu.

Quick brown foxes have long been ousted by cozy lummoxes. ABC can begin to grate, as can QWERTY. An utterly arbitrary policy, or lack of one, has developed in the choice of which letters or words were to be immortalized in Photoshop's withering glare. Some of the chosen few are crushingly obvious, others slightly exotic (to an English speaker), still others downright bizarre. Monsieur Thollois, inventor of the 19th-century alphabet game shown here, did not dither so; he went straight for "friend" and "fatherland."

Type Manipulation

The hard part is already nearly over. Assuming you can wrestle the Commit button to the ground and have a reasonable selection of robust fonts (see page 25 for likely candidates), the rest is easy. The only remaining fork in the road reads "Vector" to the left and "Bitmap via Rasterize" to the right. This is a historic junction for Photoshop users. Letters are now created using vector-based type outlines, just as they always were in most drawing applications. Though these shapes necessarily appear to be made up of pixels on your screen, they are actually capable of being mightily enlarged without loss of definition. With the help of Photoshop's Layer Style dialog (see

pages 20–21), you can keep straight on down the vector path, producing billboard-sized lettering effects, editable right to the last minute, without degrading a single pixel. The controls shown on this spread are all available prior to the moment of rasterization, and not at all afterward.

There are, however, large territories that remain inaccessible to vector-based type. If you want, for example, to operate on letters in detail rather than globally on words, create perspective effects, colorize or use filters, then the rasterized (bitmapped) road is the way to go. A general guide to the possibilities is on pages 22–23.

The character palette (above) shows the changed kern value. Possible figures run from +1,000 to -1,000; the latter value puts the second character in front of the first. Tread carefully.

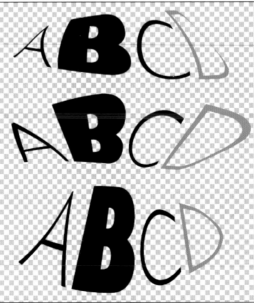

The point of (nearly) no return (above). This querulous box encourages you to check your text before it will allow bitmap operations. Use the spell checker (Edit > check spelling), having chosen from the 17 language variations on offer.

In the Character palette you can change kern values (left). Kerning only works between adjacent characters. The default is "Metrics" when the font has built-in kerning rules, or zero if there are none.

In the interests of completeness rather than recommendation, these are three of the effects obtainable through the warp type button in the options bar (left). From top to bottom: Bulge, Shell Upper, and Fish Eye, all with a small amount of horizontal and vertical distortion. In a bizarre twist, the warp function refuses, fortified by technical considerations or typographic taste, to operate on type that has already been styled with faux bold or italic. Small mercies.

Working only in the options bar, you can change font, style (where available), size, and color (above). There is also an opportunity to vary antialiasing all the way from None to Smooth, though this is only significant if you are working with small type sizes or if the work is to be displayed online.

The type-styling options in the Character pop-up menu are repeated as icons at the foot of the main palette. The choice of language variations is accessed here as well, offering spellchecking and hyphenation conventions for 17 language groups.

To the right of the Character palette, you can alter the leading value. Working with lines of capital letters, as above, it's useful to be able to close up unnecessary space, though Photoshop will allow values down to zero, planting the second line on top of the first.

Clicking on the arrow at the top right of the Character palette brings up a pop-up menu (or you can click on the icons). You can choose faux bold and italic effects here, as well as the usual small caps and so on. In the example above, the letter A is untreated, B is faux bold, C is faux italics, and D is both.

The tracking control (below "leading" in the Character palette) enables you to close up or add more space between characters (above). Any number of characters can be selected, and the values, as before, run from +1,000 to –1,000. In this case, the top line has no tracking and the lower one is set to -80.

Toward the bottom of the Character palette are the vertical and horizontal scale controls. In the example above, the letter B is scaled 30% in the vertical axis, the C 150% in the horizontal. The D is scaled horizontally and vertically, and is also baseline-shifted.

With paragraph type (in a bounding box) you can use the controls in both the Character and Paragraph palettes (above). Edward Fitzgerald's *Rubáiyát of Omar Khayyám* translation is here treated to several variations (below). The drop cap (and its attendant apostrophe) are scaled horizontally and vertically and baseline-shifted. The first few words are styled as small caps. They proved excessively small, so they were also scaled in both axes. Lines two and four are indented, the whole composition arbitrarily rotated, and "wave" applied. There is time for a break with lesser machines as a window announces that the type is being rendered. A screen image is being built–there is no rasterization going on–so there is still an opportunity to reverse some or all of these distortions.

Some typefaces don't benefit from tracking (or kerning). These curlicues are meant to stay together forever (above). When in doubt, recall the local blacksmith with his intractable materials–and forswear.

'TIS ALL A CHEQUER-BOARD of Night and Days, Where Destiny with Men for Pieces plays: Hither and thither moves, and mates, and slays, And one by one back in the closet lays.

SHAPES OF THINGS TO COME

NOW WE HAVE finely-wrought type on the screen. If you were a Gutenberg or a Caxton, you would by now be inking up your type and polishing your platen. Why delay further? Take a moment to consider the suite of additional tools at the disposal of the Photoshop operator. First, there is a practically unlimited stack of artwork layers, each of which can interact with its neighbor. These interactions range from the familiar acetate analogy, with the upper layer more or less obscuring the lower, through to modes where color and luminance values combine or compete with each other. In addition, these layers can be assigned variable opacity.

Type can be transformed into a mask or alpha channel, or even set directly for the same result. Letterforms can be saved as paths—and shapes, like cookie cutters, can be generated from type to cut through backgrounds or other characters. All of this is achievable while the type is still in a resolution-independent, and more importantly, editable state.

Once the type is set, it's easy (in the Paths palette) to create a work path based on the letterforms. All the usual path tools are then available for editing. Above, the direct selection tool is being used to lengthen a letter stroke. The type has been dimmed to make this clearer. Such a path can be stroked with the paintbrush or airbrush tools.

In the Paths palette (above), the new path appears as a thumbnail, saved and named if required.

Alternatively, if you choose *Layer > Type > **Convert to Shape***, the result in the image window appears the same, but in fact there are two developments. In the Layers palette (right), a new solid black area appears, linked (shown by the chain symbol) to a clipping path. The latter appears also in the Paths palette (right). When the shape is selected (with a double line around the thumbnail as here) you can go to the *Edit* menu and choose **Define Custom Shape**.

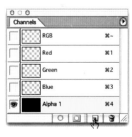

The Shape Name dialog (above) confirms the selection with a thumbnail.

New RGB documents have three channels. In the Channels palette (left) you will see the composite channel (which provided the image in the Layers palette) and the three constituent color channels. Clicking on the new channel icon at the foot of the palette will produce a new channel, filled with black, and named by default Alpha 1.

Choose type color white, and key text directly into the alpha channel. When you hit Enter (or click the Commit button), the type appears as a filled white selection (above). Though this negative image may seem perverse, it's actually far more useful than the equivalent black-on-white characters that we're more familiar with. Like the selection, the alpha channel cannot be edited, and is no longer resolution-independent.

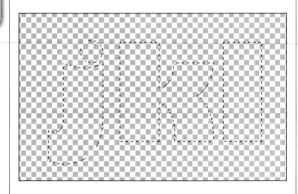

Use of the type mask/selection tool (second from the left in the option bar when the type tool is selected) produces an active selection in the shape of the letterforms (above). This area can be filled, stroked, and manipulated like any other selection. The selection is obviously no longer editable, but, less obviously, is no longer resolution-independent either.

The collation on the left shows each of the previous maneuvers put to some limited use. From the top: the original type; the work path stroked with a soft blue paintbrush; the shape layer with its original solid black fill changed in the *Layer* menu via **Change Layer Content** to a pattern fill (satin from the Photoshop default set); the saved custom shape selected from the Shapes menu, planted in a layer and filled with orange; a selection made from the alpha channel, feathered to soften the edge and filled with black; and, finally, the direct selection produced by the type tool in mask/selection mode and filled with frantic brushstrokes.

The scribbled selection is set to **Screen** blend mode, after which the pattern shape is set to **Hard Light** (this layer had to be merged with a blank layer to allow transparency in the background area); and the blue stroked path is set to **Multiply** (above).

Four of the layers (above) from the previous collation have been pressed into service to try out various layer blending modes. In the examples (left), all layers are at 100% opacity except the alpha channel feathered selection, which is offset and used as a makeshift background shadow layer at 35%.

Shown above are the same four layers, the shadow still at the base, but with the blue stroked path at the top set to **Color Burn** blend mode, next, the scribbled selection set to **Overlay**, and then the pattern shape set to **Difference**.

The final variation (above) sees the same four layers in use as follows: uppermost, the pattern shape and the blue stroked path, which are both set to **Overlay**; and the scribbled selection, which is set to **Darken**. Many more combinations are obviously available, but life is simply too short.

A TOUCH OF STYLE

THOUGH WE MAY AFFECT to prefer whole-wheat bread, very dry white wine, and sugarless coffee, what we would really like is a big candy bar and a bright red strawberry milkshake. Self-indulgence of this sort is available right out of the candy-striped, metallic-foiled, beveled and satin-covered container called Layer Style. If you can't find what you want in this Pandora's box of delights, then go ahead and make a Style of your own, name it My Particular Style and apply it to everything that doesn't move. Layer Style operates on vector type, though more flexibility comes when type has been rasterized. And of course it can be applied to any and every item on the screen. It largely replaces manual shadow making, and offers quick two-and-a-half dimensional effects, lighting management, textures, and glows. Now, what to do with all that extra leisure time?

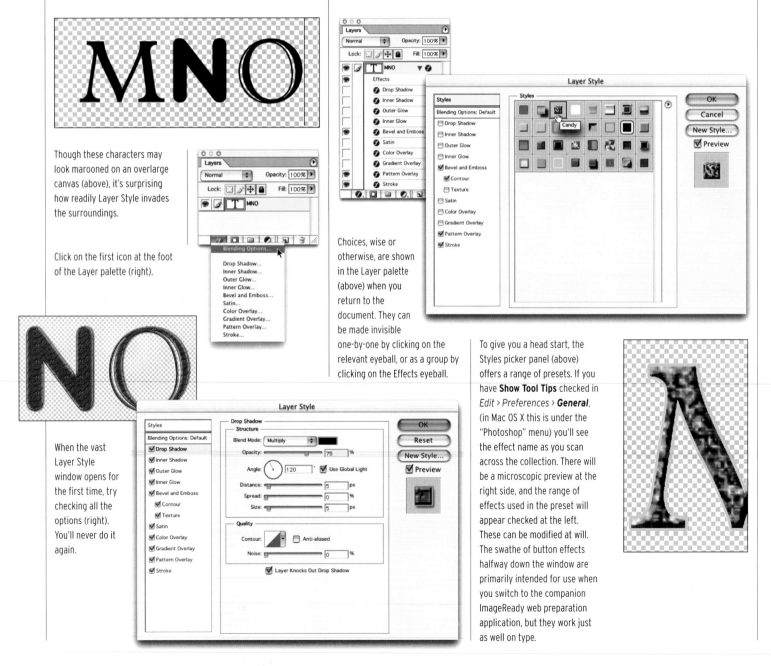

Though these characters may look marooned on an overlarge canvas (above), it's surprising how readily Layer Style invades the surroundings.

Click on the first icon at the foot of the Layer palette (right).

Choices, wise or otherwise, are shown in the Layer palette (above) when you return to the document. They can be made invisible one-by-one by clicking on the relevant eyeball, or as a group by clicking on the Effects eyeball.

When the vast Layer Style window opens for the first time, try checking all the options (right). You'll never do it again.

To give you a head start, the Styles picker panel (above) offers a range of presets. If you have **Show Tool Tips** checked in *Edit > Preferences > General*, (in Mac OS X this is under the "Photoshop" menu) you'll see the effect name as you scan across the collection. There will be a microscopic preview at the right side, and the range of effects used in the preset will appear checked at the left. These can be modified at will. The swathe of button effects halfway down the window are primarily intended for use when you switch to the companion ImageReady web preparation application, but they work just as well on type.

Drop Shadow (above), the badge by which electronic typography is known, comes naturally at the top of the heap. The default setting offers quite a restrained result–for more strength, drag out the distance and size sliders as here (the exact settings for the best results will depend on the size of your lettering). Ignore the Quality panel for now.

The initial settings give a relatively hard result. This can be softened by increasing the Size value slightly, and/or reducing the opacity of the effect (above right). There's also an opportunity to select an entirely different color for the shadow. A white layer has been added underneath to make the effect clearer.

With **Inner Glow**, as with Outer Glow, you will need to change the default settings to achieve an effect. The Source option buttons (right) allow you to flip the effect from the center to the edge of the letter stroke. You can also use a gradient instead of a solid color. Decisions on color and blend mode depend on the original color of the letters under treatment.

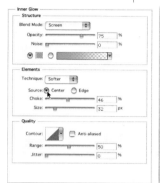

In the example above, the capital M has just enough width of stroke to show an effect, though it's more apparent with a fatter letterform. The chiseled O shows almost no effect.

Inner Shadow This useful function replaces the maneuvering necessary in older Photoshop versions to get a "cutout" effect (above).

Again, I have increased the default settings (right) for Distance and Size. For obvious reasons, this effect is of no help on black type.

The **Bevel and Emboss** function (right) is by far the most powerful tool within Layer Style. Used in conjunction with the Contour picker, it offers a huge range of effects. The settings shown here are little changed from the default–depth and size have been increased–but this is just a beginning. These effects are explored in greater detail on the next two pages.

Even at the basic settings, there is an effect of roundness with convincingly balanced highlight and shadow areas. Black type has to wait for the application of additional effects (above).

For **Outer Glow** (above), the default blend mode is **Screen**, and the default color light yellow, neither of which is any help on a white background. To get a result, the blend mode has been changed to **Normal** and the color to red. Spread and Size have also been increased. In the Quality panel, there is a choice of contours–experiment with these

to vary the appearance of the glow.

The change of Contour setting (right) proves subsequently to be the most influential move. Using the default contour will produce a more conventional glow.

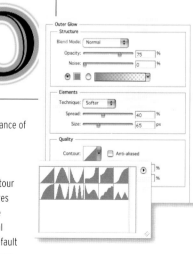

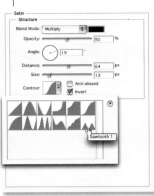

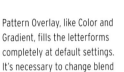

Satin The Photoshop designers themselves offer this effect in rather diffident terms: "Satin ... to apply shading to the interior of a layer that reacts to the shape of the layer, typically creating a satiny finish." The subtle effect of the default settings can be enlivened by increasing the Distance value and choosing an alternative contour–"Sawtooth 1" in this case (right).

The edges of the character are greatly displaced by the large Distance setting and overlap each other (above). The "Sawtooth 1" contour generates the double line.

The blank pastures of the **Color Overlay** panel (right) offer a rare chance to bring the dusty old **Dissolve** blend mode into play (above).

The Color Overlay function is unremarkable used by itself, but offers great flexibility in conjunction with one or more other Layer Style effects (see next two pages).

Gradient Overlay It's unusual for default settings to give an instantly usable result (above).

Appearing through the mist ... just one move gets a result that would otherwise involve blending layers. And the gradient itself can be changed in a mere moment (right).

Pattern Overlay Here you can choose from the default patterns, import other examples, or use your own. The crucial control is the Scale slider (right) to adjust the pattern pitch to work with the width of letter stroke. Snap to Origin ensures that the pattern begins in the top left corner of the document–a useful feature if you are combining two or more patterns in different layers of the document.

Pattern Overlay, like Color and Gradient, fills the letterforms completely at default settings. It's necessary to change blend mode and /or opacity levels to see elements of the original color or texture (top).

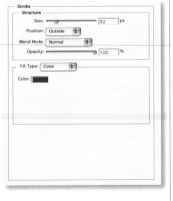

Stroke (right) is a useful function for defining edges and smoothing out jagged selections. Curious effects are obtainable by choosing Gradient or Pattern in the Fill Type panel.

From left to right in the composite view (above): default Stroke settings but increased stroke width; as before but with "Outside" selected as Position and Gradient as Fill Type; and, finally, Center as Position and Pattern (this is Nebula) as Fill type.

CARVING OUT A CAREER

Many of the techniques in this book are concerned with creating the illusion that type is three-dimensional. Our aim is to lift it off the page or screen and invest it with more power and immediacy. Of all the Photoshop functions, **Bevel and Emboss** is foremost in helping to break out of the confines of two dimensions. It's all a trick of the light, of course. The illusions depend on your familiarity with parallel appearances in the real world. If you had never previously seen a carved stone inscription, or an embossed shop sign, none of this would count for anything. **Bevel and Emboss** should be equipped with an on-screen plea for moderation. Not every word needs glossy treatment and a drop shadow too, but the megalomania that comes with the possibility of pushing a global sun across a digital sky is certainly pleasurable, and probably harmless.

With the basic **Bevel and Emboss** settings, the paneled letter benefits from lighting from the top left. The freestanding letter's shape is emphasized by highlight and shadow that accurately follow its form (above).

This composite window (right) points out the two most powerful controls: the Style choice in the Structure panel, and the Angle and Altitude disk that defines the direction of shading. It's more useful to think of this disk as a hemisphere, with movements of the cursor dragging a light source over its surface. Unlike

the **Lighting Effects** filter, there is only one light source, though the Use Global Lighting checkbox offers the opportunity, if unchecked, to have different lighting directions operating on different layers in the same document.

The target is formed of one letter embedded in a panel and another that is freestanding (above). A white layer has been inserted under the working examples to make the effects clearer.

The two subsidiary picker panels (above) are found within **Bevel and Emboss** function. **Contour** offers a selection of shapes that influence the sculptural qualities of the embossed form. Ridges and valleys appear in the fill, following the curves of the contour. If the presets don't provide you with what you're looking for, you can create your own contour by drawing. **Texture** uses the default or any other pattern as a (monochrome) map to create repeating shadows and highlights within the fill.

Default settings (**Inner Bevel**) with Size increased and light source shifted to lower right (above).

Style–**Emboss**; Technique–Chisel Hard (below).

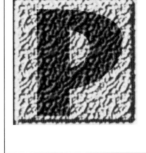

Style - **Outer Bevel**; Technique - Chisel Hard (above).

Clicking on the Contour function shows an immediate change in the nature of the highlighting and shading of both letters. Even with the default "straight" curve (Photoshop calls it "Linear"), there is already a marked difference (above).

It's possible, though hardly worth the trouble, to combine different shading, contour and texture options in all three areas of **Bevel**

and Emboss. Here, the Gaussian curve is used in Shading; "Cone - Inverted" in Contour; and Metal Landscape in Texture (above).

Style - **Pillow Emboss**. The next move in this logical sequence is to use Stroke Emboss, but the effect is so marginal that it can be ignored (above).

Contour changed to Ring; Lighting Altitude moved to almost overhead. As in the Shading panel, you can draw your own curves to make more complex effects (above).

Using fewer than half of Layer Style's ten options yields an interesting result on these letters, which started out bright red. First, a purple **Drop Shadow**, increased in Size and Distance; Pillow Emboss in **Bevel and Emboss**, with Chisel Hard selected; Sawtooth 1 chosen in the Contour picker; default black foreground to white background gradient used with Difference mode in the **Gradient Overlay** panel; and finally, **Pattern Overlay** with "Wrinkles" scaled and set to Luminosity for the blend mode.

Bright red letters again, with a default **Drop Shadow**, increased in Size and Distance; simple Emboss in **Bevel and Emboss**, with Chisel Soft; Cove Deep in the Gloss Contour picker in the Shading panel; the "Ring - Double" contour selected in the Contour Elements panel; Bubbles, used inverted, as the Texture; a yellow **Color Overlay** set to Screen mode; and an Orange, Yellow, Orange fill in **Gradient Overlay**, set to Hard Light and angled at 30° (above).

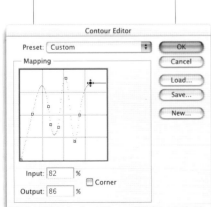

Moving to the Shading panel, this is the effect of changing Gloss Contour to "Ring - Double" (above).

The final area of **Bevel and Emboss** contains an option for adding texture as a shading element. The usual default textures can be used (this is the over-familiar Optical Checkerboard), providing a range of highlights and shadows. Each texture needs to be scaled to work well with the letterform, or the result will be an indecipherable porridge.

Click on the selected contour icon to bring up the Contour Editor. If you want dramatic divisions, check the "Corner" box as you redraw the curve (left).

Contour Editor

Preset: Custom

Mapping

OK
Cancel
Load...
Save...
New...

Input: 82 %
Output: 86 %
☐ Corner

The **Copy Layer Style** and **Paste Layer Style** functions allow speedy shortcuts. Two new letterforms, this time cut out of a bright red background, are treated with the identical Layer Style combination used in the last example (above).

JUST MY TYPE

PHOTOSHOP FAVORS the fat face. Thin faces slip too easily through the cracks in the system. But there is a place for serif, curlicued, chiseled, incised, inline and outline as well, since many effects are enlivened by contrasts in stroke width. The niceties of typeface choice should still operate. And what if the allure of 4,000 typefaces begins to pall? Then draw freehand with a fat brush, fire up a type design application or scavenge outside in the real world for inspiration (see pages 26–29).

Even in adversity there is quick and dirty salvation. When the font management utility can't or won't render the chosen typeface on screen, the mangled letter can still be rescued. Here the last Layer Style from the previous page gets pressed into service.

The remaining letters on these two pages are rasterized to allow for bitmap editing, and they all start off blue. First, the ubiquitous Arial Bold is selected, then stroked with a fat, contrasting line. You could continue stroking the letter with increasingly fat lines of different colors to produce a simple multiple outline effect.

The same selection (above), but this time the reduced area is colored. The face is Memphis Extra Bold, Egyptian (square-serif) style.

Calvert (above) is also Egyptian style, but with half-size slab serifs. The reduced selection is re-used, but feathered to give a soft edge, then filled with color,

A treatment for Lithograph Bold; the selection marquee is moved rightwards and then filled with a contrasting color set to **Multiply**.

Here the selection is expanded outside the letterform, feathered to give a soft edge, and filled with color (set to **Hard Light**). Futura is available in a wide range of styles and weights; this is Extra Bold Condensed.

With a similar technique, the selection is reduced in size before being stroked (above). The face is Berkeley Black, with characteristic thick and thin strokes.

The cryptic X (above) is from Engravers' Old English. The letterform selection has been changed to a path, which allows it to be stroked with many of the toolbox tools. Here it is stroked with the airbrush in a contrasting color, and set to **Soft Light**.

Chiseled or open-face fonts offer possibilities for differential treatment. Here, Cloister Old Face is colorized, then the colorless groove in the stroke is selected with the magic wand tool and filled with another color.

Where the letterform is broken by intersecting lines, it's easy to treat isolated areas separately. Vineta (above), has shadow blocks colorized, and the main strokes colorized, selected and reduced, with a fill of Satin set to **Color Burn**.

Another useful command is found in *Select > Modify > Border*. Here the X from Traffic has been given a large border selection filled with a contrasting color set to **overlay**. The color thus acts on the edges of the letter as well as creating a halo.

This curiosity uses individual selections which are provided by the fragmented style of Eileen Caps. Each area, originally completely black, was selected with the magic wand, then colorized. A paintbrush set to **Difference** mode, with Wet Edges checked, was then scribbled over each section, changing brush color from time to time. The drop shadow is made by choosing *Layer > Layer Style > Drop Shadow*.

Bermuda Squiggle provides the basis for this tubular effect. The background layer, filled with color and blurred noise, has been treated with *Filter > Render > Lighting Effects* to achieve a three-dimensional effect, using an enlarged, feathered and gray-filled selection of the letterform itself as an alpha channel texture map. On the top layer, the character was colorized and given a feathered highlight in the center of its axis; then the feathered area was treated with Photoshop's own **Chrome** filter. **Lens Flare** was added in small amounts, and finally upper and lower layers were separately treated in **Layer Style** to obtain a drop shadow and a beveled edge respectively.

LOOKING FOR CLUES

AROUND EVERY CORNER in your brain lurks a typographic diversion. Somewhere in your subconscious are half-remembered letters: a fairground poster flapping in the wind; two names incised into a tree; enamel words on a window promoting ancient confectionery; the way the government logo looks on a tax-demand envelope; the doodling around the title page of a school exercise book, or the engraving on your front-door key. If none of the above applies, then proceed directly to the techniques beginning on page 32; otherwise dwell awhile on these pages of fragments snatched from the typographic maelstrom.

Gloriously rising from the squalor under the elevated section of the M4 highway of west London, 1000 Great West Road deserves better surroundings (left). Home in the 1980s of the then-mighty Wang Laboratories, scourge of IBM, it now houses the part of the Comdisco Corporation which "provides global technology services to help its customers maximize technology functionality, predictability and availability while freeing them from the complexity of managing their technology."

Inside the Ritz hotel, London, the décor is extraordinarily opulent, they say. Outside, 66 ordinary bulbs of various wattages serve to project its image down Green Park (far left). This is the quintessence of corporate *chutzpah*, borrowing the language of the fairground to speak of chic. Half a mile westwards, Leicester Square boasts many more bulbs, and moving images too, on Van Wagner's frantic news and promo screen (left).

There is still romance on British railroads. Charles Rennie Mackintosh, designer, architect, visionary, and essential Glaswegian is commemorated in cast aluminum (above) on both sides of an obsolescent electric locomotive, which perversely, is restricted to humble duties at Edinburgh's Waverley station. The lively collectors' market in nameplates leads to sophisticated fixing methods. Things were less covert in the Danish system. Was it luck or good design that allowed the conscientious fixer of the caboose (guard's van) letters (above right) to avoid the gaps between the slats and still arrive at a passable letter spacing? By the way, you can buy an affectionate Rennie Mackintosh font very economically at www.artworksuk.com.

In Cambridge, Peck's chemist's sign (above) also employs signwriter's Belle Époque, including a voluptuous ampersand, to commemorate the original foundation. Though years of weather and bird life have not been kind, a devotee still ascends to gild the lily now and then. In 1912, the Bristol Hippodrome opened with the spectacular staging of a "water gala." From a pit below the stage, hydraulic pistons raised a watertank containing a lady and a genuine horse for the audience's pleasure. Although not original, the quasi-Art Nouveau stained-glass marquee (below) makes a welcome change from the habitual neon tube.

Stare fixedly at the enlarged R (above), and deduce whether it is carved into or stands proud of the wood. Employ parafoveal vision (the one where you focus on infinity like a wartime air-raid spotter) and pretty soon your original conviction will be overturned. Turn the book upside-down and try again. Enough. Hairdressing is a rather gentle art, so it's surprising to find it being pursued behind a six-foot balk of timber (top right). In this London salon, you can divert yourself while waiting for your highlights to take hold.

Vermorel used to make spraying equipment for the French wine industry. Their standard backpack, filled with copper sulfate solution, would stop mildew in its tracks. The sprayers are now reduced to domestic decoration, and usually polished to a high sheen, the ornate transfers disappearing in the process. This 1957 example (left) somehow escaped most of this abrasion, and now serves as a useful Photoshop exercise. So, after three: *File* > *New* > *Type* > *Warp* > *Drop Shadow* > *Craquelure* > *Dissolve*, and again ...

In Bury St. Edmund's Cathedral graveyard (above) we unlearn the adage that virtue is its own reward. And that some Words deserve Capital letters more Than others. Faced with such a harrowing tale, it's hard to concentrate on the issues of non-lining numerals and the stonecutter's skill (right).

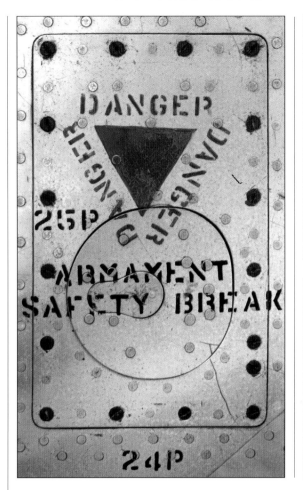

Though this street sign (below) looks to have been simply painted, the underlying letters are actually cast. We should be grateful that we, unlike Britain's Georgian ironfounders, have an unlimited supply of the rarer letters in our toolbox.

If soldiers had chromium-plated Rolls-Royces, they would still stencil all over them. This fearsome collection of rivets (above and top right) is luckily grounded at the Imperial War Museum, London. Lettering on aircraft is now mostly achieved with computer-cut vinyl, though of a more robust quality than that supplied for the average grocery delivery truck. Two grades are available: permanent, for airlines with a firm design policy and a dominant CEO, and semi-permanent, for airlines not so blessed, and those offering aircraft on contract hire to larger airlines. The latter need to change their stripes overnight– the only way to be really sure who you're flying with is to look for a logo on the little paper bag.

This technique is simple vandalism in real life (left), and utterly vulgar in Photoshop.

THE EFFECT IS STARTLING

LEFT ALONE in Photoshop's basement areas, it's easy to fall prey to the deadly sin of pressing too many buttons. The mathematics of this plethora of choices suggests a billion permutations and rising. Not all of these are useful; if they were, this book would have eighteen wheels. The examples here result from deliberate attempts at bad behavior, but they speak equally eloquently of retreat from blind alleys blocked with unpleasant combinations of pixels. Following this erratic pathway, you can keep an escape route open by saving a copy of the last state of your document before major leaps into the darkness. You could step back by using the History palette or *Edit* › **Step Backward**, but the byways are so seductively extensive that you will soon run out of History states. (You can allow up to a hundred with the setting in the General area of Preferences, but be aware that a such a high figure has a negative effect on computer performance—and is hard on the brain.)

Recipe for a life on the open road–part-time signwriter and cage cleaner. Fill a layer with a circular spectrum gradient, take one font (Posse Regular will do), set the type, hide the type layer, select its outline, return to the colored layer, and create a Work Path. Select a small, soft paintbrush and set it to **Difference** mode. Choose a new foreground color (red will do) and stroke the path with it; increase the brush size, choose a new foreground color, and stroke the path again. Continue until nausea sets in. Open the Curves dialog and redraw the graph line with as many switchback curves as you can manage. Hit OK. Reselect the type outline, and then copy and paste to make a new layer containing only the letterforms. Open the Layer Style dialog and poke feverishly at the **Bevel and Emboss** controls. Add a drop shadow while you're there. Use **Lens Flare** to add extraordinary glamor. Merge the visible layers, and stroke the path again with a sharp brush of a bright color set to **Screen** mode. A career in law is more remunerative and combat duty less dangerous.

A pungent combination of distortions. The original type (Miami Nights) was warped by the Wave function. It shows as the lighter swathe. Combined with a colored background, it was then treated with the Twirl filter. The effect of Twirl was Faded, and the blend mode changed to the hardly-ever-used **Luminosity**. The hues in the window were then reversed with Invert.

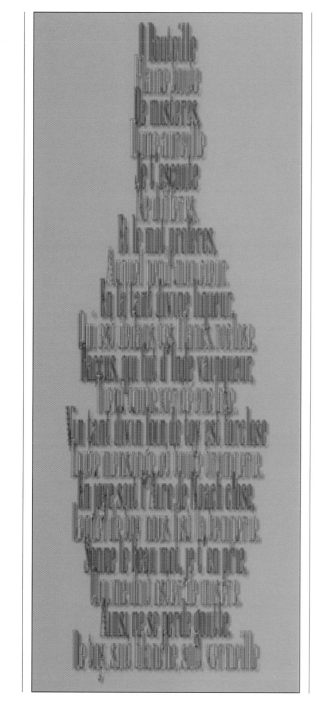

Rabelais' hymn to the "Dive Bouteille" (divine bottle), expressed in his invented French dialect, is remanufactured here with negative leading, character scaling, and Layer Styling.

An English translation bravely reproduces the sentiments, but not the shape:

> O Bottle! whose mysterious deep
> Does ten thousand secrets keep,
>   With attentive ear I wait;
> Ease my mind, and speak my fate.
>   Soul of joy, like Bacchus, we
>   More than India gain by thee.
> Truths unborn thy juice reveals,
>   Which futurity conceals.
>   Antidote to frauds and lies,
> Wine, that mounts us to the skies,
>   May thy father Noah's brood
>   Like him drown, but in thy flood.
>   Speak, so may the liquid mine
> Of rubies or of diamonds, shine.

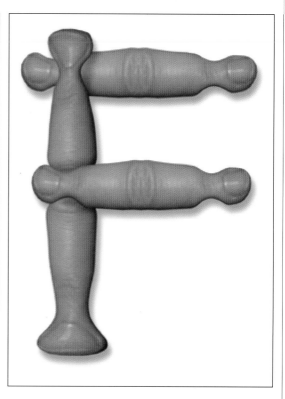

Many taboos are at risk when Liquifying body parts as type components. There are plenty of precedents for whole, clothed figures—children's primers full of harlequins and jesters acrobatically reenacting the alphabet—but fingers in scanners? Maybe, but only with gloves on.

THE EFFECTS

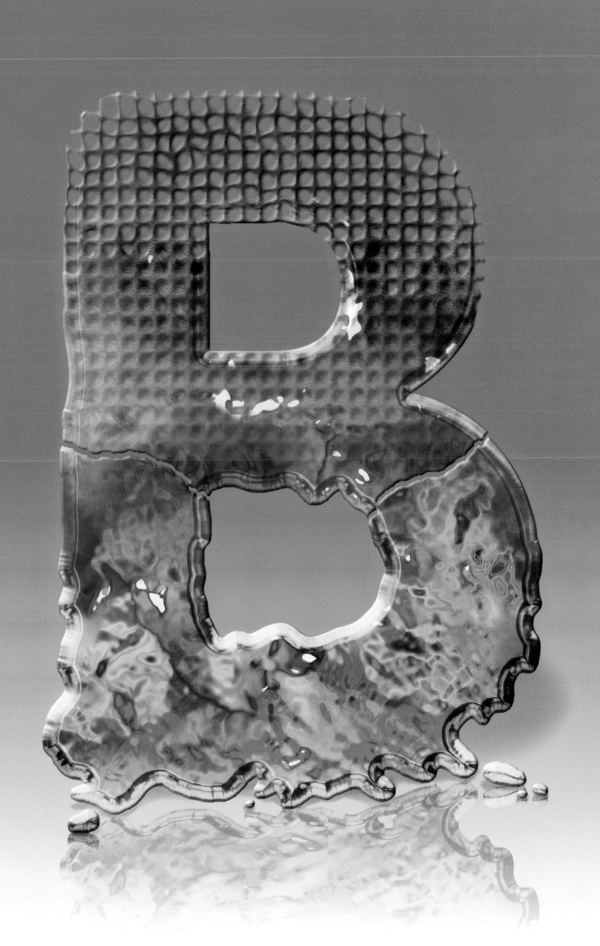

POLISHED
CHROME

THE PUREST of all type effects —the letterform is described only by the reflected world. You could almost see your face in it, and if you choose a self-portrait to serve as the reflected image, you will. The illustration above shows the example after the drop shadow has been applied in the final step. The result can be developed further by using Layer Style—try Pillow Emboss with a Sawtooth contour, for example. Dark glasses are useful too.

CHOOSING THE RIGHT IMAGE

Choose the image that will form the reflection on the type with care–plenty of cloudless sky is usually best. Avoid fussy, detailed images since these may end up looking very grainy, spoiling the effect. For example, although the image left has smooth sky, when it is applied to type as a reflection (bottom left) the foreground forest creates too much "noise," reducing the chrome effect.

Chromium plate

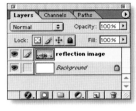

1 Create a new RGB document and call it "chrome lettering." Paste the reflection image as a layer above a white background layer. Name the image layer "reflection image."

2 In the Channels palette, create a new channel and set the type into it. This will be Channel #4–call it "type mask." Deselect.

3 Duplicate the type mask channel by dragging it onto the **Create new channel** icon on the palette. This is Channel #5–call it "blurred type." Apply a Gaussian Blur (*Filter > Blur > Gaussian Blur*) of 4 to the channel.

4 Duplicate the "blurred type" channel (#5) as in step 3 and call the new channel "masked blur." Load the "type mask" channel (#4) as a selection (*Select > Load Selection*)–make sure you check the **Invert** box in the dialog box. Fill the selected area with black (*Edit > Fill > Black*). This makes a trimmed blur (detail below).

5 Save the "masked blur" channel as a separate document (*Select > Select All, Edit > Copy, File > New, Edit > Paste*) in Photoshop format, naming it "Displacement map."

6 Return to the "chrome lettering" document and deselect. Click on the RGB channel in the Channels palette to activate the reflection image. Apply the "Glass" filter (*Filter > Distort > Glass*) using the settings shown in the illustration at left. For the texture, load the masked blur "displacement map" file that you saved in step 5. This applies the type to the reflection image, giving it the glasslike effect shown above.

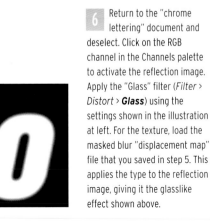

7 In the Layers palette, create a new layer, "emboss." Fill this layer with white. Then go to *Filter > Render > **Lighting Effects***. Load the "masked blur" channel as a texture channel, checking the **White is High** box. Position five Omni lights around the image–do this by dragging the lightbulb icon onto the image, then choose Omni from **Light Type** menu. Give each of the five lights a pale color by clicking on the **Light Type** color swatch. In **Properties** box, apply similar settings to those illustrated above–but you'll have to experiment to get a result resembling that shown.

8 Change the "Emboss" layer's blending mode to **Overlay**. This gives the reflection image increased shininess by combining the highlights and shadows of the "Emboss" layer (top) with the glassy effect of the reflection image layer (right).

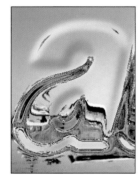

9 Additional specular highlights can be applied by using the *Plastic Wrap* filter (*Filter > Artistic > **Plastic Wrap***). Values set at maximum (above) usually give the best results, although you may need to experiment. Compare the image above with that of step 8.

10 To remove the excess background image, load the original "type mask" (channel #4) as a selection (*Select > **Load Selection***), checking **Inverse** in the Load Selection dialog. Click on the "emboss" layer in the Layers palette to activate it, then press the Delete key on your keyboard. Repeat the same procedure on the "reflection image" layer. Deselect.

11 Now apply *Lighting Effects* to the white background layer (*Filter > Render > **Lighting Effects***), using a single blue spotlight and loading the "blurred type" channel as the texture channel–but uncheck the **White is High** box.

12 Finally, apply a drop shadow (*Layer > Layer Style > **Drop Shadow***) to the "reflection image" layer–try settings of 50% shadow with a 15-pixel distance and size, although your choice of settings will depend on the size of your image.

POSITIONING THE TYPE ON THE IMAGE

Be careful to position the type at the appropriate height on the reflection image. The type above is positioned too high on the image, providing insufficient detail for the reflection.

If the type is positioned too low on the image, too much detail is reflected, lessening the chrome effect (above).

This shows the position of the type used in our example on these pages.

BOLD AS BRASS

BRASS IS AN ALLOY of copper and zinc. The more copper (up to 60%), the yellower the metal. It is resistant to corrosion but not to the abrasive attentions of energetic cleaners. This example attempts to mimic the style of door-plate favored by British enterprises of a certain standing in the 19th and 20th centuries. The legal requirement is for the company name to be displayed outside the registered office; cast or engraved brass is overtaken by aluminum for the junior entrepreneur and by stainless steel for multinationals.

Polished brass

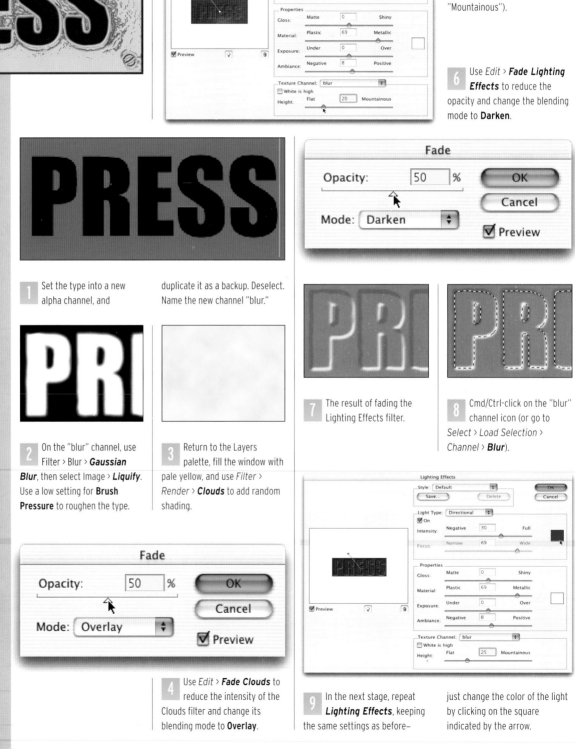

5 Use *Filter > Render > **Lighting Effects*** with the "blur" channel selected for texture. Uncheck "White is high" and use a small value in the Height slider (nearer "Flat" than "Mountainous").

6 Use *Edit > **Fade Lighting Effects*** to reduce the opacity and change the blending mode to **Darken**.

1 Set the type into a new alpha channel, and duplicate it as a backup. Deselect. Name the new channel "blur."

2 On the "blur" channel, use *Filter > Blur > **Gaussian Blur***, then select *Image > **Liquify***. Use a low setting for **Brush Pressure** to roughen the type.

3 Return to the Layers palette, fill the window with pale yellow, and use *Filter > Render > **Clouds*** to add random shading.

7 The result of fading the Lighting Effects filter.

8 Cmd/Ctrl-click on the "blur" channel icon (or go to *Select > Load Selection > Channel > **Blur***).

4 Use *Edit > **Fade Clouds*** to reduce the intensity of the Clouds filter and change its blending mode to **Overlay**.

9 In the next stage, repeat **Lighting Effects**, keeping the same settings as before– just change the color of the light by clicking on the square indicated by the arrow.

10 Use *Edit* > **Fade Lighting Effects** and change the blending mode to **Hard Light** to get this result. Deselect.

11 To embellish the plaque, make a new alpha channel and draw a screwhead in each corner. (Use the elliptical marquee tool to create a circular selection, selecting *Edit* > **Stroke** to create a white circle. Then use the pencil tool to draw the diagonal line: click where you want it to start, then Shift-click where you want it to finish.

Deselect.) Blur the channel slightly. Ctrl/Cmd-click in the "blur" channel, return to the Layers stack, invert the selection, and apply **Lighting Effects** once again (but with the light color reset to white, and with the new alpha channel, containing the screwheads, set as the texture channel).

12 The result should look similar to this. After applying the filter, leave the selection active.

13 Apply *Filter* > *Sketch* > **Chrome** at maximum settings.

14 Use *Edit* > **Fade Chrome** to reduce the opacity and change the blending mode to **Hard Light**. Deselect.

15 If you have patience and a graphics tablet, make an additional alpha channel to simulate scratch marks. Choose the smallest brush and energetically scribble white lines all over, then go to *Image* > *Adjustments* > **Invert** to produce black lines, and add a small amount of noise (*Filter* > *Noise* > **Add Noise**).

16 Return to the Layers stack, reload the "blur" selection, go to *Select* > **Inverse** and apply *Filter* > *Render* > **Lighting Effects** with the new scribbled channel selected for texture. Reduce the effect in *Edit* > **Fade Lighting Effects** by choosing blending mode **Darken** at a very low opacity value. *Select* > **Inverse** once again.

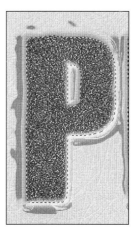

17 Apply *Filter* > *Pixelate* > **Pointillize** at a low setting to disturb the lettering infill.

18 Then use *Edit* > **Fade Pointillize** to reduce the opacity and change the blending mode to **Color Burn**. Invert the selection.

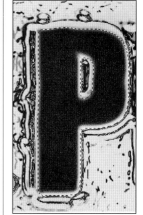

19 Use the Chrome filter (*Filter* > *Sketch* > **Chrome**) again, but this time at minimum settings.

20 Fade the Chrome effect to 50%, and change the blending mode to **Hard Light**.

21 Finally, add a small beveled edge using Inner Bevel from the Layer Style dialog.

GOOD AS GOLD

Gold effect

WHERE would we be without gold? Indestructible, malleable, and equipped with a mountain of mythological baggage, gold takes pride of place in the typonaut's armory of effects. Scarcely less precious is Photoshop's native Clouds filter which rewards the user with apparently random blotches. It's a vital weapon in the endless campaign to soften the computer screen image and achieve a naturalistic appearance.

"Carat" is from the Greek *keration*, a carob bean. Also vital to know: the world's entire production of gold since the Stone Age is estimated at 100,000 tons—that's enough to fill the long-suffering tennis court to the height of a two-story house.

1 Set the characters into an alpha channel and name it "type"; deselect.

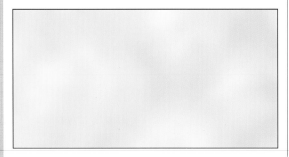

2 Return to the **Layers** palette and choose a light yellow to fill the frame. Use *Filter > Render > **Clouds*** to produce a random mottling, then reduce the effect (*Edit > Fade > **Clouds***) by around 50%. Apply a small amount of Gaussian blur.

3 Make a selection of the type channel and go to *Filter > Sketch > **Chrome***. The effect is almost imperceptible in the preview window.

4 The result of the first application of the *Chrome* filter.

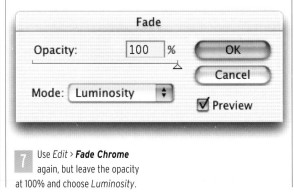

5 Reduce the filter effect, choosing *Hard Light* from the *Edit > **Fade Chrome*** menu.

6 Apply the *Chrome* filter again at the same settings —just press Cmd-F (Mac)/Ctrl-F (Windows). You should begin to see some variation appearing in the characters.

7 Use *Edit > **Fade Chrome*** again, but leave the opacity at 100% and choose *Luminosity*.

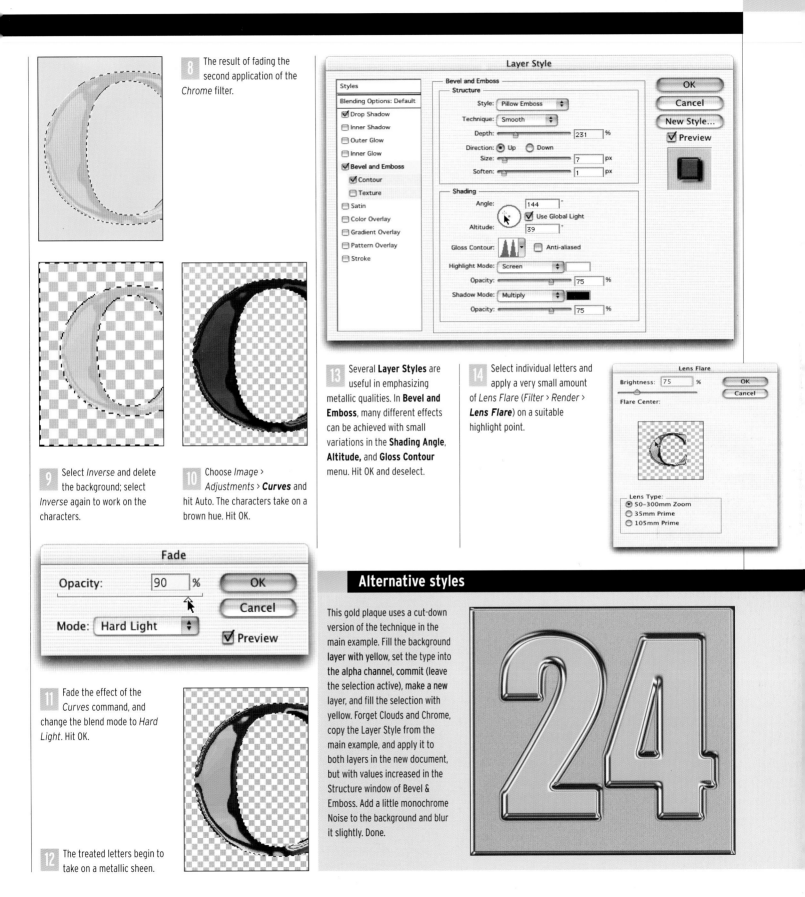

8 The result of fading the second application of the *Chrome* filter.

9 Select *Inverse* and delete the background; select *Inverse* again to work on the characters.

10 Choose *Image* > *Adjustments* > **Curves** and hit Auto. The characters take on a brown hue. Hit OK.

11 Fade the effect of the *Curves* command, and change the blend mode to *Hard Light*. Hit OK.

12 The treated letters begin to take on a metallic sheen.

13 Several **Layer Styles** are useful in emphasizing metallic qualities. In **Bevel and Emboss**, many different effects can be achieved with small variations in the **Shading Angle**, **Altitude,** and **Gloss Contour** menu. Hit OK and deselect.

14 Select individual letters and apply a very small amount of *Lens Flare* (*Filter* > *Render* > **Lens Flare**) on a suitable highlight point.

Alternative styles

This gold plaque uses a cut-down version of the technique in the main example. Fill the background layer with yellow, set the type into the alpha channel, commit (leave the selection active), make a new layer, and fill the selection with yellow. Forget Clouds and Chrome, copy the Layer Style from the main example, and apply it to both layers in the new document, but with values increased in the Structure window of Bevel & Emboss. Add a little monochrome Noise to the background and blur it slightly. Done.

POLISHED METAL

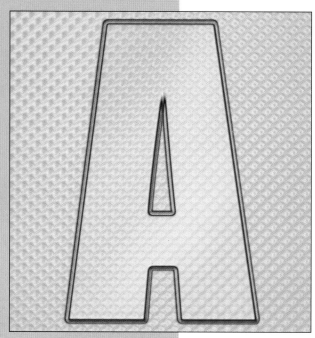

METAL refracts light, producing spectrum effects. The fine grating of interference patterns in holographic printing achieves the effect on a microscopic scale of fractions of a wavelength of light. At a larger size, the effect shown here links metallic finishes from different sources. The familiar "fish scale" appearance of decorative metal is achieved by machine-grinding and polishing. In the days of steam-powered railroads this task fell to the apprentice engine driver who used an oily rag to polish an entire locomotive. Think of him when you next hit Cmd-Z (Mac)/Ctrl-Z (Windows), and be thankful.

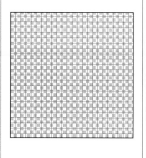

1 Set a suitably fat character into a new alpha channel. Commit the type and deselect. Return to the **Layers** palette.

2 Set up a grid that gives 25 squares per side. The exact pitch is not critical—the more squares, the more detailed will be the finished pattern. Select *View > Snap To > Grid*.

Scaling and polishing

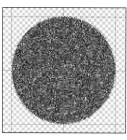

3 Zoom in to around 300% magnification, and use the ellipse tool, while holding down Shift, to make a circular selection. Fill with **50% Gray** and apply a small amount of noise.

Radial Blur

Amount   20   OK

Cancel

Blur Center

Blur Method:
● Spin
○ Zoom

Quality:
○ Draft
○ Good
● Best

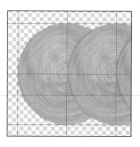

4 Apply *Filter > Blur > Radial Blur*.

5 You may need to reapply the filter to the center of the disk. Use a feathered selection to get a smooth result.

Hue/Saturation

Edit: Master

Hue: 196
Saturation: 24
Lightness: 30

OK
Cancel
Load...
Save...

☑ Colorize
☑ Preview

6 Deselect, and open the **Hue/Saturation** dialog in the **Image > Adjustments** menu. Check the **Colorize** box and adjust the sliders to obtain a metallic hue.

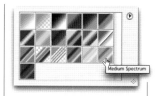

7 Select the gradient tool and choose **Medium Spectrum** in the **Gradients** menu. (Be sure you have Spectrums.grd loaded first. Do this by using the flyout menu accessed using the arrow on the top right of the Gradients window.) In the options bar, set **Screen** as the mode at 50% opacity.

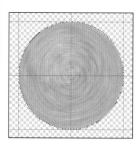

8 Drag the gradient tool diagonally across the upper left quadrant of the disk.

9 Deselect, and use the move tool with Option/Alt pressed to duplicate the disk while moving it one square to the right. Repeat this operation to make another disk. There should now be three layers in the document. Merge all the layers.

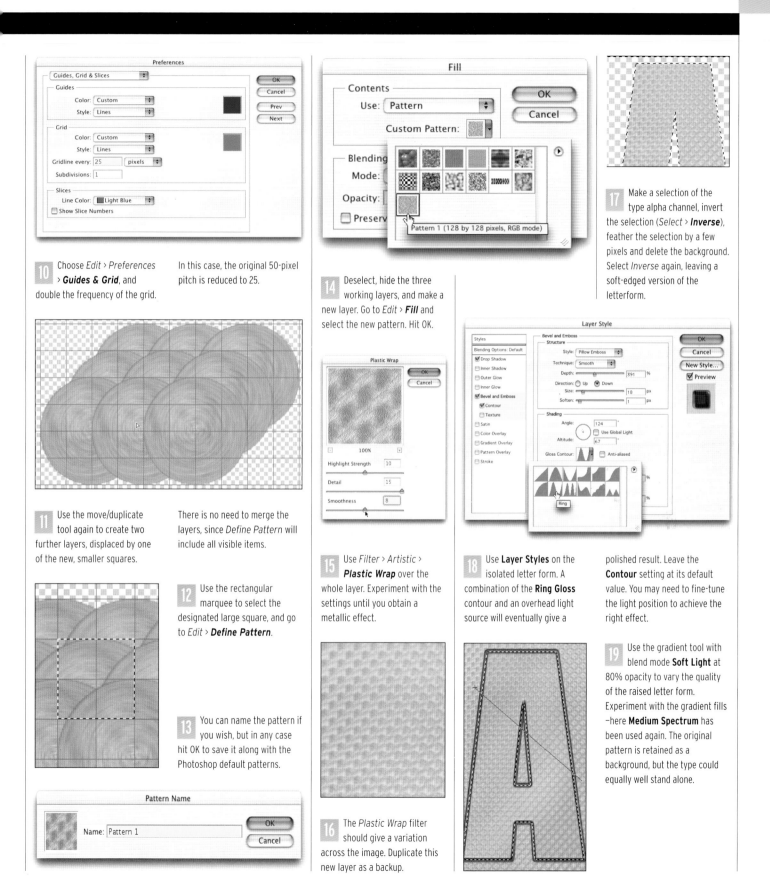

10 Choose *Edit > Preferences > Guides & Grid*, and double the frequency of the grid.

In this case, the original 50-pixel pitch is reduced to 25.

11 Use the move/duplicate tool again to create two further layers, displaced by one of the new, smaller squares.

There is no need to merge the layers, since *Define Pattern* will include all visible items.

12 Use the rectangular marquee to select the designated large square, and go to *Edit > Define Pattern*.

13 You can name the pattern if you wish, but in any case hit OK to save it along with the Photoshop default patterns.

14 Deselect, hide the three working layers, and make a new layer. Go to *Edit > Fill* and select the new pattern. Hit OK.

15 Use *Filter > Artistic > Plastic Wrap* over the whole layer. Experiment with the settings until you obtain a metallic effect.

16 The *Plastic Wrap* filter should give a variation across the image. Duplicate this new layer as a backup.

17 Make a selection of the type alpha channel, invert the selection (*Select > Inverse*), feather the selection by a few pixels and delete the background. Select *Inverse* again, leaving a soft-edged version of the letterform.

18 Use **Layer Styles** on the isolated letter form. A combination of the **Ring Gloss** contour and an overhead light source will eventually give a polished result. Leave the **Contour** setting at its default value. You may need to fine-tune the light position to achieve the right effect.

19 Use the gradient tool with blend mode **Soft Light** at 80% opacity to vary the quality of the raised letter form. Experiment with the gradient fills –here **Medium Spectrum** has been used again. The original pattern is retained as a background, but the type could equally well stand alone.

20/20 VISION

THE ACID TEST for mime artist duos is to manhandle a large and imaginary sheet of plate glass across a crowded street. Successful performers score points for stopping the traffic. They trade on our inability to resolve the optical signals offered by the glass surface. So the world is divided into two groups: those who have walked at speed into a glass door—and the rest. Clean glass viewed in subdued light shows no reflections; the imperfections due to surface dirt or abrasion are the only clues.

1 First choose the image you want to reflect, and then create a document in the same proportions as this image. Set the type into a layer, commit it, and rasterize.

2 Click on the "Add a layer style" icon at the foot of the Layers palette (or go to *Layer > Layer Style*), and select **Bevel and Emboss**. With the "Pillow Emboss" style selected, increase the "Size" value, then choose "Cove–Deep" from the Gloss Contour picker in the Shading panel. Next, check "Contour," make sure the Contour row is selected, and choose "Ring–Double" from the Contour picker in the Elements panel. Hit OK.

3 Here is the result of applying **Bevel and Emboss**. A neutral-colored layer has been inserted below the type to show the effect more clearly; this isn't part of the technique.

4 Use *Image > **Image Size*** to make your reflecting image slightly bigger than the type document. This will allow for some flexibility when aligning it with the letterforms. Copy the image to the clipboard.

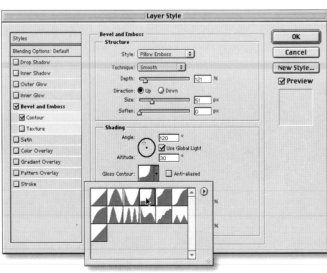

5 Make a new layer, then Cmd/Ctrl-click in the type layer's thumbnail to select the lettering. Feather this selection by a few pixels.

6 Choose *Edit* > **Paste Into**; a new layer will appear with the reflecting image masked to the shape of the letters. Cmd/Ctrl-click once again on the type layer icon, feather, and go to *Select* > **Inverse**.

7 Choose *Edit* > **Paste Into** a second time, and the empty area will be filled with the reflecting image. You will see a faint outline of the original type.

8 Move the new layer to the bottom of the stack.

9 Working on the top (type infill) layer, make sure that there is no link symbol between the image and the mask icon in the layer stack. Use the move tool to displace the image within the letters. Try the same move with the link symbol active (click between the icons) and you'll see the difference.

10 To enhance the effect, Cmd/Ctrl-click on the mask icon in the top layer, and use *Image* > **Liquify** (PS6) or *Filter* > **Liquify** (PS7) to distort the image. The red areas in the Liquify dialog window indicate the "frozen" (not selected) areas. Try the same technique on the bottom layer. A little liquefaction goes a long way.

Alternative styles

Insert a backgound. Choose the type tool with color set to midgray. Set the type, commit, and rasterize, then set the Lasso to zero pixels and cut the characters; chop the characters into large chunks first, then subdivide the result. Now select individual shards with the magic wand and rotate some. Next, open the Layer Style palette, choose Stroke, increase stroke size to maximum, and check the following: position–inside; mode–screen; fill type–gradient; style–shape burst. Move to the Bevel & Emboss section, choosing Pillow Emboss and Chisel Hard. Check Ring-Double in the shading dialog, and move the light source around until the broken pieces appear lighter than the background. Add a little Drop Shadow. Finally change the layer blend mode to Hard Light.

GLASS EYE

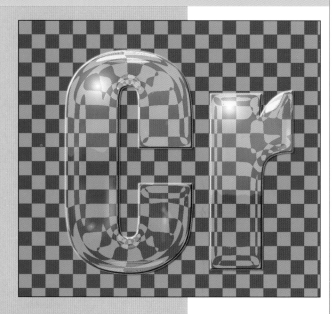

GLASS IS CURIOUS STUFF. It's not even properly solid—technically it's a supercooled liquid. Its properties are tantalizingly difficult to imitate. Opaque glass just reflects energetically; these effects are the preserve of the very shiny world of 3D modeling applications where reflections of reflections are commonplace. Transparent glass reflects; but, shaped into even a basic lens, it refracts light as well. Photoshop offers the "Glass" filter to do the basic distortion, but the image always needs additional treatment to achieve a realistic effect.

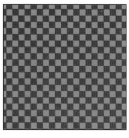

1 Make a background by drawing or importing an image, or by defining a pattern as shown here.

2 Make a new alpha channel, name it "type," and set the type in it.

Glass lens

3 To provide a suitable subject for reflection in the letterforms, either import a photograph with high contrast values or paint an all-purpose landscape as here, and paste it into a new layer in the main document.

4 In the **Channels** palette, duplicate the "type" channel and blur it with a little Gaussian blur.

5 Still working in the **Channels** palette, make a selection from the original sharp letterform (*Select > Load Selection*), invert it, and use it to fill the background of the blurred letterform channel with black (e.g. with *Edit > Fill*). This sharpens the edge of the type by removing the outer blur, leaving the inner blurred effect. Deselect.

6 With the duplicate channel ("type copy") still active, go to the **Channels** pop-up menu, choose **Duplicate Channel** and save the blurred letterform as a new Photoshop document. (You may need to use *File > Save As* to ensure the new file is saved in the correct format.)

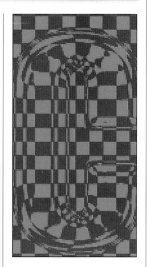

7 Return to the main document, duplicate the background layer, and apply *Filter > Distort > **Glass***. Go to **Load Texture** and load the Photoshop document you made earlier from the blurred type channel. Select maximum distortion and medium smoothness.

8 This is the result of applying the distortion. Note that the effect is applied over the whole background layer and not on the type selection only.

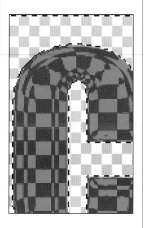

9 In order to trim away the excess background, go to the original type channel, select it and invert the selection, return to the distorted layer, and cut away the background.

10 Apply a selection of the standard Photoshop layer effects (such as Inner Bevel) to the newly trimmed letterforms to create the first of many possible glass effects.

11 Duplicate the layer you created in step 3 as a reflection image, and run the glass filter again at the same settings. This produces text containing reflections of your landscape or photo.

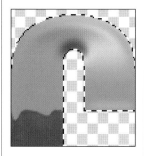

12 Load a selection from the original sharp type channel, select *Inverse* and then use that selection to remove surplus background by hitting Backspace (Mac) or Delete (Windows).

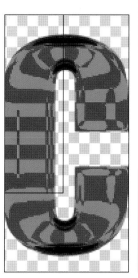

13 Duplicate the type layer, delete the effects by dragging them to the trash, and with no selection run the glass filter three or four times at exactly the same setting as before.

14 With foreground color black, go to *Select > **Color Range***. Make a new layer and fill the selected areas with white. Name the layer "highlight."

15 Set the mode of the "highlight" layer to **Overlay** and an opacity of about 85%, and set the reflection image layer to **Soft Light** at 100% opacity.

16 Further highlights can be introduced using *Filter > Render > **Lens Flare*** (not too much); you can use the dodge tool to simulate internal reflections.

Alternative styles

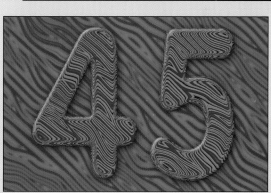

You can give the laws of optics a helping hand as follows: use steps 1-11 above (don't bother with the landscape) but make a blurred copy of the background. Insert the blurred layer under the treated cut-out letters. This miracle focusing glass beats the Hubble telescope on all counts.

RIVER AQUA

"APPLE HUMAN INTERFACE engineers labor painstakingly over every pixel you encounter," it says boldly on the Apple OS X Web page. Since an average screen contains over three quarters of a million pixels, that's a lot of pain. And do they not feel pain in Seattle too? Share in this laborious task—use our example to redecorate your screen in the currently voguish watery style. If you routinely use Windows, you may wonder what all the fuss is about, as a Mac user still wavering in older systems, you had better get used to it; warm rivers of Aqua are stealthily creeping across the landscape, and will eventually engulf you in their soft embrace.

1 Set the foreground color (in the Tools palette) to R190/G221/B251, and the background color to white. Fill with the foreground color, then apply *Filter > Sketch > **Halftone*** **Pattern**, using the settings shown here. This pattern is very popular at the moment and will go well with our Aqua effect type.

2 Type the text on a new layer choosing a serif font for the best results. Fill the text with R0/G51/B222, and name this layer "type 1."

3 Cmd/Ctrl-click in this layer to create a selection, then choose *Select > Modify > **Contract*** to reduce the selection by 7 pixels.

4 Make a new layer called "Multiply," and fill the selection with R31, G82, B255.

5 Deselect (Cmd/Ctrl-D) and then duplicate "Multiply" layer and name the new copy "gel."

6 In the "gel" layer, apply *Filter > Blur > **Gaussian Blur*** set to a radius of 5 pixels.

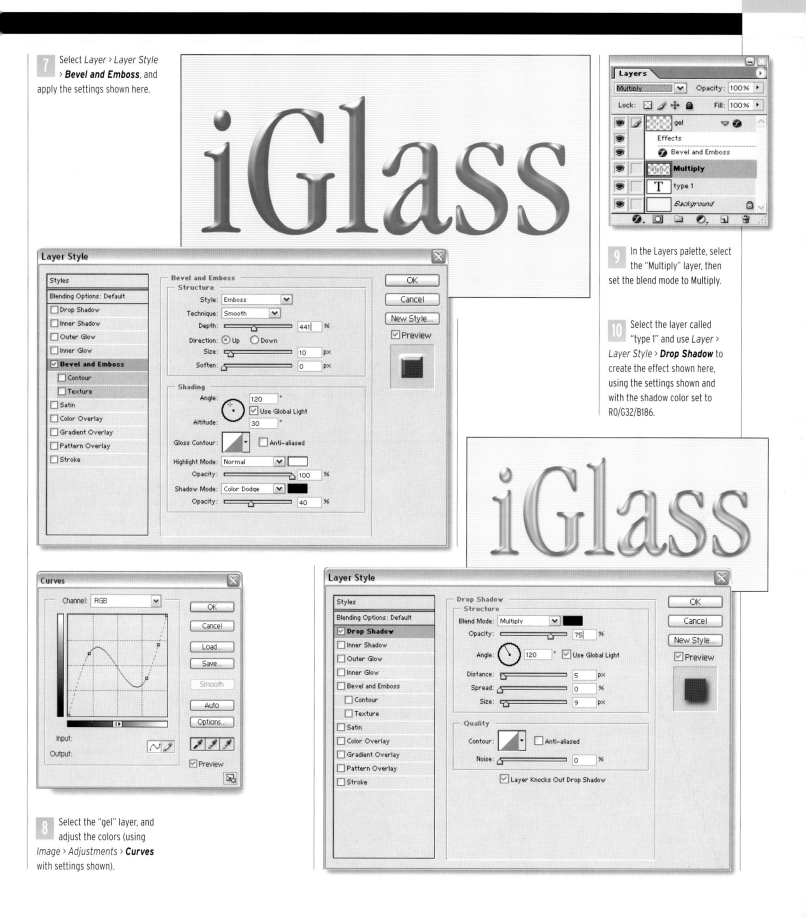

7 Select *Layer > Layer Style > Bevel and Emboss*, and apply the settings shown here.

9 In the Layers palette, select the "Multiply" layer, then set the blend mode to Multiply.

10 Select the layer called "type 1" and use *Layer > Layer Style > Drop Shadow* to create the effect shown here, using the settings shown and with the shadow color set to R0/G32/B186.

8 Select the "gel" layer, and adjust the colors (using *Image > Adjustments > Curves* with settings shown).

RAISE A GLASS

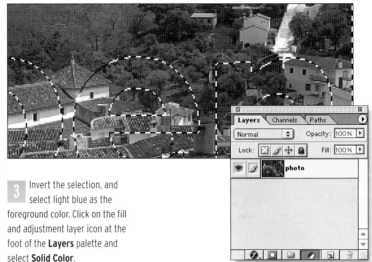

3 Invert the selection, and select light blue as the foreground color. Click on the fill and adjustment layer icon at the foot of the **Layers** palette and select **Solid Color**.

ETCHED AND FROSTED GLASS have intriguing associations. The inner mysteries of Victorian British temples of drink were obscured by shoulder-high panels of acid-etched and engraved glass. Outsiders could read of the glorious liquors and other comforts on offer inside, but could not identify individual consumers. Insiders needed only enough daylight to know whether their time was up. Funeral parlors, grocers to the aristocracy, gentlemen's outfitters, and Scottish barbers' shops were all decked out in florid capitals. Most of this opulence has been destroyed, though any window can now benefit from a thin layer of frosted, laser-cut, self-adhesive vinyl.

1 Select an image to use as the background layer.

4 This is the result of the previous move.

2 Set the type into a new alpha channel. Switch to the RGB layer and move the resulting selection to fit the image better.

5 Cmd-click (Mac)/Ctrl-click (Windows) on the icon of the mask in the "Color Fill" layer, then go to *Filter > Noise > **Add Noise*** and select 50% Gaussian noise (monochromatic).

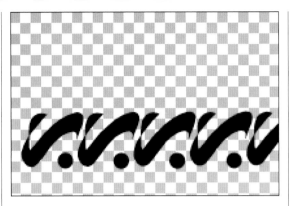

10 Now work on the background photograph: having selected the nonlettering area, it is possible to reduce the saturation of the color using *Image > Adjustments > **Hue/ Saturation***, and also to add some filtering, in this case *Filter > Distort > **Ripple***.

6 You can modify the "Color Fill" layer by importing drawn images from outside Photoshop and using them to effectively cut through the "Color Fill" layer. The underlying principle is that the darker the color in the "Color Fill" layer, the less the layer's effect on the underlying image. These curlicues were drawn in Illustrator, imported as an EPS file and combined in an alpha channel with the Photoshop type.

9 This is the result of the previous step.

11 Finishing touches courtesy of some third-party filters– the Sucking Fish filters (Japanese shareware) and Frame Curtain filters–and some work with the dodge tool.

7 Select the background photograph, and Cmd-click (Mac)/Ctrl-click (Windows) in the "Color Fill" layer to select the non-lettering area. Then choose background color black and

delete the selected area. You can now experiment with the density of the "Color Fill" layer and continue to act on it with filter effects and color change until you achieve the desired result.

8 Still working in the "Color Fill" layer, Cmd-click (Mac)/Ctrl-click (Windows) on the channel icon to select the non-lettering area and apply a very small amount of drop shadow using the **Layer Style** dialog.

Alternative styles

As an alternative, take an animated background such as this busy hotel courtyard scene. The built-in perspective effect helps to reinforce the illusion of depth and mystery, and the variety of shapes and color makes a good target for the beveled edges of the letterforms.

LIQUID ASSETS

Glass bottle

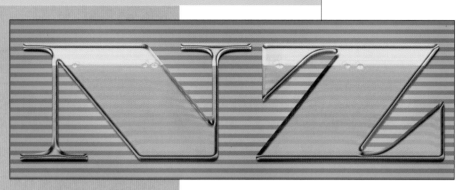

THIS EXAMPLE imagines fashionable New Zealand Pinot Noir bottled in souvenir letters. The refractive index of wine is presumably similar to water—more research is needed here. The typeface is Madrone, designed by Barbara Lind and based on wood letters in the Smithsonian Institution in Washington, DC. This kind of letterform, with enormously exaggerated differences in stroke width, is favorite prey for the type-effects enthusiast, but indigestion beckons.

1 Set the type into a new alpha channel and commit it. Deselect.

2 Select all the contents of the alpha channel, copy, go to *File* > **New**, and make a new document. When the dialog box opens, name the document "map." The copied material in the clipboard will automatically determine the other characteristics of the new document, so hit OK. Click to bring the Channels palette to the front, and paste. Save this new document to disk as a Photoshop file.

3 Duplicate the alpha channel, and name the result "blur."

4 Go to *Filter* > *Blur* > **Gaussian Blur** and apply about 15 pixels of blur to this channel.

5 Cmd/Ctrl-click in the thumbnail of the original type channel to select the letterforms, then choose *Select* > **Inverse**.

6 With the "blur" channel still selected, fill the selection with black to resharpen the edges of the type. Make the original channel invisible. Save the document in this state.

7 Return to the main document, choose new foreground and background colors–blue and turquoise in this example–and select *Filter* > *Sketch* > **Halftone Pattern** set to Line and High Contrast. Duplicate the layer.

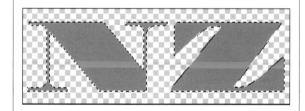

8 Hide the striped layers, create a new layer, make a selection of the type alpha channel, and fill it with color. Call this layer "Filled."

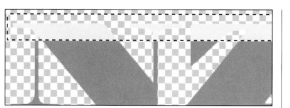

9 Select the upper part of the letters, and use *Image > Adjustments > **Hue/Saturation***, adjusting the Lightness slider to reduce color and intensity. You will need to adjust this area more carefully at a later stage. Deselect. Change the blending mode to Hard Light and reduce the layer's opacity to around 70%.

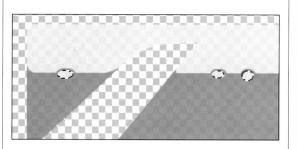

10 Cmd/Ctr-click on the layer thumbnail to select the letterforms, and use the smudge tool at a small brush setting to imitate the curve of liquid at the edge of a glass. Deselect.

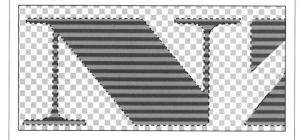

11 Try drawing small ellipses at the liquid surface; stroke them a couple of pixels with the "liquid" color, and fill them with the "glass" color.

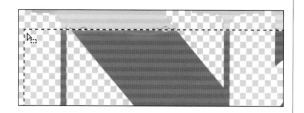

12 Make the "Background copy" layer active and hide the others. Use the inverse of the original type selection to cut away the surplus striped area. Deselect.

13 Make the "Filled" layer visible as a guide, and select the filled part of the letters, leaving the "Background copy" layer active.

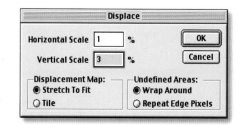

14 Choose *Filter > Distort > **Displace***. It's worth experimenting with the horizontal and vertical scale settings–the default values of 10% are generally too violent in their effect. Hit OK, and, when the next dialog opens, navigate to your "map" document to achieve the displacement.

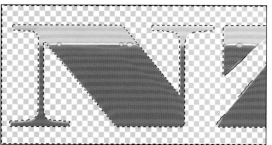

15 Here is the result of one application of the Displace filter. It may be useful to reapply it one or more times; just hit Cmd-F. The fringing at the letters' edges is not significant, it can be trimmed away later. When the distortion is nearly sufficient, deselect and apply the filter one more time to the whole image.

16 The aim is to apply greater distortion in the "liquid" than in the "unfilled" area. Use the inverse of the type selection to trim the letters again.

17 Make the top layer active and open the Layer Style menu. A setup like the one shown here will give a reasonable result. As usual in the **Bevel and Emboss** dialog, the crucial settings are the shading altitude and the gloss contour. Additionally, a spectrum gradient has been applied at a low opacity in **Gradient Overlay**, and a red tint in **Outer Glow**.

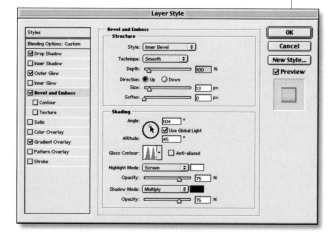

POND LIFE

THIS PROCEDURE is divisive. If you have no camera, digital or otherwise, and live in a landlocked area without easy access to open water, or have an aversion to clipart, please excuse this heartless exclusion. The vital ingredient is an image of rippling water. These particular ripples were acquired in the evening gloom of a London canal. Prerequisites: a high shutter speed and considerable patience while waiting for discarded computer packaging to clear the shot.

CHOOSING THE RIGHT RIPPLES

What's required is an image showing high contrast and a well-defined ripple structure. These breaking waves won't do. Equally, avoid puddles and tsunami.

3 Go to *Image* > **Canvas Size** and double the height of the canvas, with the original image at the foot of the frame.

4 Create a new layer under the existing one, change the foreground color to blue, and use the gradient tool (foreground to background) to insert a "sky." Use the entire image area for the gradient fill.

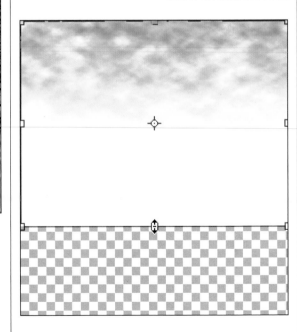

1 Import a suitable scan or digital photograph to form the background layer.

2 Save the document, then select the entire image and copy it. Select *File* > **New**, set the background to transparent, and click OK. Paste the image into the resulting document.

5 Treat the sky area with *Filter* > *Render* > **Clouds**, and reduce the effect by choosing *Edit* > **Fade Clouds** and changing the blend mode to **Screen**. Select this new layer and scale it vertically to half its depth (*Edit* > *Transform* > **Scale**).

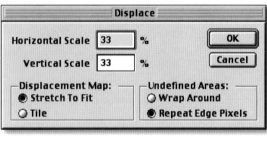

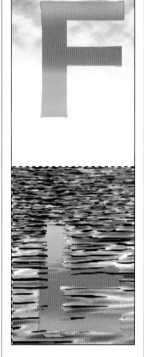

7 Still working in the flipped type layer, Cmd-click (Mac)/Ctrl-click (Windows) in the "sea" layer to select its rectangular shape. This is necessary to ensure that the eventual displacement of the letters coincides with the surface shape of the ripples.

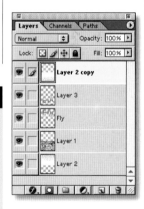

Displace

Horizontal Scale   33   %

Vertical Scale   33   %

OK   Cancel

Displacement Map:
- ● **Stretch To Fit**
- ○ **Tile**

Undefined Areas:
- ○ **Wrap Around**
- ● **Repeat Edge Pixels**

---

6 Choose a contrasting color for the type, and set the characters above the "sea" area. Rasterize the type and apply some variation with the dodge tool; then use Alt+Cmd (Mac)/Alt+Ctrl (Windows) drag to duplicate the letters in the lower half of the frame. Select *Edit >*

Transform > Flip Vertical and hit Enter. Cut the flipped letters from this layer and Paste them into a new one. Ensure that the flipped letters are an equal distance below the horizon. Change the blend mode on the letters to **Screen** at around 70% opacity.

8 Go to *Filter > Distort > Displace* and select 33% scale in both axes. Hit OK, and when the dialog box opens, choose the very first reflection image as the displacement map. Hit OK. Deselect.

9 The flipped and displaced letters should sit neatly in the ripple shapes.

Alternative styles

When the foreground water won't cooperate, make your own. Duplicate the city image, increase the canvas depth, and flip the duplicate vertically. Apply vertical motion blur. Fill a new alpha channel with 50% gray in the "water" area, apply noise and horizontal motion blur. Load this channel as a selection, move to the Layers window. Create a new top layer and fill the selection with black. Set white type along the horizon, change the Blend mode to Overlay at 50%, duplicate the layer, flip the type vertically, and position it under the original. Reset the Blend to Soft Light at 80%. Home and dry.

10 Finally, duplicate the "sky" layer and drag the duplicate to the top of the layer stack. Flip the image vertically as before, trim it to size, shift it to coincide with the sea area, and set the blend mode to **Hard Light** at around 30% opacity. Return to the "sea" layer and run the smudge tool along the horizon a few times until it begins to look more natural.

BOLD CONDENSED

CONDENSATION can occur at any temperature. Airborne water vapor condenses when it contacts a cooler surface and, since cool air can hold less vapor than warm air, droplets form. Bearing all this in mind, you can use this technique to apply condensation to any suitable surface. Perspiration may look similar, but its origins are entirely different and need not concern us here. Careful manipulation of the Layer Styles dialogs, especially the Shading values and Gloss Contour (both in Bevel and Emboss), is the key. There are so many combinations that it is worthwhile duplicating the main lettering layer to test the effects. Similarly, the "droplet" layer may be colorized and/or set to an alternative blending mode. Some perspiration may occur.

1 Set the type into a layer, commit it, and rasterize (*Layer > Rasterize > **Type***).

Condensation

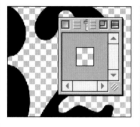

2 Make a new, square document about one-tenth the height of the main type document. Name it "drip," for example.

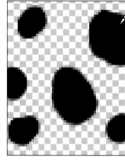

3 Zoom in on the new document, and use the ordinary paintbrush to paint some blobs; these will form a repeating pattern, so don't touch the edges of the frame.

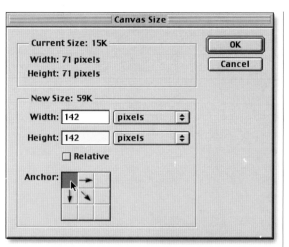

4 Go to *Image > **Canvas Size*** and double the canvas size in both dimensions; click in one corner of the **Anchor** box to establish the position of the existing image. Hit OK.

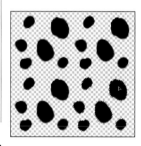

5 Reduplicate the image by Cmd-clicking/Ctrl-clicking in the **Layers** palette, then using the move tool with the Option/Alt key pressed.

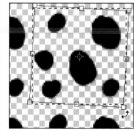

6 Use the various options under *Edit > **Transform*** to rotate and flip the components of the image until a more random appearance is achieved.

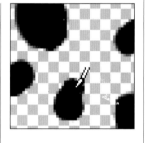

7 Use the paintbrush again to develop a few more shapes; move some of the existing blobs around as well.

8 Change the black image to gray using *Image > Adjustments > **Hue/Saturation***, and add highlights with the dodge tool set to a soft-edged brush style. Make the highlights in the top left-hand area of each blob.

Alternative styles

Expiring of thirst, and still half a day before happy hour begins? This example echoes the monastic brewing tradition of Belgium, where more or less silent monks have been fermenting extraordinary beers for over a thousand years. Choose a conventionally colored ground for the regular stuff, change to misty yellow-white for wheat beer, and to red-brown for "oud bruin."

Canvas Size dialog:

Current Size: 15K
Width: 71 pixels
Height: 71 pixels

New Size: 59K
Width: 142 pixels
Height: 142 pixels
Relative
Anchor:

OK
Cancel

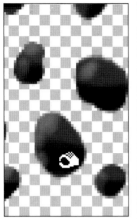

9 Switch to the burn tool and treat the lower part of each shape, this time with a hard-edged brush style.

10 You can increase the area of the pattern document by repeating steps 4 and 5, but don't flip or rotate, otherwise the highlight direction will be lost. Move and reshape a few blobs along the edges of the original blocks of blobs. Deselect and go to *Edit* > **Define Pattern**.

Pattern Name

Name: drip.psd

OK
Cancel

11 When the **Pattern Name** dialog opens, name the pattern "drip" and hit OK.

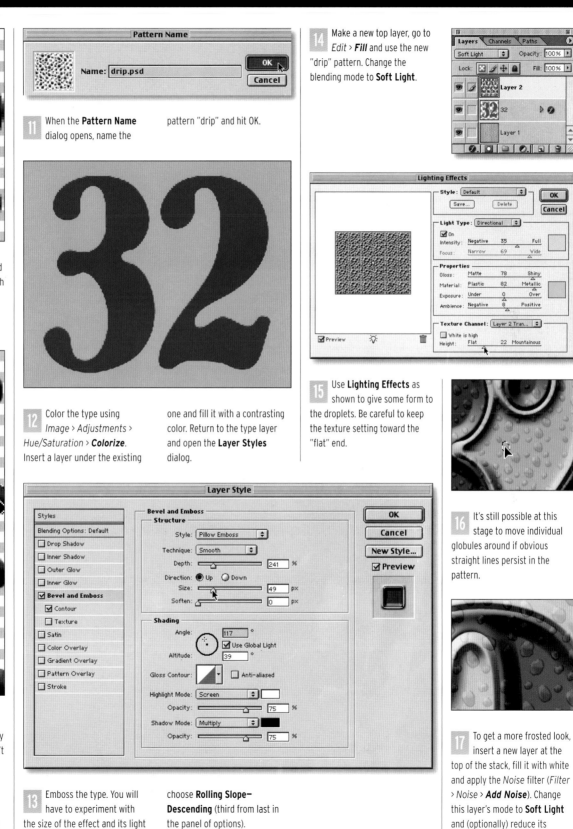

12 Color the type using *Image* > *Adjustments* > *Hue/Saturation* > **Colorize**. Insert a layer under the existing one and fill it with a contrasting color. Return to the type layer and open the **Layer Styles** dialog.

Layer Style

Styles

Blending Options: Default
☐ Drop Shadow
☐ Inner Shadow
☐ Outer Glow
☐ Inner Glow
☑ **Bevel and Emboss**
  ☑ Contour
  ☐ Texture
☐ Satin
☐ Color Overlay
☐ Gradient Overlay
☐ Pattern Overlay
☐ Stroke

Bevel and Emboss
Structure
Style: Pillow Emboss
Technique: Smooth
Depth: 241 %
Direction: ● Up ○ Down
Size: 49 px
Soften: 0 px

Shading
Angle: 117 °
☑ Use Global Light
Altitude: 39 °
Gloss Contour: ☐ Anti-aliased
Highlight Mode: Screen
Opacity: 75 %
Shadow Mode: Multiply
Opacity: 75 %

OK
Cancel
New Style...
☑ Preview

13 Emboss the type. You will have to experiment with the size of the effect and its light direction. Click on **Contour**, and choose **Rolling Slope–Descending** (third from last in the panel of options).

---

14 Make a new top layer, go to *Edit* > **Fill** and use the new "drip" pattern. Change the blending mode to **Soft Light**.

Layers ╲ Channels ╲ Paths
Soft Light   Opacity: 100%
Lock: ☐ ✎ ✚ 🔒   Fill: 100%
👁 ✎   Layer 2
👁   32
👁   Layer 1

Lighting Effects

Style: Default
Save...   Delete

Light Type: Directional
☑ On
Intensity: Negative 35 Full
Focus: Narrow 69 Wide

Properties
Gloss: Matte 78 Shiny
Material: Plastic 82 Metallic
Exposure: Under 0 Over
Ambience: Negative 8 Positive

Texture Channel: Layer 2 Tran...
☐ White is high
Height: Flat 22 Mountainous

☑ Preview

OK
Cancel

15 Use **Lighting Effects** as shown to give some form to the droplets. Be careful to keep the texture setting toward the "flat" end.

16 It's still possible at this stage to move individual globules around if obvious straight lines persist in the pattern.

17 To get a more frosted look, insert a new layer at the top of the stack, fill it with white and apply the *Noise* filter (*Filter* > *Noise* > **Add Noise**). Change this layer's mode to **Soft Light** and (optionally) reduce its opacity.

FIRE OPAL

Precious stone

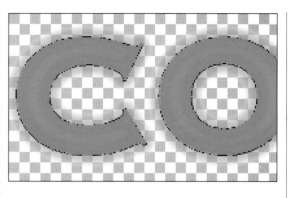

COOBER PEDY is in the middle of Australia, 530 miles (850 km) north of Adelaide and 430 miles (690 km) south of Alice Springs, and is named from the Aboriginal phrase "Man in a Hole." The men in question were, and still are, mining for opal. The gemstone's sparkling flakes are composed of minute spheres of tightly aligned silica and put the opal squarely in the drawer marked "Subjects with which the 4-color process printer would prefer not to deal." The rainbow colours are the result of a diffraction grating effect—substantially the same as those seen in a printed foil hologram.

1 Set the type into a layer and commit it (hit the check-mark button in the options bar).

2 Choose *Layer > Type> **Create Work Path**. A thumbnail of the letterforms will appear in the Paths palette.

3 Rasterize the type (*Layer > Rasterize > **Type***), load the lettering as a selection from the Paths palette (choose *Make*

Selection from the Paths pop-up menu), and fill it with turquoise (R40, G170, B210 or similar). Deselect.

4 Choose a contrasting foreground color (purple in this case—R220, G80, B255), select the paintbrush tool, and set its mode to *Difference* in the options bar. Choose a soft brush around half the width of

the letter stroke and set it to 50% opacity. In the Paths palette, click on the Work Path still selected, then on *Stroke Path* in the Paths pop-up, and choose *Paintbrush* in the subsequent dialog box.

5 The result of the brush application.

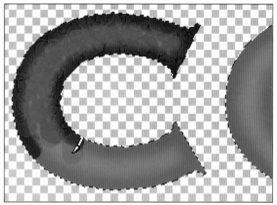

6 Cmd/Ctrl-click on the Work Path icon to turn the path into a selection, go to *Select > Inverse*, and delete the unwanted background. Invert the selection again. Choose a third strong color (this brush is orange, using R235, G155, B0) and apply successive small strokes with the same paintbrush as in Step 4, with *Difference* mode still selected, at around 80% opacity. Experiment with the *Wet Edges* option turned on or off.

7 Apply a little Gaussian Blur (*Filter > Blur > **Gaussian Blur***) to soften the brush strokes. Next try shifting the color values, as here, with the Hue function in *Image > Adjustments > **Hue/Saturation***.

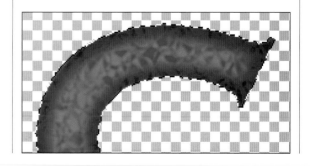

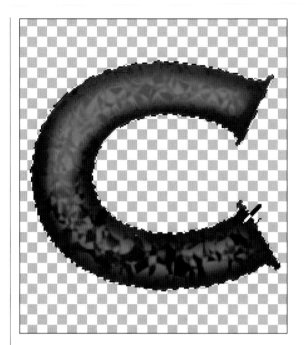

8 There are infinite possibilities for further color variations. Here an airbrush about the width of the letter stroke, and still set at **Difference**, is used to shift the color range—I used a cyan spray (R:0 G:255 B:255) at very low pressure (just 5%).

Alternative styles

The groundwork is already done for you. To get this result, set the type, commit, and open the Layer Style dialog. Click on Styles at the top left corner, and select Blue Glass (the middle one in the top row). Three changes are necessary; add Drop Shadow; change Smooth to Chisel Hard in the Structure panel of Bevel & Emboss; and change the existing gradient in Gradient Overlay to Orange/Yellow/Orange (click just to the right of the gradient image to access the gradient presets). That's it.

9 Further short puffs of the airbrush result in a deep red tone overall.

10 Persisting with the airbrush, with a much larger brush size (at least twice the width of the letter stroke), eventually yields an imitation of the characteristic fire opal appearance.

11 A black background treated first with *Filter > Noise >*. **Add Noise** (using Gaussian distribution and selecting Monochromatic), and then with a small amount of *Filter > Blur > Motion Blur* (3 pixels) helps to make the lettering stand out. The letters themselves have **Bevel and Emboss** (*Layer > Layer Style > Bevel and Emboss*) applied.

SLIPPERY WHEN WET

RECYCLING DIRECTIVES in the automobile industry now demand that components should be clearly marked with the name of the material from which they are made. This applies equally to plastics, so that the organized dissection of the life-expired family sedan gives rise to a hundred neatly labeled piles, ready for renaissance. The plastic in this example is unluckily unidentifiable—somewhere between blister-pack and nonslip carpet overlay.

1 In the toolbox, choose two dissimilar colors for foreground and background. Hit the X key to toggle between them. Fill a new window with the foreground color, then use *Filter > Sketch > **Halftone Pattern*** with Pattern Type: Line selected to produce stripes like these.

2 Hit the D key to return foreground and background colors to default, and set the type into a new layer.

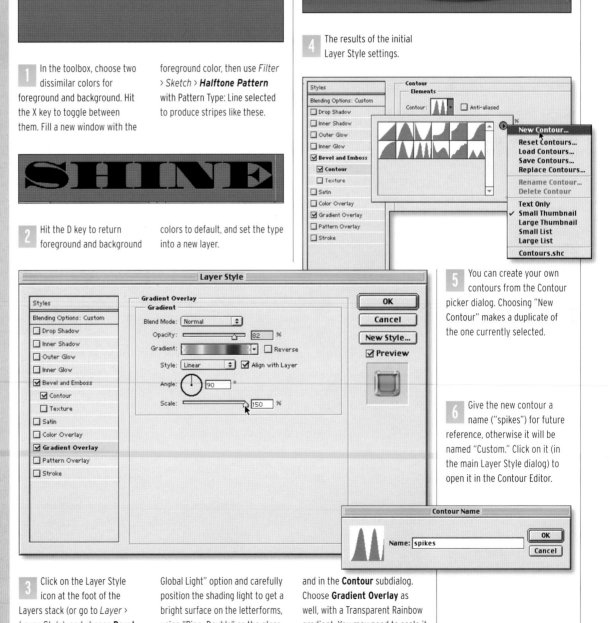

4 The results of the initial Layer Style settings.

5 You can create your own contours from the Contour picker dialog. Choosing "New Contour" makes a duplicate of the one currently selected.

6 Give the new contour a name ("spikes") for future reference, otherwise it will be named "Custom." Click on it (in the main Layer Style dialog) to open it in the Contour Editor.

3 Click on the Layer Style icon at the foot of the Layers stack (or go to *Layer > Layer Style*), and choose **Bevel and Emboss**. Switch off the "Use Global Light" option and carefully position the shading light to get a bright surface on the letterforms, using "Ring–Double" as the gloss contour both in the main dialog and in the **Contour** subdialog. Choose **Gradient Overlay** as well, with a Transparent Rainbow gradient. You may need to scale it to cover the characters completely.

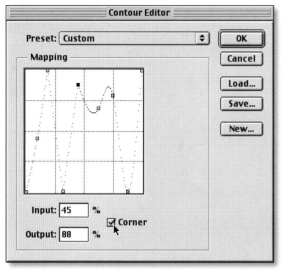

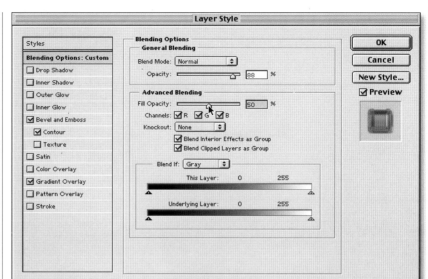

7 Add points by clicking on the graph line. To obtain sharp peaks, check "Corner" as you create or move points (this checkbox appears when you click on a point). The finished profile has several well-defined peaks and troughs. Unfortunately as soon as you modify the contour its name changes back to "Custom"; click the "New" button to name it "spikes" again.

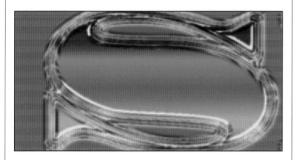

8 The initial result of using the new contour in the Shading panel of the main dialog and in the **Contour** subdialog. There is now a wider margin where the background can show through, though the highlights need attention.

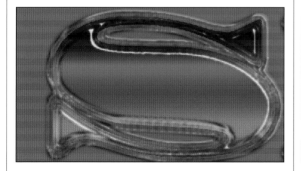

9 Moving the shading light can produce a better result.

10 Click on **Blending Options: Default** at the head of the Layer Style dialog to influence the degree of transparency of the effect. Make sure "Blend Interior Effects as Group" is checked, then move the "Fill Opacity" slider.

11 Reducing the Fill Opacity allows the background layer to show through the whole letterform, though the highlights are not affected.

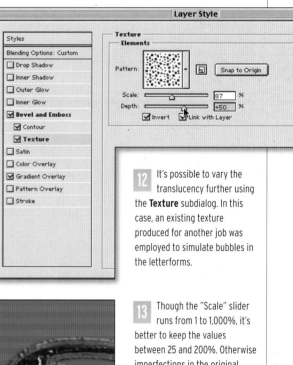

12 It's possible to vary the translucency further using the **Texture** subdialog. In this case, an existing texture produced for another job was employed to simulate bubbles in the letterforms.

13 Though the "Scale" slider runs from 1 to 1,000%, it's better to keep the values between 25 and 200%. Otherwise imperfections in the original texture will become obtrusive. In the final version, small drop shadows and inner shadows have been added in the Layer Style dialog to help define the characters.

SOFT PLASTIC

Plastic: translucent

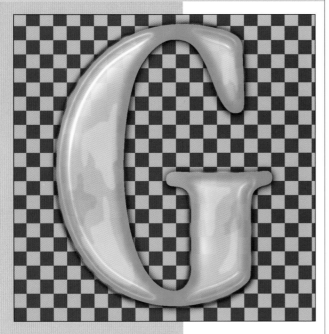

G IS FOR GARAMOND Bold Condensed, the cheerful, all-purpose fat friend of indecisive typographers looking for uncontroversial solutions for middling headlines. Claude Garamond designed the original roman version in 1530, but later complained, "I gained very little profit from my work of carving and casting type … those who can only cut letters make little progress … they (only) build comfortable nests for booksellers, they bring them honey."

CHOOSING THE RIGHT BACKGROUND

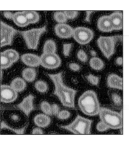

The pattern in the main example is made from *Filter* > *Sketch* > **Halftone Pattern**, with large high-contrast dots colorized, overlaid with a colored layer. If your taste is more exotic, try **Texture Explorer** in KPT Filters 3.0. This is Golden Eggplant Blend from the Metal menu (see pages 168–173 for more KPT effects).

1 Create a suitably complex background by dropping and importing an image, or creating a pattern from scratch, as here.

2 Make a new alpha channel and set the type in it.

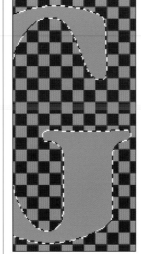

3 Make a new layer and fill the selection with a color.

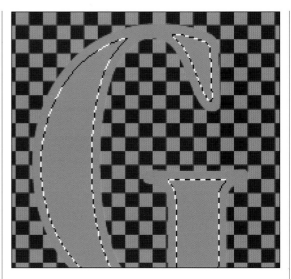

4 Go to *Select* > *Modify* > **Contract** and reduce the area of the selection. Then use *Select* > **Feather** to soften the edge.

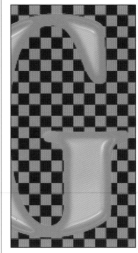

5 Use the feathered selection with *Image* > *Adjustments* > **Hue/Saturation** to lighten the internal area of the letterform, and go to *Filter* > *Artistic* > **Plastic Wrap** to produce highlights. You'll need to experiment with the slider levels to get the right result. Finally, having applied the plastic wrap effect, go to *Edit* > **Fade Plastic Wrap** and change the mode to **Overlay**.

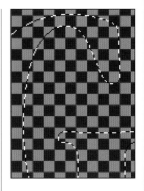

6 Cmd-click (Mac)/Ctrl-click (Windows) on the type channel to select the letter shape, then go to the background layer and press Cmd-J (Mac)/Ctrl-J (Windows) to make a new layer which contains the selection, i.e. the letterform filled with the pattern.

7 The layer stack should now look like this.

8 With the new layer still active, load the selection again and go to *Select* > *Modify* > **Contract** and decrease the selection by a few pixels. Then invert that selection and blur the resulting narrow strip around the letter. Then go to *Image* > *Adjustments* > **Hue/Saturation** and darken that edge.

9 Using the lasso tool, make a rough selection of one of the major strokes of the letterform.

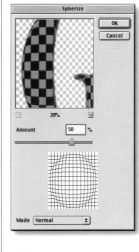

10 Refine the selection by using the nudge command (hold down the Cmd [Mac]/Ctrl [Windows] key and tap the left cursor key followed by the right key).

11 Go to *Filter* > *Distort* > **Spherize** to simulate the lenslike effect of the plastic.

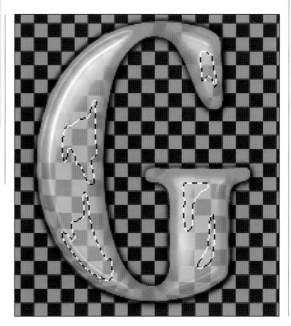

12 With all three layers visible, set the opacity of the top layer to 85%.

13 You can enhance the effect by making small feathered selections to represent reflections, and making them lighter or darker.

Alternative styles

To join in this festival of excess, do the following: set and commit the type (blue will do); rasterize, and select the characters; choose a medium paintbrush in a contrasting color, set to Difference mode and with Wet Edges. Paint horizontal stripes across the characters, changing colors from time to time. Deselect and use all the tools in Image > Liquify to distort the type. Hit OK, and select the characters again. Return to the Liquify dialog and use the same tools at lower settings to stir up the colors. Because the background area is "frozen" this time, the distortion is confined to the interior of the letters. A little Drop Shadow and Bevel and Emboss (Inner Bevel, increased in size) with Contour selected, brings the affair to an oleaginous conclusion. You may care to continue with Chrome, Plastic Wrap, etcetera, or not.

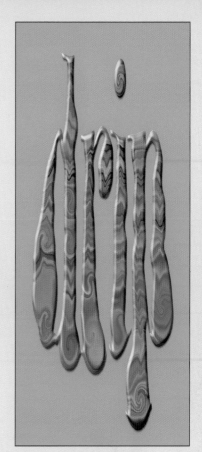

BOILERPLATE

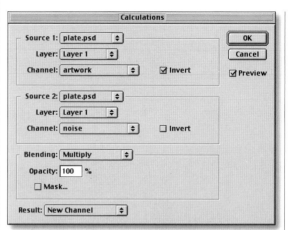

FOR MAXIMUM authenticity, carve a wooden master (all in reverse), press firmly into a shallow tray of casting sand, remove, and carefully fill the impression with molten brass. Allow to cool, and remove from the tray. Paint the sunken areas to taste, and grind and polish the raised lettering. Or try the shortcut described here.

1 This artwork was scanned in, cleaned up, and embellished with four screw-heads. (It could equally well be drawn from scratch.)

2 Copy this layer and paste it into a new alpha channel. Then go to *Image > Adjustments > Invert* to interchange the white and black pixels. Name this channel "artwork."

3 Make another alpha channel, fill it with **50% Gray**, and apply noise using the noise filter (*Filter > Noise > Add Noise*). Call this channel "noise"; it will form the basis for the cast background of the plate.

4 Using the *Calculations* function under the *Image* menu, merge the two alpha channels as shown in this dialog box.

5 Name the resulting channel "merged" and apply a few pixels of blur.

6 Return to the **Layers** palette, make a new layer, fill it with a suitable color for the background of the casting, then go to *Filter > Render > Lighting Effects* and use the new "merged" channel as the texture channel.

7 This shows in close-up the result of applying the *Lighting Effects* filter.

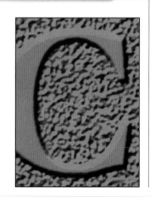

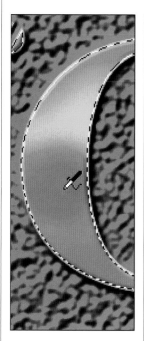

8 Select a suitable foreground color, which will become the surface of the raised lettering, make a new layer, and load the selection from the "artwork" channel. Go to *Select > Modify > **Contract*** and reduce the area of the letterforms by one or two pixels. Then fill with the chosen color.

11 In the finished version, a magic wand selection made from the edge of the "artwork" channel has been used to cut the plate out of its background, and a smaller selection was used to introduce a colored channel around the edge of the plate. The effects sprayed on the letterforms were reduced and slightly blurred to give a more natural appearance.

9 Reduce the selection still further to leave a bright edge around the letterforms, choose a contrasting color, in this case green, and spray with the airbrush set to a low pressure value in mode **Multiply**.

10 Reflections can be introduced using several methods. In this case the lasso selects a possible area of reflection, and *Image > Adjustments> **Hue/Saturation*** is used to darken and desaturate that area. You can equally well use the airbrush tool set to mode **Multiply** to spray layers of contrasting color.

Alternative styles

Four alpha channels together contributed to the representation of old movable type (above). A basic character (reversed for authenticity) was heavily blurred, and the result was merged (in the Calculations menu) with a light covering of noise. The merged channel started out with overall noise, but a selection of the original character was used to remove the texture from the face of the character. Two areas of black served to represent the gaps between adjoining characters. In the Layers palette, an area of plain gray was filtered using Lighting effects with the fourth channel used for the texture map. Using the original character selection, a soft red airbrush set to Dissolve simulated the beginning of inking-up.

PACKING A PUNCH

MOVABLE TYPE DATES from the 15th century, when the vital punch-making techniques were founded in the jewelry trade. First, you carve the letter in reverse out of a steel block. Start with something manageable like 144pt so you can see what you're doing. When satisfied, strike the punch firmly into a block of copper. Melt a mixture of lead, tin, and antimony and pour into the copper mold. Allow to cool. Ink up and print. In Photoshop, the Lighting Effects filter fills most of this labor. And there's a bonus: if you leave out the Mask function when doing the Calculations, you'll be rewarded with convincing casting marks around the letter edges.

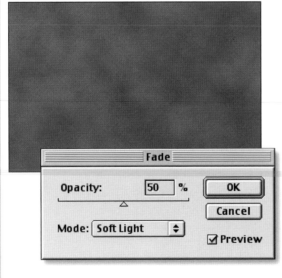

1 Create a new document and fill it with a dull metal color, the one used here is made up by mixing R140, G150, B160.

2 Use *Filter > Render > **Difference Clouds*** to vary the surface. Decrease the intensity of the effect with *Edit >* **Fade Difference Clouds** as shown here. This creates a now slightly mottled surface on which you can overlay the text.

3 Choose foreground color white, create a new alpha channel and set the type, commit and deselect. Duplicate the alpha channel. Name the duplicate "blur" and apply *Filter > Blur > **Gaussian Blur***.

4 Use the magic wand tool, set to a low tolerance value, to isolate the purely white parts of the letterforms.

Uncheck "Contiguous" in the options bar to ensure the selection of all the white areas.

5 With the selection still active, create another channel (a new one, not a duplicate) and name it "white."

Hit key "D," then "X" to make the foreground color black and the background white. Press Delete and deselect. Blur very slightly.

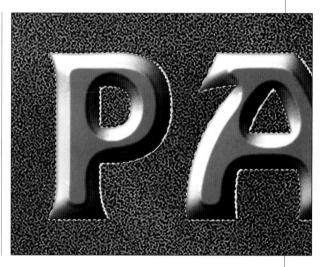

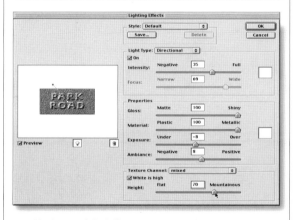

6 Use *Image* > **Calculations** to blend the "blur" and "white" alpha channels. Choose *Screen* as the blend mode, and select the original type channel (Alpha 1) as the mask. Name the resulting channel "mixed." Create the embossed effect with *Filter* > *Render* > **Lighting Effects.** Use the Shiny and Metallic sliders at maximum settings and choose "mixed" as the texture channel.

7 To smooth the edge between the letters and the background, select the blur tool and give it a small soft brush setting. Go to the Channels palette and Cmd/Ctrl-click on the thumbnail of the Alpha 1 channel to get a selection of the original letterform. Open the Paths palette, select *Create Work Path* in the popup menu and accept the default setting. Choose *Stroke Path* in the same menu. The blur tool will appear—hit OK.

8 To treat the background, use the same alpha channel selection, invert it (*Select* > *Inverse*), feather it slightly (*Select* > *Feather*) and use *Filter* > *Sketch* > **Reticulation** at low values. Fade the filter effect to around 10% of its original strength (*Edit* > **Fade Reticulation**).

Alternative styles

If you travail further in the Calculations menu, you'll see that it's possible to achieve stranger combinations. These colliding forms started out in the same style as the main example (but as type on two separate layers), then the subsequent channel merging took a different direction. Selecting the default Multiply at the foot of the Calculations dialog inevitably means that overlapping black areas obscure each other completely. In this case, Invert was chosen alongside each channel and Difference selected as the Blend mode. The result was an intersecting grayscale image on a white ground. Select Invert, and the result is a channel (light image on a black ground) that can be used as a texture map in Lighting Effects, simulating both convex and concave surfaces.

NUMBERPLATE

NOT ALL METAL is chrome. Less theatrical metallic effects are easily made with subtler textures and glows. This humble street numberplate evokes aspects of the enameler's art, and also demonstrates that the shape and style of the background is often just as important as the letterforms themselves.

CHOOSING THE RIGHT TYPEFACE

Three nonrunners in the inlaying stakes. From the top: Decorated–too grim; Chromatic–too shiny already; Preternatural–too crazy. What's required is a fat, mannered face with plenty of meat on the bone. Falstaff, for example.

1 Make a new alpha channel, naming it "type," and set the type.

2 With the selection still active, go to *Select* > *Modify* > **Contract** to reduce the selection area.

3 Make a second new alpha channel, and fill the selection with white. Name this channel "infill."

4 With the "type" channel visible, use the elliptical marquee tool to draw a shape around the character. Make a new alpha channel, naming it "border." Go to *Edit* > **Stroke** and stroke the selection with white to produce a fat outline. Deselect the selection.

5 The channels palette should look something like this.

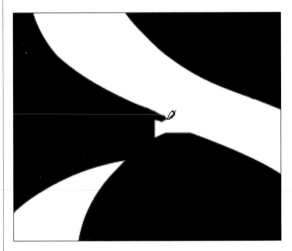

6 If necessary, use a small brush to clean up the "infill" channel.

7 Use the magic wand tool to isolate the center of the "border" channel, make a new channel (name it "back"), fill the selection with **50% Gray**, and apply *Filter* > *Pixelate* > *Mezzotint* > **Fine Dots**. Apply a slight blur.

8 Once again, select the center of the "border" channel. Return to the **Layers** palette and fill the selection with the chosen color. With the selection still active, go to *Select > **Load Selection***, choose the "type" channel, and choose **Subtract from Selection**. Click OK, then go to *Select > Modify > **Contract*** to reduce the selected area. Finally, feather the selection by a few pixels.

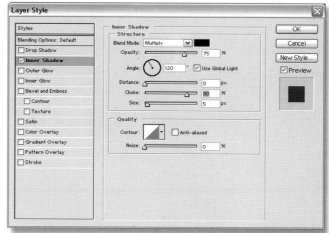

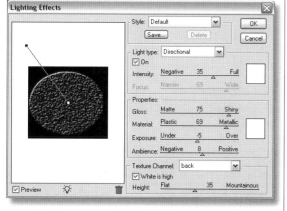

9 Apply *Filter > Render > **Lighting Effects***, using the "back" channel for the texture effect. Experiment with the light type and direction, as well as with the **Properties** section of the dialog.

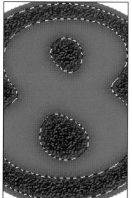

10 After applying *Lighting Effects*, go to *Edit > **Fade Lighting Effects*** and choose **Darken** as the mode.

11 Apply a little motion blur to the ellipse, make a new layer, make a selection of the "type" channel, and add the "border" selection as well (*Select > Load Selection > **Add to Selection***). Fill the selection with a contrasting color. Name this layer "type layer."

12 Apply layer styles to the new layer. Use "Inner Shadow" with a high choke setting to define the raised area.

13 Having applied layer styles, work with the dodge tool to vary the surface of the raised area.

14 Make a further new layer, load the "infill" channel as the selection, fill it with a new foreground color, and apply a small amount of noise. Apply a little motion blur to soften the effect, and choose *Layer > Layer Style > **Inner Shadow***. Finally, change the layer's blend mode to **Color Burn**. If necessary, you can return to the "type" layer and add detailed highlights by hand with the dodge tool.

EROSION

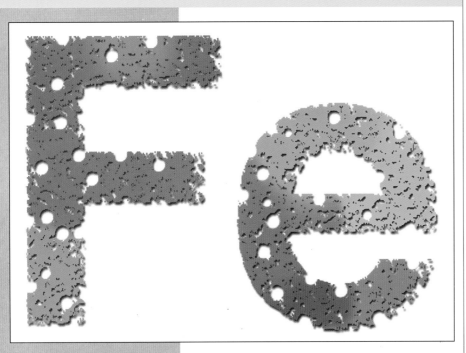

STAINLESS STEEL is the material of choice for your architectural sign. Even so, the shiny surface may be attacked by corrosive airborne chemicals, opportunistic gunmen may pepper the sign with buckshot, thoughtless birds may roost uninvited. Far better, then, to adopt the wily strategy of prewashed and worn-out denim, and do the damage yourself before the enemy gets a chance. This example tries to mimic the ever-present threat of machinegun fire and general deterioration, overlaid with a mysterious and strangely charming colored patina. Go to *Image > Mode > **Grayscale*** for the truly urban grit effect.

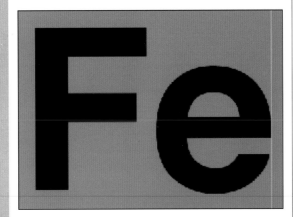

1 Set the type into a new alpha channel.

2 Now duplicate this type channel.

Metal: eroded

3 Deselect the type. Go to *Filter > Pixelate > **Mezzotint*** and apply the **Grainy dots** filter. Repeat the filter until the lettering is broken up to the desired degree.

4 It's a good idea to name the two alpha channels.

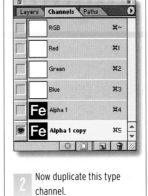

5 Create a new layer. Go to *Select > **Load Selection*** and choose the filtered channel.

6 In order to remove the unwanted background texture, go once again to *Select > Load Selection*; choose the clean channel and check **Invert** and **Subtract from Selection**.

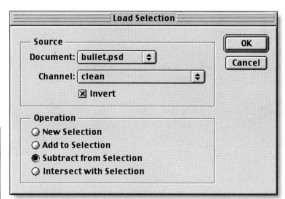

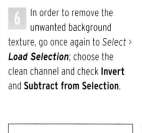

7 This is the result of combining the two selections.

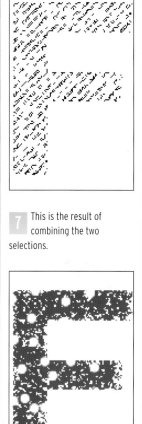

8 Fill the selection with the chosen foreground color by pressing Option-Delete (Mac)/Alt-Delete (Windows). Then, using the eraser at different brush diameters, place a number of bullet holes in the lettering. It's important to use the eraser rather than the white paintbrush to make the holes, for the benefit of the subsequent steps.

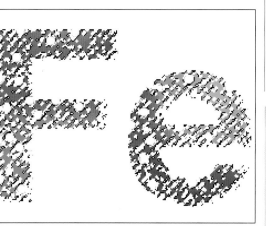

9 Activate the painted area by Cmd-clicking (Mac)/Ctrl-clicking (Windows) in the layer. You can then use the soft paintbrush set to **Color Dodge** or **Difference** to modify the color of parts of the lettering.

10 By this stage the image should appear as above.

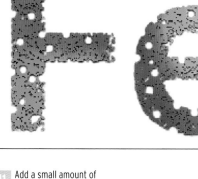

11 Add a small amount of **Drop Shadow** from the **Layer Style** dialog to make the edges crisper.

Alternative styles

Famously hard-wearing, though not (yet) bullet-proof, denim makes a handy background for a violently abused logo. Select the type layer, enlarge and feather the selection, and use it to desaturate the background fabric. All far easier than sitting in the bathtub for hours.

QUICK SILVER

MERCURY won't stand up, and it won't lie down either, but Photoshop can suspend the laws of physics and shepherd it into useful shapes. Real mercury reflects the environment absolutely, but this example ignores the science and concentrates only on internal reflections. There is a small principle wobbling around in here. Many Photoshop filters are so powerful and spectacular in their effect that it's tempting just to apply them at full strength to the whole image, and move on. In this example, global application of the *Chrome* filter at the usual settings would result in a grim metallic porridge. Though that may one day find an application as a cover treatment for some as yet unpublished book, in this case the better trick is to be cooly moderate, selective, and subtle.

1 Set the type into a layer. Choose a bold face and use the **Tracking** feature in the **Character** palette to close up the letters. Commit the type and rasterize it.

2 Use the rectangular marquee to select the lower part of the letters and the empty foreground area. Feather this selection by a few pixels.

3 Choose *Image* > **Liquify** (Photoshop 6) or *Filter* > **Liquify** (Photoshop 7) to disturb the letterforms. The pink tint denotes the "frozen" area where distortion will not occur. When you are finished, hit OK and deselect.

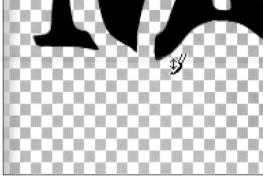

4 Zoom in and use a small paintbrush set to **Hard Light** to add globules and introduce further distortion to the letters.

5 With painting complete, duplicate the layer as a backup, Cmd-click (Mac)/Ctrl-click (Windows) in the **Layers** palette to select the image, and fill it with **50% Gray**. Deselect.

6 To get the best result, use the lasso set at zero pixels to select a part of the artwork. Hold down the Cmd/Ctrl key and nudge the image left and right with the cursor keys to isolate just one section.

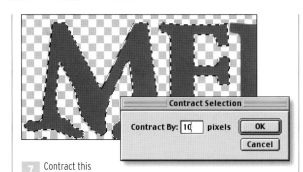

7 Contract this selection by a few pixels (*Select* > *Modify* > **Contract**). As a guide you should aim at around 75% of the original stroke width.

11 Toward the end of the process you may need to run **Auto Curves** (*Image* > *Adjustments* > *Curves* > **Auto**) on the image to increase the brightness and contrast.

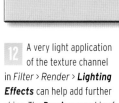

8 Feather this reduced selection by a few pixels, and use *Image* > *Adjustments* > **Hue/Saturation** to darken the interior of the letters. Leave this selection active.

9 Use *Filter* > *Sketch* > **Chrome** at maximum settings. Using just a couple of characters means that the reflections are limited to those between the two characters. Otherwise the filter tends to produce many confusing lines.

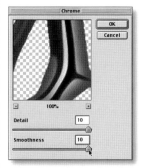

12 A very light application of the texture channel in *Filter* > *Render* > **Lighting Effects** can help add further shine. The **Preview** panel is of no help, so be prepared for several attempts.

13 To give the characters some extra warmth and depth, **Layer Effects** have been used, particularly **Gradient Overlay** at a low value. There is also a small amount of **Drop Shadow** and **Bevel and Emboss**. Feathered selections have additionally been treated with *Filter* > *Render* > **Lens Flare**.

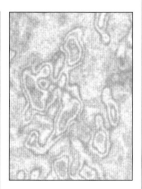

10 The result of treating the first two characters.

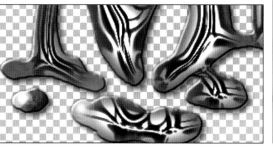

14 To make a matching background, fill the frame with **50% Gray**, apply *Filter* > *Render* > **Clouds**, then *Filter* > *Sketch* > **Chrome** at maximum settings. The result will be too dark–use *Image* > *Adjustments* > **Hue/Saturation** to lighten it.

FREEZER

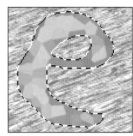

GIVE YOURSELF a break and choose a face where half the work's been done already. Ragged armies of type designers have labored for over 400 years to supply a cornucopia of fonts—flick through from Aachen (no need to linger there) to the works of Hermann Zapf (not only Dingbats, but Optima, Melior, and Palatino). Though you'll find many where painful labor might usefully have been avoided, there are truckloads of two-dimensional designs that cry out loudly for re-birthing in the round.

3 Make a new layer, load the selection from the type channel, fill the selection with light blue, go to *Select* > *Modify* > **Contract** to reduce the selection by a few pixels, then lighten this interior area of the letterforms using *Image* > *Adjustments* > **Hue/Saturation**. Deselect.

4 Select all the contents of this lettering layer, and apply *Filter* > *Pixelate* > **Crystallize**. Experiment with the cell size to get the maximum number of cells to appear within the letterforms using the preview function.

6 Apply *Filter* > *Artistic* > **Plastic Wrap** at high values to the letterforms. Then go to *Edit* > **Fade Plastic Wrap**, change the mode to **Multiply** and slightly reduce the opacity value, i.e. the strength of the filter.

1 Make a new alpha channel and set the type in it.

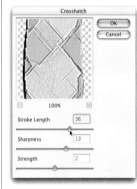

5 Run *Filter* > *Brush Strokes* > **Crosshatch** on the new layer. Experiment with the settings to maximize the effect.

7 To increase the effect, use *Filter* > *Distort* > **Glass** with texture **Frosted**. Then re-apply *Plastic Wrap* once again, using the fade function to finesse the effect.

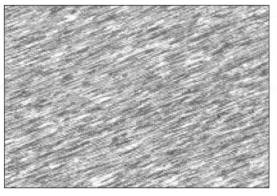

2 Import or create a suitable background layer. In this case, the noise filter (*Filter* > *Noise* > **Add Noise**) was applied at a high value to a plain gray background. Motion blur was applied at an angle, and then *Filter* > *Render* > **Lighting Effects** was used to add a crystalline quality.

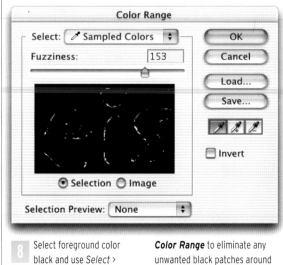

8 Select foreground color black and use *Select* > **Color Range** to eliminate any unwanted black patches around the edge of the letterforms.

9 Set the layer's opacity to about 90% to allow some of the background to show through, and then work on the highlights with the dodge tool. At this stage you can experiment with the **Layer Style** dialog. In this case the standard drop shadow has been added.

10 Finally, go to *Image* > *Adjustments*> **Hue/ Saturation** and use the saturation slider to take out most of the color from the lettering.

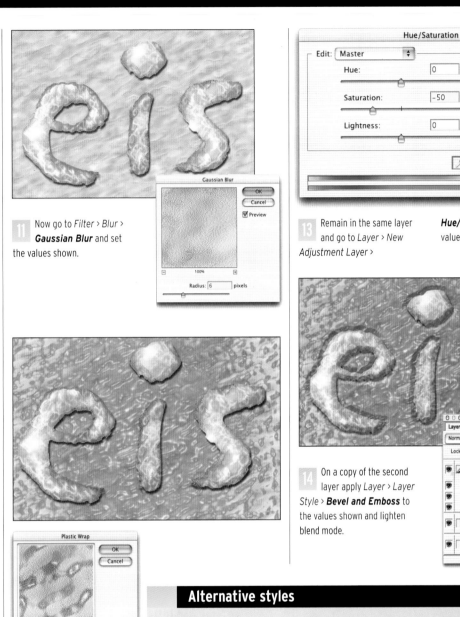

11 Now go to *Filter* > *Blur* > **Gaussian Blur** and set the values shown.

12 Next, apply *Filter* > *Artistic* > **Plastic Wrap** to the values shown above.

13 Remain in the same layer and go to *Layer* > *New Adjustment Layer* >

Hue/Saturation and apply the values shown above.

14 On a copy of the second layer apply *Layer* > *Layer Style* > **Bevel and Emboss** to the values shown and lighten blend mode.

Alternative styles

Change the foreground color to light blue and the background to light grey. Run *Filter* > *Render* > **Clouds**, then follow steps 4 to 7 of the main example. Attack the principal type with Clouds, then with Plastic Wrap; finally apply Bevel & Emboss with a small Chisel Hard edge in Pillow Emboss. The subtitle is solid grey type on a low-opacity Color Burn layer. Position the new layer above the type and background layers and experiment with the sliders.

CUT IN STONE

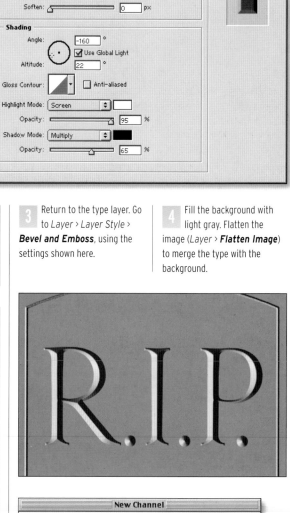

IN THE PURSUIT of permanence and a lasting memorial, take up your virtual mallet and chisel. Real carvers draw, pounce, and cut the unforgiving stone in an abrasive cloud of health-threatening chips. You can still wear the hat, though. To resemble Eric Gill in full memorial-cutting regalia, take a piece of white paper around 16 inches (400mm) square, fold in all four edges by two inches (50mm), then open up the folds to obtain a kind of paper tray. Staple or glue the corners, invert, close the curtains and try for size.

1 Set the type in a shade of gray on a white background.

3 Return to the type layer. Go to *Layer > Layer Style > **Bevel and Emboss***, using the settings shown here.

4 Fill the background with light gray. Flatten the image (*Layer > **Flatten Image***) to merge the type with the background.

2 Select the rectangle tool. With the "Create new work path" option selected in the options bar, draw a box around the text. Use the "Add anchor point" tool (a variant of the pen tool) to add a new anchor point in the middle of the top of the box; move the point up and adjust the direction points to create a smooth curve. Make sure the background layer is selected in the Layers palette, and then (in the Paths palette) stroke the work path with an appropriately thick line.

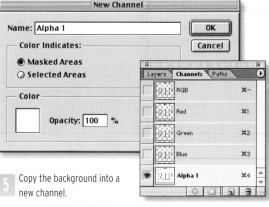

5 Copy the background into a new channel.

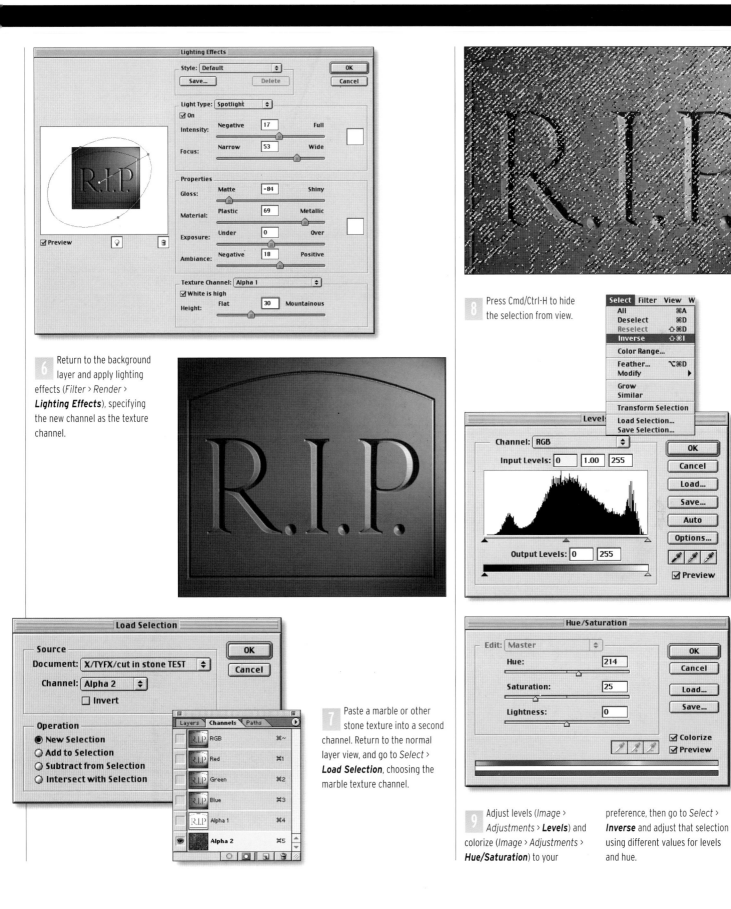

6 Return to the background layer and apply lighting effects (*Filter* > *Render* > **Lighting Effects**), specifying the new channel as the texture channel.

7 Paste a marble or other stone texture into a second channel. Return to the normal layer view, and go to *Select* > **Load Selection**, choosing the marble texture channel.

8 Press Cmd/Ctrl-H to hide the selection from view.

9 Adjust levels (*Image* > *Adjustments* > **Levels**) and colorize (*Image* > *Adjustments* > **Hue/Saturation**) to your preference, then go to *Select* > **Inverse** and adjust that selection using different values for levels and hue.

LET'S ROCK

ROUGH-HEWN rocks can provide a welcome contrast to elegant letter-cutting (see previous page). Imagine yourself as Mount Rushmore sculptor John Gutzon Borglum, abseiling down the face of a half million-point high limestone cap. Dynamite, pneumatic rock-drills, plaid shirts, and bold gestures are on the menu. Knock out a couple of handholds, spit on your hands (optional), and fire away.

1 Type the letters in white on a gray background, using different point sizes and adjusting the baseline. Duplicate the type layer and hide the duplicate for now.

2 Make a selection of the type by Cmd/Ctrl-clicking in the type layer in the Layers palette, and expand the selection by 32 pixels (*Select > Modify > **Expand***).

3 Make a new layer, drag it under the type layer, and fill the selection with black.

4 Use *Edit > **Transform** > Distort* to create a shadow shape. Deselect.

5 Rasterize the type layer, and go to *Filter > Distort > **Displace***. Choose a rocklike texture for the displacement map.

6 Repeat the filter for the shadow layer (Cmd/Ctrl-F).

Lighting Effects

Style:	Default
	Save... / Delete
Light type:	Spotlight
☑ On	
Intensity:	Negative 35 Full
Focus:	Narrow 69 Wide
Properties:	
Gloss:	Matte 0 Shiny
Material:	Plastic 69 Metallic
Exposure:	Under 0 Over
Ambience:	Negative 8 Positive
Texture Channel:	rock Transparency
☑ White is high	
Height:	Flat 100 Mountainous

☑ Preview

Layer Style

Styles	Bevel and Emboss
Blending Options: Default	**Structure**
☐ Drop Shadow	Style: Outer Bevel
☐ Inner Shadow	Technique: Smooth
☐ Outer Glow	Depth: 86 %
☐ Inner Glow	Direction: ● Up ○ Down
☑ Bevel and Emboss	Size: 23 px
☐ Contour	Soften: 0 px
☐ Texture	**Shading**
☐ Satin	Angle: 73 °
☐ Color Overlay	☑ Use Global Light
☐ Gradient Overlay	Altitude: 30 °
☐ Pattern Overlay	Gloss Contour: ☐ Anti-aliased
☐ Stroke	Highlight Mode: Screen
	Opacity: 75 %
	Shadow Mode: Multiply
	Opacity: 75 %

OK / Cancel / New Style... / ☑ Preview

7 Apply *Filter > Render > **Lighting Effects*** to the type layer. Set the texture channel to the current layer's transparency ("ROCK Transparency").

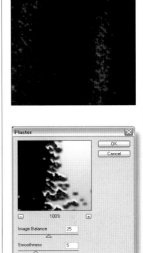

8 Make the second type layer visible, and position it below the main type layer. To the main type layer apply *Layer* > *Layer Style* > **Bevel and Emboss**, using the settings shown in step 7.

11 On a new layer, above the rest, apply *Filter* > *Render* > **Clouds**.

13 Apply *Filter* > *Texture* > **Grain**, with Grain Type Contrasty. Go to *Edit* > **Fade Grain** and change the blend mode to Soft Light. Go to *Filter* > *Distort* > **Displace**. Choose a rough texture for the displacement map.

14 Go to *Filter* > *Sketch* > **Plaster**. Go to *Edit* > **Fade Plaster** and reduce the opacity to 30%, with blend mode Color Burn.

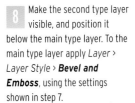

12 Apply *Filter* > *Blur* > **Motion Blur** with a high Distance setting and an almost vertical angle. (Warning: if you use too high a value for Distance, the layer may become transparent.)

9 Change the main type layer's opacity to 75%, and the shadow layer's opacity to 70%.

10 Rasterize the lower type layer and use the rectangular marquee tool to select the "O." Go to *Image* > *Adjustments* > **Hue/Saturation** and reduce the lightness. Deselect.

15 Apply a drop shadow to the top type layer (*Layer* > *Layer Style* > **Drop Shadow**).

CAPITAL BUILDING

PHOTOSHOP strives to leap out of plain two-and-a-half dimensional space into fully-rounded 3D. In the Transform menu, you find Perspective; a noble gesture which needs a little help from the neighboring Scale function to get a satisfactory effect. In the Filters menu, Spherize gives you bumps; Pinch gives you pits,while 3D Transform just results in depression. So, in this example of brickwork, the rules of perspective are ignored in favor of an elementary 30° projection. Speculative shadows are an optional extra, added on a final top layer, set to Multiply. If you aim to create more than one such character in a working lifetime, invest in a 3D modeling program.

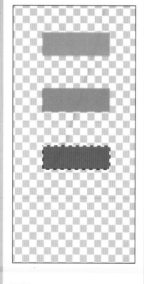

1 In a large document, use the Marquee tool to draw an area in the proportion 3:1, (300 x 100 pixels in this case) and fill it with a brick color (we used R255, G82, B33). Use the Move tool with Alt held down to duplicate the colored area, and use *Image* > *Adjustments* > **Hue/ Saturation** to darken it slightly. Repeat the process once more. Leave the selection active.

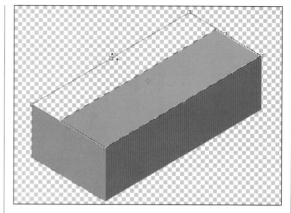

2 Choose *Edit* > **Free Transform**. When the Options bar appears you will see three angle control boxes at the right side. Enter -30° in the last box on the right (angle of vertical skew). Leave the others untouched and click the tick button to confirm.

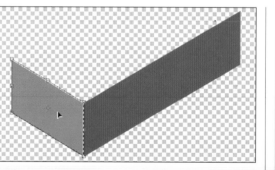

3 Select the next area with the Magic Wand tool, and go once again to *Edit* > **Free Transform**. This time enter 47% in the width (W) box (to avoid later pain while bricklaying) and 30° in the vertical skew angle box. Plant the cursor in the middle of the skewed area and drag it to coincide with the first face of the "brick." Try to match the edges exactly. Though the Zoom tool is not available during the transformation process, you can still enlarge the image using Cmd/Ctrl-+ and scrolling to the most useful position. When you are satisfied, press the tick button to apply the transformation.

4 Treat the last face in a similar way, but enter -60° in the "rotate" box (third from the right in the Options bar) and 30° in the last box. Leave the center one at 0°. Drag and resize as necessary to create the top face of the brick.

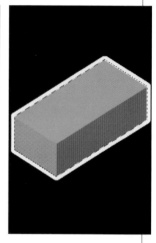

5 Select the whole brick; choose a light foreground color for the "cement joints," and select *Edit* > **Stroke** set to 10 pixels to create an encircling line. A black background has been inserted here to make the line more apparent.

6 Cmd/Ctrl-click again to select the brick with its new joints, and apply some noise (*Filter* > *Noise* > **Add Noise**) using the settings shown. Copy the brick to a new document (Cmd/Ctrl-C > Cmd/Ctrl-N > OK > Cmd/Ctrl-V) as a backup. Return to the original window.

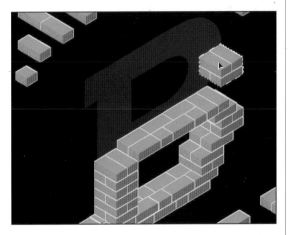

10 Once you have made a collection of bricks, gather them in unused corners of the screen. To create bricks that run in the opposite direction, just flip them horizontally. Or, if you are feeling virtuous and wish to retain the lighting setup, return to the beginning of this example and start over with angle values reversed. Insert a guide character, skewed to the correct angle, under the construction layer and reduce its opacity. Then start building at the lowest, most distant point of the scene.

11 As the character takes shape, useful combinations of bricks can be formed to speed up the process.

7 Reduce the brick to a manageable size. The shortest edge of this one is 30 pixels tall (including the joint). The document is 1200 pixels tall, so there could be 40 courses of bricks. In practice, the "perspective" effect and simple exhaustion reduce this to around 25.

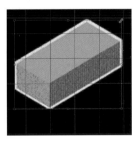

8 You can display a grid (*Edit > Preferences > Guides & Grid*) to help guide the vertical spacing of the bricks, but don't choose Snap to Grid or the task will become impossible. This image is enlarged 300% to help achieve the right dimensions.

9 To speed up bricklaying, you can duplicate individual bricks to make rows. With a brick selected, the Move tool with Alt depressed will duplicate the brick on the same layer, but you will have to be accurate when aligning. Alternatively you can duplicate without selecting. This will generate a brick on a new layer, so you can nudge it around before merging with the layer below. Incidentally, it's easy to make different color bricks using *Image > Adjustments > Hue/Saturation*. The lower row shows how to make a half-, or any other fraction, of a brick. Just roughly lasso the rear

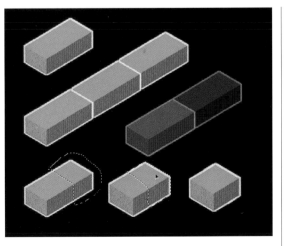

section and drag it forward with the Move tool. If the brick is still too big, repeat the process. At this stage, it is vital to check that two half-bricks equal one whole brick.

12 Selecting the whole structure, inverting the selection, nudging it slightly, and then using the Eraser can remove spurious cement joints at the brick edges. Shift the selection as necessary as you move around the image.

NUMBER TILE

Ceramic effect

3 Holding down the Option/Alt key, begin dragging the circle to the other corner; as you drag, press and hold the Shift key. This will allow you to copy the circle to the other corner while keeping it level. Do this for the other two corners as well. Draw two more small circles for the fastening holes. Commit the shape, then go to *Layer* > *Rasterize* > **Shape**.

4 Use the magic wand tool to select the shape; cut it and paste it into a new alpha channel.

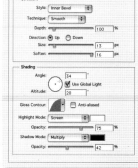

THERE'S NO Ceramic filter in Photoshop (though Mosaic lurks in the Pixelate menu and Mosaic Tiles are available as a texture). Glass and metal are well-represented, even plaster gets a mention. Where are Porcelain (with sliders from matt to gloss), Meissen, Matt Terra-cotta, Ming Dynasty Dribble, Automatic Delftware, Ancient Potsherd, Unwanted Vase, and Crazed Bathroom? Let's hope that these shortcomings will be addressed in future releases.

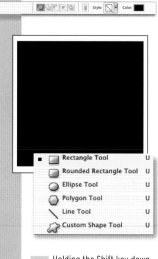

Texturizer dialog showing Texture: Sandstone, Scaling 100 %, Relief 3, Light Dir: Top Right.

7 Apply *Filter* > *Texture* > **Texturizer** with the sandstone texture set to the values shown.

Drop Shadow dialog — Blend Mode: Multiply, Opacity: 60 %, Angle: 34, Use Global Light, Distance: 5 px, Spread: 10 px, Size: 5 px, Quality — Contour, Anti-aliased, Noise: 0, Layer Knocks Out Drop Shadow.

New Channel dialog — Name: tablet, Color Indicates: Masked Areas / Selected Areas, Color Opacity: 50 %.

1 Holding the Shift key down, use the rectangle tool to draw a square box to occupy most of the document. Make sure that "Create filled region" is selected in the options bar.

Tool menu: Rectangle Tool U, Rounded Rectangle Tool U, Ellipse Tool U, Polygon Tool U, Line Tool U, Custom Shape Tool U.

5 Return to the shape layer. Load the selection from the alpha channel (*Select* > *Load Selection*) and invert it (*Select* > *Inverse*).

Load Selection dialog — Source Document: X_TYFX_number tile_l..., Channel: tablet, Invert, Operation: New Selection, Add to Selection, Subtract from Selection, Intersect with Selection.

Smooth Selection dialog — Sample Radius: 7 pixels.

2 With the "Subtract from shape area" option selected, use the ellipse tool to draw a circle centered on one corner of the box (hold the Option/Alt and Shift keys down).

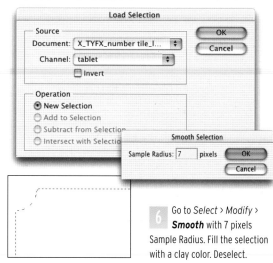

6 Go to *Select* > *Modify* > **Smooth** with 7 pixels Sample Radius. Fill the selection with a clay color. Deselect.

Bevel and Emboss dialog — Structure: Style: Inner Bevel, Technique: Smooth, Depth: 100 %, Direction: Up / Down, Size: 13 px, Soften: 16 px. Shading — Angle: 34, Use Global Light, Altitude: 28, Gloss Contour, Anti-aliased, Highlight Mode: Screen, Opacity: 75, Shadow Mode: Multiply, Opacity: 42 %.

8 Use **Bevel and Emboss** and *Drop Shadow* layer styles for shading (*Layer* > **Layer Style**).

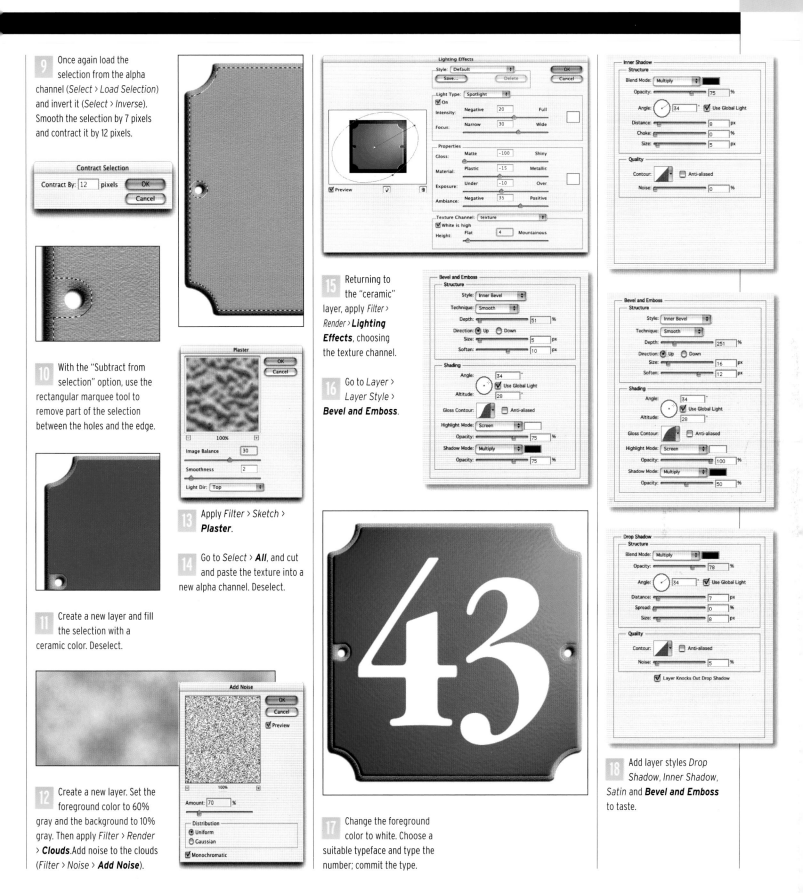

9 Once again load the selection from the alpha channel (*Select > Load Selection*) and invert it (*Select > Inverse*). Smooth the selection by 7 pixels and contract it by 12 pixels.

Contract Selection
Contract By: 12 pixels

10 With the "Subtract from selection" option, use the rectangular marquee tool to remove part of the selection between the holes and the edge.

11 Create a new layer and fill the selection with a ceramic color. Deselect.

12 Create a new layer. Set the foreground color to 60% gray and the background to 10% gray. Then apply *Filter > Render > Clouds*. Add noise to the clouds (*Filter > Noise > **Add Noise***).

Plaster
Image Balance 30
Smoothness 2
Light Dir: Top

13 Apply *Filter > Sketch > **Plaster***.

14 Go to *Select > **All***, and cut and paste the texture into a new alpha channel. Deselect.

Add Noise
Amount: 70 %
Distribution
○ Uniform
○ Gaussian
☑ Monochromatic

Lighting Effects
Style: Default
Light Type: Spotlight
☑ On
Intensity: Negative 20 Full
Focus: Narrow 30 Wide
Properties
Gloss: Matte -100 Shiny
Material: Plastic -15 Metallic
Exposure: Under -10 Over
Ambiance: Negative 35 Positive
Texture Channel: texture
☑ White is high
Height: Flat 4 Mountainous

15 Returning to the "ceramic" layer, apply *Filter > Render > **Lighting Effects***, choosing the texture channel.

16 Go to *Layer > Layer Style > **Bevel and Emboss***.

Bevel and Emboss
Structure
Style: Inner Bevel
Technique: Smooth
Depth: 51 %
Direction: ● Up ○ Down
Size: 5 px
Soften: 10 px
Shading
Angle: 34
☑ Use Global Light
Altitude: 28
Gloss Contour: □ Anti-aliased
Highlight Mode: Screen
Opacity: 75 %
Shadow Mode: Multiply
Opacity: 75 %

17 Change the foreground color to white. Choose a suitable typeface and type the number; commit the type.

Inner Shadow
Structure
Blend Mode: Multiply
Opacity: 75 %
Angle: 34 ☑ Use Global Light
Distance: 8 px
Choke: 0 %
Size: 5 px
Quality
Contour: □ Anti-aliased
Noise: 0 %

Bevel and Emboss
Structure
Style: Inner Bevel
Technique: Smooth
Depth: 251 %
Direction: ● Up ○ Down
Size: 16 px
Soften: 12 px
Shading
Angle: 34
☑ Use Global Light
Altitude: 28
Gloss Contour: □ Anti-aliased
Highlight Mode: Screen
Opacity: 100 %
Shadow Mode: Multiply
Opacity: 50 %

Drop Shadow
Structure
Blend Mode: Multiply
Opacity: 78 %
Angle: 34 ☑ Use Global Light
Distance: 7 px
Spread: 0 %
Size: 8 px
Quality
Contour: □ Anti-aliased
Noise: 5 %
☑ Layer Knocks Out Drop Shadow

18 Add layer styles *Drop Shadow*, *Inner Shadow*, *Satin* and ***Bevel and Emboss*** to taste.

FRET NO MORE

ATTRACTIVE, warm to the touch, easily manipulated … a block of wood is a highly satisfactory thing. Equipped with a fretsaw from the Photoshop Junior Carpenter's Kit, one can carve one's name (or social-security number) with pride. All the real-world woodworking functions are there: for Stain, read Colorize; for Polish, read Layer Style; for Oh Dear, I've Cut That Wood Too Short, read Undo.

1 Choose an informal face (this is Reporter 2) and set the type into an alpha channel.

Commit it and deselect.

2 Return to the Layers palette and import a suitable texture. This is a home-made scan of an odd length of pine. Duplicate the layer and name it "skew."

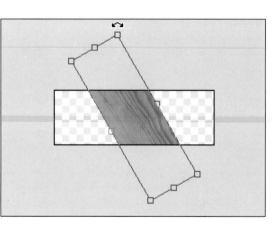

3 Reduce the view to a small percentage, and drag out the edges of the frame to reveal the gray rebate. Working on the "skew" layer, go to Select > **All** and then Edit > Transform > **Rotate**. Hold down the Shift key while rotating to ensure you can achieve an exact 45˚ angle. Hit OK.

4 Duplicate the skewed slice to fill the frame and merge all the skewed layers.

5 You should now have two layers–one with a horizontal grain, and a second skewed at 45˚. Go to Image > **Trim** to remove the unseen surplus outside the working area. This has no immediate effect on the image, but relieves the program of the burden of keeping these additional pixels in memory.

6 Make a selection of the type channel, and delete it from the skew layer. Deselect.

7 Use Image > Adjustments > **Hue/Saturation** to darken and desaturate the skew layer.

Use the move tool to shift the whole layer a few pixels up and leftward.

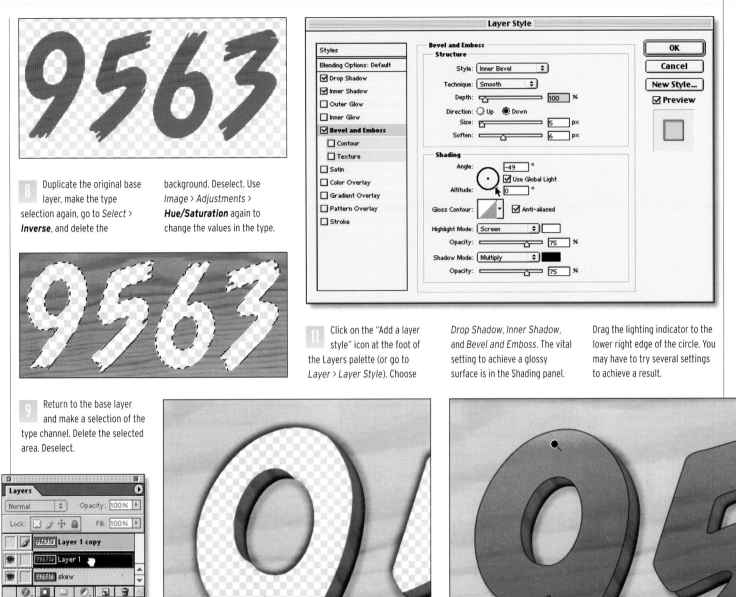

8 Duplicate the original base layer, make the type selection again, go to *Select* > **Inverse**, and delete the background. Deselect. Use *Image* > *Adjustments* > **Hue/Saturation** again to change the values in the type.

11 Click on the "Add a layer style" icon at the foot of the Layers palette (or go to *Layer* > *Layer Style*). Choose *Drop Shadow*, *Inner Shadow*, and *Bevel and Emboss*. The vital setting to achieve a glossy surface is in the Shading panel. Drag the lighting indicator to the lower right edge of the circle. You may have to try several settings to achieve a result.

9 Return to the base layer and make a selection of the type channel. Delete the selected area. Deselect.

10 Move the base layer above the skew layer.

12 When viewed with the skew layer, the original base layer should now resemble this view. Make the top layer active, and nudge the letterform to fit exactly on its base.

13 To ensure that there are no unwanted white edges, add a thin stroke in the Layer Style dialog. Here, a small amount of highlighting has been applied with the dodge tool.

UTTERLY ROUTED

Wood: routed

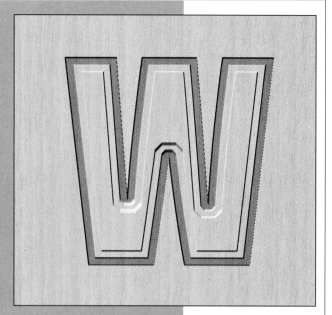

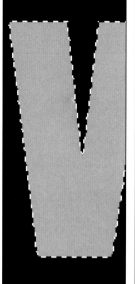

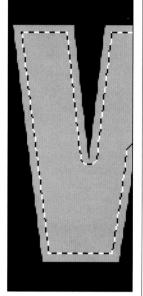

THE TIMBER here is from a clip-art collection, but it would be just as good, more realistic, and cheaper, as a scan from a real chunk of wood (not too heavy). Clip-art textures come from a world where moth and rust (or woodworm) doth not corrupt. The routing business, which supports a magazine publishing industry of its own, would like routing to become a recognized art-form, or possibly an Olympic discipline. They will supply an alphabet template set which will enable you to carve letters neatly and repeatably into decorative plastic laminates. Please don't.

1 Make a new alpha channel and use the type tool to set the character.

3 This is the result of the previous step.

4 With the selection still active, go to *Select > Modify > **Contract*** and set a value of about 8 pixels.

6 Return to the normal layer view. Open a file containing a suitable texture–in this case a wood veneer from a clipart CD–copy it and paste it into your document.

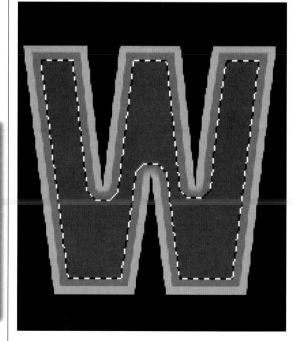

2 With the selection still active, go to *Edit > **Fill*** and fill the selection with black at opacity 15% and set to **Multiply**.

5 Continue in this way, contracting the selection and filling it with the same fill

until the letterform is filled and the selection has contracted to nothing.

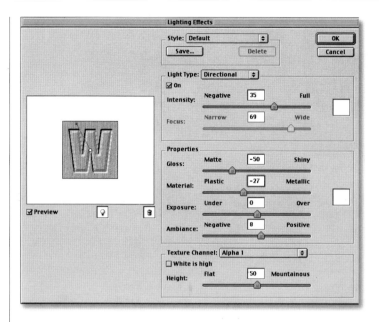

Alternative styles

Using the techniques outlined in the main example, you can easily vary the relationship between the surface wood and the routed letterforms. Use the alpha channel selection to subdivide a copy of the initial routed result into "routed" and "un-routed" layers. Set both layers to a lesser opacity and juggle with the blend modes above the base layer. In this case, the un-routed layer gives a rich tone by being set to Color Burn at 80% opacity. Go a stage further by colorizing one or both of these upper layers—try inverting the image for more unnatural effects.

7 With the newly pasted layer selected, go to *Filter > Render > **Lighting Effects*** and set up the options as shown, selecting the alpha channel as the texture channel.

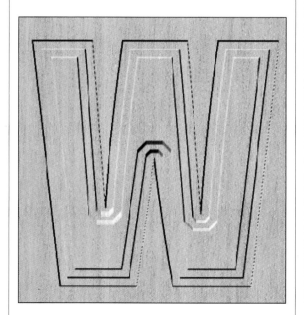

8 This is the result of the previous step.

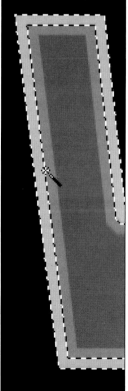

9 Returning to the alpha channel, choose the magic wand tool with low tolerance and select the outermost band of gray.

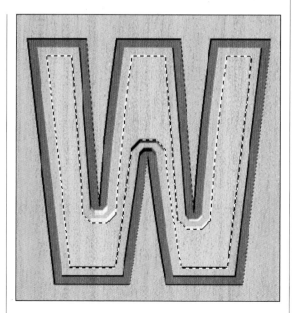

10 The new edge selection can be used with *Image > Adjustments > **Hue/Saturation*** to change the color of the outside area to simulate staining.

SANDS OF TIME

GIVE THANKS for *Canvas Size*. When dealing with the perspective of trackless desert, it helps to start with a broad canvas. Photoshop allows a maximum area of 30,000 pixels square—this equates to a single-layer file-size of 2 gigabytes, and a grisly task for the average machine. Even on a more realistic and modest scale, it's still less troublesome to start with an oversize area than to clone chunks of scenery in the corners when you run out of image.

The city of Khartoum sits at the confluence of the Blue and White Niles; the surrounding desert is noted for its mirages.

1 Create a canvas about four times deeper than your final image size. Fill with yellow and apply a small amount of monochromatic noise (*Filter > Noise >* **Add Noise**). Then apply *Filter > Render > **Clouds*** and immediately go to *Edit > **Fade Clouds***, and change the mode to **Multiply**.

2 Change the foreground color back to black. Fill a new layer with **50% Gray** and apply *Filter > Sketch > **Halftone Pattern***. Try various combinations of size and contrast.

Desert illusion

3 Change the mode of the striped layer to **Soft Light** and reduce its opacity.

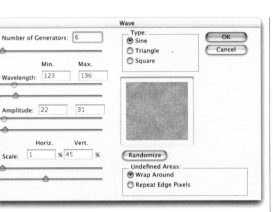

4 Merge the two layers, and use *Filter > Distort > **Wave*** on the merged layer. With so many variables, it's useful to keep a written note of successive trial settings.

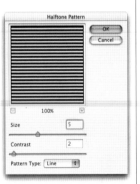

5 Reduce the view to a smaller size, then click and drag the window edges to reveal the gray "rebate" outside the working area. Select the whole layer, go to *Edit > Transform > **Perspective*** and drag the lower handles outward. The moiré effects you may see are just screen artifacts and do not affect the full-size image. Press Enter to commit the transformation.

6 Keeping the same view, choose *Edit > Select All*, followed by *Edit > Transform > **Perspective***, and transform again (*Edit > Transform > **Scale***), this time simply using the central lower handle to scale the image vertically. Incidentally, the apparently oversize selection shows that Photoshop is still retaining image information from outside the working area. This can be deleted by going to *Image > **Trim*** with **Based On Transparent Pixels** selected.

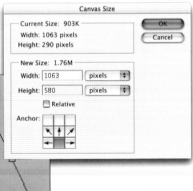

7 Having cropped the "sand" to remove any unwanted edge effects, double the canvas height by selecting *Image > **Canvas Size***, with the original image anchored at the foot.

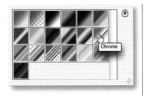

8 Create a new layer. Select the gradient tool, and choose the **Chrome** gradient from the default gradients palette.

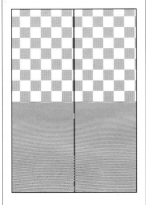

9 Drag the working window to reveal the rebate again, hold down the shift key and apply the gradient from top to bottom. Be careful to make sure that the gradient starts exactly at the top and ends exactly at the foot of the canvas. In this way, the two horizons will coincide.

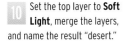

10 Set the top layer to **Soft Light**, merge the layers, and name the result "desert."

11 Set the type so its baseline is just below the horizon,

and rasterize it (*Layer* > *Rasterize* > **Type**).

12 Duplicate the type layer, then select the type and choose *Edit* > *Transform* > **Flip** **Vertical**. Hit OK, and then move the flipped type down below the original type.

13 With the type still selected, choose *Edit* > *Transform* > **Perspective** and drag the lower corner handles outward. Hit OK and name the layer "shadow."

14 Select all but the upper part of the shadow, feather the selection strongly (in this case 30 pixels), and apply *Filter* > *Blur* > **Gaussian Blur**.

15 Use *Image* > *Adjustments* > **Hue/Saturation** to introduce some color to the shadow, then set the layer mode to **Hard Light** at about 75% opacity.

16 Return to the original ("khartoum") type layer, and use *Image* > *Adjustments* > **Hue/Saturation** to color the lettering. At the same time, introduce some transparency by changing the layer mode to **Multiply**.

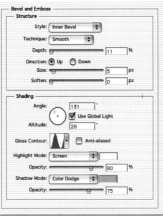

17 Apply *Layer* > *Style* > **Bevel and Emboss** to the "khartoum" type layer. Here, the shading angle proves to be the most significant factor in influencing the appearance of the type.

18 The result of applying the **Bevel and Emboss** style.

19 Move the "shadow" layer below the "khartoum" layer. Select the "desert" layer. To soften the horizon, make a feathered selection along its length, and use the *Image* > **Liquify** command at low strength to vary the contour. Use the same selection to introduce a few pixels of blur. Merge the "shadow" and "desert" layers, and use the *Liquify* effect on the rest of the terrain as well.

INTO THE FIRE

THE FASCINATION OF fire rests on its perpetual movement and shifts in color. So it's an uphill struggle to give it life on a static page or screen. The best one can hope for is to spur some ancient memories in the viewer. Old television enthusiasts might remember the titles of Roald Dahl's "Tales of the Unexpected," with equally artificial flames but enlivened by the presence of a dancing siren. Books, according to Ray Bradbury in Fahrenheit 451, burn at 451°F (232°C).

1 Create a new document and fill the image area with orange.

2 Run *Filter* > *Render* > **Difference Clouds** on the whole area. Repeat up to 15 times, or until a thoroughly variegated effect appears with a variety of red/orange hues. The following frames show the progress of the filtration.

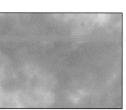

3 Duplicate the layer, naming the lower one "smoke" and the upper one "flame."

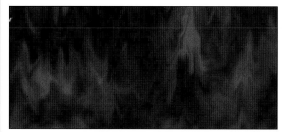

4 Hide the "flame" layer and use the various tools in *Image* > **Liquify** (PS6) or *Filter* > **Liquify** (PS7) to tease out the lighter colored patches in the "smoke" layer. Hit OK.

5 Use *Image* > *Adjustments* > **Hue/Saturation** with **Colorize** checked to reduce the color values and darken the image. Hit OK. You may need to use *Color Balance* additionally to increase the yellow content.

6 Make the "flame" layer active, and use the lasso tool to select the upper part of the image. Choose *Select* > **Feather** and insert a large value (40 pixels in this case) to soften the selection. Hit OK.

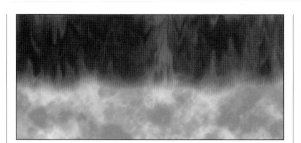

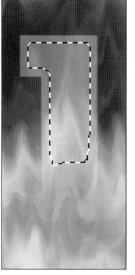

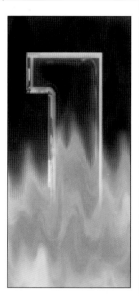

7 Hit the Delete key to remove the selection, deselect, and use *Image > Liquify* (PS6) or *Filter > Liquify* (PS7) as before to bring up the lighter parts of the image, thereby creating flames.

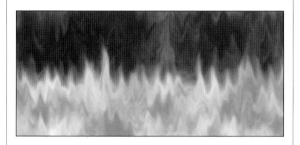

8 Change the layer blending mode to **Screen**.

11 Cmd-click (Mac)/Ctrl-click (Windows) on the type layer icon, go to *Select > Modify > Contract* and reduce the selection slightly, feather it, and delete it. Deselect.

12 Run the Chrome filter (*Filter > Sketch > Chrome*) on the remaining part of the letterforms.

13 Final adjustments include: darkening the "smoke" layer to give more contrast; and on the type layer: using *Filter > Render > Lighting Effects* to introduce minor reflections; applying *Filter > Artistic > Plastic Wrap*; and cloning (with a small brush setting) some of the flame colors into the letterforms. Apply this cloning to the flame layer only– the colors will then change in concert with any hue changes made to the main flame image,

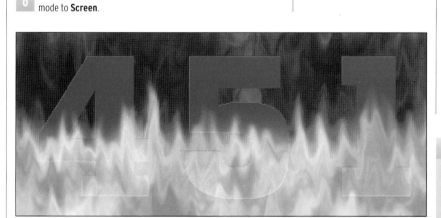

9 Select the type tool and choose a midtoned color (the actual hue is not significant). Set the type, commit it, and move the resulting layer in between the "smoke" and "fire" layers. Rasterize the type (*Layer > Rasterize > Type*).

10 Draw a selection with the lasso tool. Go to *Select > Feather* with a high value, and delete the lower part of the letterforms. Change the layer's blend mode to **Hard Light**. Deselect.

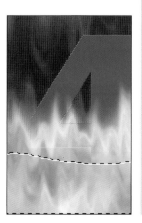

Alternative styles

It's simple to run *Image > Adjustments > Hue/Saturation* on the flame layer for a radical color change.

ABSOLUTE ZERO

The long-running "400 Eskimo words for snow" myth is systematically destroyed with linguistic authority at www.ling.ed.ac.uk/linguist/issues/5/5-1239.html. The phenomenon of Photoshop snow, however, is little understood. There are typographic issues which need unraveling—the difficulty of getting snow to settle on a cap A, for example. Equally problematic is the business of obtaining highlights on a white background, and whether the addition of a sprig of holly constitutes poor taste. We may be some time.

1 Create a new file of approximately 800 x 500 pixels. Create a background to simulate a sky by laying a graduation that runs from light blue (R120, G183, B244) to dark blue (R36, G79, B128). Create some type on a new layer–use a large, heavy font for the best results–and fill it with 20% gray.

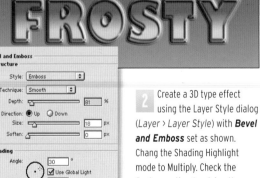

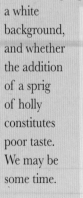

2 Create a 3D type effect using the Layer Style dialog (Layer > Layer Style) with **Bevel and Emboss** set as shown. Chang the Shading Highlight mode to Multiply. Check the Contour option (applying the "Rounded Steps" contour), the Satin option (set to Screen with a "Cone" contour), and the Gradient Overlay effect (set to Reverse and with an opacity of 50% and a scale of 50%).

3 Next, Cmd/Ctrl-click on the type layer in the Layers palette to load it as a selection, and choose Select > Modify > **Expand** set to 4 pixels. Choose Select > **Save Selection**, naming your selection "type 1." Now select the alpha channel called "type 1" and stroke (Edit > **Stroke**) the selection by 14 pixels, choosing the color white and the Center location. Deselect.

4 Create a new layer above the type layer, call it "Snow" go to Select > **Load Selection** and load "type 1." Transform the selection vertically, reducing its height to 70%. (Select > **Transform Selection**).

5 With the selection still active, subtract the original type layer by holding down Option/Alt and Cmd/Ctrl-clicking on the type layer. Expand this new selection by 7 pixels. Smooth the selection by 3 pixels (Select > Modify > **Smooth**). Save this selection as a new channel named "type 2." Deselect.

6 Apply Filter > Blur > **Gaussian Blur** to the "type 2" channel. Set Radius to 1.8. Apply Filter > Stylize > **Diffuse**.

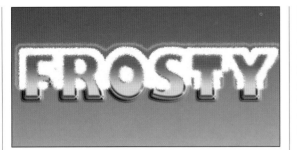

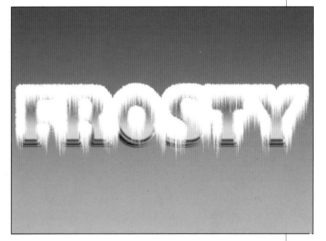

Using *Image* > *Image Size*, reduce the image to 50% of its size. Duplicate the layer called "Snow" (producing a new layer called "Snow copy"), and apply *Filter* > *Stylize* > **Wind** to this layer. Go to *Image* > *Rotate canvas* > **90° CCW**. Delete the original "Snow" layer.

7 Go to *Select* > **Load Selection** and load "type 2." Select the layer called "Snow" and fill the selection with white. Set *Select* > **Feather** to 2 pixels and again fill the selection with white. Subtract "type 1" from your selection (hold down

Option/Alt and Cmd/Ctrl-click in the "type 1" channel). Delete the resulting selection from the layer, and deselect. Now go to *Filter* > *Noise* > **Add Noise**, set to about 8%. Go to *Filter* > *Stylize* > **Diffuse**, and apply the Diffuse filter again.

11 Duplicate the "Snow copy" layer and apply *Filter* > *Stylize* > **Diffuse** to it.

8 In the "Snow" layer, load the "type 1" channel, expand the selection by 2 pixels,

then choose *Select* > **Inverse** and delete this selection. Deselect again.

9 Go to *Image* > **Image Size** and size the image to 200%, then choose *Image* > *Rotate Canvas* > **90° CW**. Select the "Snow" layer and apply *Filter* > *Stylize* > **Wind** with the settings shown here.

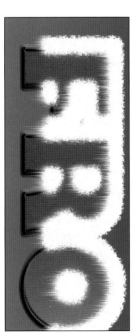

Alternative styles

A Dingbats asterisk dreams of being a snowflake. Try Layer Style with some or all of the following: Inner Shadow in Screen mode with white selected; Color Overlay in very pale blue, set to Dissolve; Pattern Overlay with Clouds selected (scale much increased) at 50% opacity, and a thin white Stroke. A generous shot of Lens Flare and a light covering of painted, drop-shadowed snow complete the scene against a radially-blurred gradient.

IS IT A BIRD?

Vapor trails

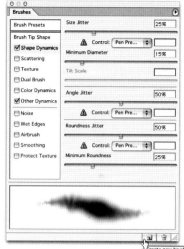

HEALTH AND safety issues, crowded airspace, and lowered advertising budgets find today's skywriting pilot with his feet up in the hangar contemplating a vanished history. Some practitioners persist. Wayne Mansfield wrote "War is over if you want it Happy Xmas from John and Oko" over Toronto in 1970. The smoke is made from dropping liquid paraffin onto the plane's hot exhaust pipe. Typically the stroke width is 75 feet (23 m) and the letter x-height 1,320 feet (400 m). In type terms this lettering is around 1,500,000 points, taking the body height as 1,800 feet (550 m). Serifs are not usual, typos are left uncorrected, but the most difficult part is writing backward so that the earthbound audience gets the point. Mansfield suggests taping the reversed letters to your instrument panel before takeoff.

1 Create a small, square document—say 100 pixels across—and paint in black with a soft-edged brush. Break up the shape with the eraser tool at a similarly soft setting. At this scale, both tools are easier to use with a pressure-sensitive stylus.

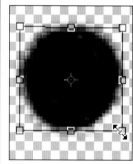

2 Use the blur tool to selectively soften parts of the disk.

3 Use the transform tool while holding down Shift to scale the disk to about half its original diameter. Then draw a square marquee around (but not touching) the disk, and go to *Edit > Define Brush*.

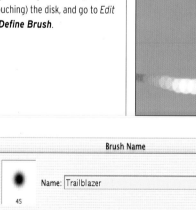

Brush Name

Name: Trailblazer   OK   Cancel

45

4 Click on the new brush in the options bar, increasing the spacing value to around 45%, and name the brush "writing."

5 There is a multitude of controls in the (PS7) Brush Dynamics dialog. With a pressure-sensitive tablet and stylus, variations in the brush stroke can be tied to tip pressure, tilt, and even the thumbwheel found on one model. The Other Dynamics dialog offers variation of opacity and "paint flow."

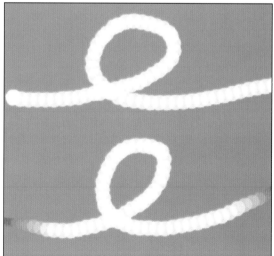

6 Make a new, larger document for the artwork, and fill Layer 1 with blue. In a new layer, with foreground color white, try out the new brush with the airbrush tool. The upper trail is produced with the mouse, the lower with a pressure-sensitive stylus. The fading color at either end of the trail is determined by the choice of background color in the toolbox.

7 Various unlikely aerobatic maneuvers are possible with the stylus and tablet.

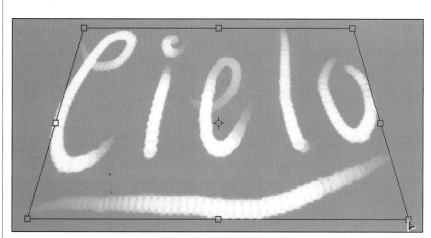

8 A more monumental effect can be achieved with *Edit > Transform > **Perspective***.

9 The underlying sky was treated with a slight blue-to-transparent gradient, then with *Filter > Render > **Clouds***, subsequently faded and changed to **Screen** mode. The central axis of *Filter > Render > **Lens Flare*** was then placed by trial and error at the dot of the "i." The trails themselves are treated with the manual blur tool, and, finally, a suitable aircraft appears.

Alternative styles

This one's not for you. Skywriting is a very public medium. This ground-based Rosie benefits by pure chance (on her birthday) from someone else's aerial largesse.

SHOWTIME

HEROICALLY SPOTLIT type strikes a masterful pose with its back to a besotted audience—they scream in adulation. How often do you see that? In the Lighting Effects dialog you can trawl the presets for theatrical lighting plots; Five Lights Up looks good for overture and sinister scenes, the yellow glow of 2 O'Clock Spotlight for the warmly romantic passages, Triple Spotlight at the big finish, and Five Lights Down for the curtain call. All these and more can be modified, named, and saved for reuse. Get into Circle of Light, for example, with its meager set of four colored lamps—shift them around, add a dozen more, save, and rename as Nothing Succeeds Like Excess.

1 Select the type tool, and type in the word, choosing an appropriate dark color (but not black) for the text. Go to *Layer > Type > Warp Text* and choose the Fisheye style with the settings shown here.

2 Use the rectangular marquee tool to select the lower part of the window, just overlapping the bases of the letters. Go to *Select >* **Load Selection** and choose "STAGE Transparency" as the channel; make sure that "Subtract from Selection" is selected. Create a new layer and fill the selection with a suitable "stage" color. Deselect. Move this "stage" layer below the type layer. Fill the background layer with black for now.

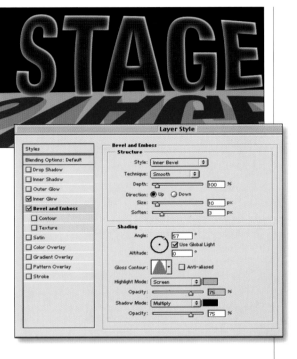

3 Duplicate the type layer, and apply *Edit > Transform > Flip Vertical*. Move the flipped type below the original, and use *Edit > Transform >* **Rotate** to match the bases of the letters. Rasterize the type (*Layer > Rasterize > Type*).

4 Use *Edit > Transform > Perspective* to create perspective on the type.

5 Copy the layer, moving this new copy under the previous one. Use *Edit > Transform > Perspective* again to slide this layer in the other direction. Set the layer opacity to 20%.

6 Apply *Layer > Layer Style > Bevel and Emboss* and *Inner Glow* to the original type layer.

7 On both shadow layers, erase the far side of the shadows with the eraser tool set to a soft round paintbrush of fairly large diameter, 50% opacity. Erase more where the shadow is cast farther away from the "figure." Blur the predominant shadow layer with *Filter > Blur > Gaussian Blur* with radius set to 4 pixels. Blur the secondary shadow layer similarly, but using a radius of 2.5 pixels.

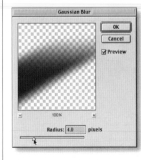

8 Use quick mask mode to make a gradient selection of the bottom half of the shadows. Exit quick mask mode

and blur each shadow layer a further 10 pixels with Gaussian blur. Deselect.

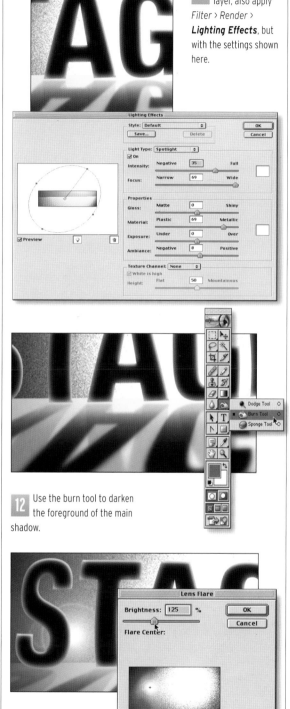

11 To the "stage" layer, also apply *Filter > Render > **Lighting Effects***, but with the settings shown here.

9 Fill the background layer with 50% Gray, and apply *Filter > Texture > **Grain*** using the settings shown here.

12 Use the burn tool to darken the foreground of the main shadow.

14 Rasterize the type layer, and then apply *Filter > Render > **Lens Flare*** at lower intensity.

10 To the background layer apply *Filter > Render > **Lighting Effects*** with the Soft Omni style.

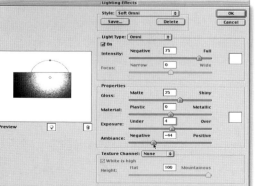

13 Return to the background layer and apply *Filter > Render > **Lens Flare***.

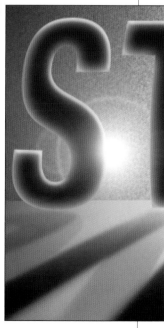

15 Darken the edges of the background layer with the burn tool if necessary.

GLOW BABY GLOW

NEON GAS exists in ordinary air in the proportion of 1:65,000. Application of current to the gas in a sealed tube results in a glow. Neon glows red, other colors are produced by mixtures of argon, mercury, and phosphor. The manufacture of the tubes is an exacting process—forming them into legible characters even more so. Pursuers in Photoshop of the utterly authentic will need to mimic this operation with a continuous stroke, obscured as necessary between adjoining characters, and garnished with clips, wires and other impedimenta. The emphasis in this example is on capturing that particular glow and, for once, the invented simulation looks better than the real thing.

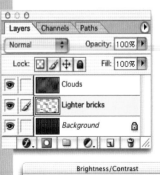

1 Create a new document. This is 590 x 354 pixels. Choose a brick red color. This is 108R 0G 10B (100M 100Y 60K). Dark colors work best for this effect. Fill the background with the brick color. Go to *Filter > Texture > **Texturizer***. Choose Brick as the texture, and use the settings shown here.

2 Create new layer, and name it "Clouds." Set the background color to 0C 100M 100Y 70K and the foreground color to 0C 100M 100Y. Select *Filter > Render > **Clouds***. Set Blend Mode to Multiply.

3 To give a more realistic effect, lighten and darken a random selection of bricks as follows: Shift-select individual bricks with the rectangular marquee tool. Go to *Layer > New > **Layer via Copy*** and name the new layer "Lighter bricks." With the new layer active, lighten using *Image > Adjustments > **Brightness/ Contrast***.

4 With the background layer active, repeat step 3 and darken. Select the type tool, and type a word ("Café") using a suitable font. This uses VAG Rounded.

5 If you want to save this word as type, create a duplicate layer. On the copy, select *Layer > Type > **Convert to Shape***. Uncheck the layer visibility of the original "Café" type layer so that it is hidden. In the Layer Styles Blending Options dialog, set Advanced Blending to 35%. Finally, set the Blend Mode of the "Café copy" layer to Multiply.

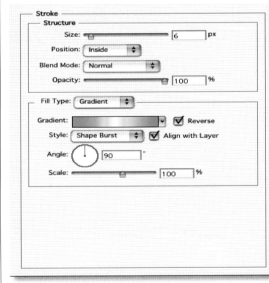

TO CREATE A BROKEN LETTER EFFECT

On the Paths palette, duplicate the "Café copy Clipping Path." Using the direct selection tool, select the letters you want to delete. Hit Delete, leaving the character(s) you want to retain. Duplicate the "Café copy" layer. Using the direct selection tool, select the character you want to "dim" and hit Delete.

Turn off the layer visibility of the "Café copy" layer. On the Paths palette, select "Path 1." Create a new layer called "Dimmed letter." With the paintbrush tool set to a 3-pixel brush and the foreground color set to 100C 50M 0Y 40K, select Stroke Path from the Paths palette pop-up menu. Select *Edit > Transform > Rotate* and rotate the letter. Apply *Layer > Layer Style > Drop Shadow* and *Bevel and Emboss*. Make sure the drop shadow falls away from the main source of light (that is the other letters).

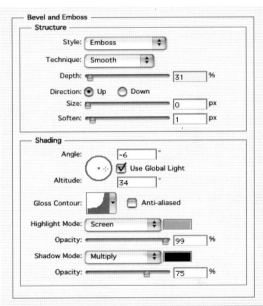

6 Apply *Layer > Layer Style > Outer Glow* and *Inner Glow* for the red glow around the shape, and *Stroke* for the yellow.

Alternative styles

The neon tube is a delicate structure–though a well-made one is said to last up to 10 years. Inevitably there will be failures, and they must be recorded. Here the dead letter shows only the glow of its functioning neighbors, through manipulation of Stroke in the Layer Style dialog.

RED HOT

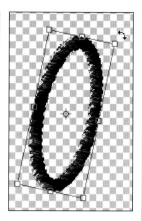

PHOTOSHOP'S NEON GLOW filter is almost always ineffectual, so the ardent pyromaniac is forced to look elsewhere. This example is an oblique tribute to David Rakoff, designer of the Crackling Fire typeface (see below), while his face is the ideal choice for every barbecue invitation—this technique lends itself more to gatherings of collectors of obsolete, and probably illegal, electrical equipment. Since this image inevitably celebrates 230 volts, the British standard, readers in other countries should adjust the figure accordingly.

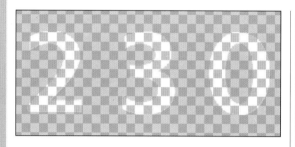

1 Select the type tool and choose type color white. Make a new alpha channel and set the type. Choose a color for the mask. This has no effect on the action of the channel; it simply makes it easier to identify and manipulate it when working in layers. Select 50% opacity for the mask color.

2 Duplicate the type channel, naming it "type blur," Cmd-click (Mac)/Ctrl-click (Windows) to select it, and expand the letterforms (*Select* > *Modify* > **Expand**). Fill the enlarged shape with white and apply blur. It is also helpful to identify this mask by color.

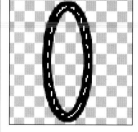

3 Return to the **Layers** palette and draw an ellipse with the elliptical marquee tool. Stroke it about one-fifth of its width (*Edit* > **Stroke**).

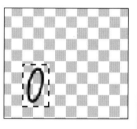

4 Treat the ellipse with the Wind filter (*Filter* > *Stylize* > **Wind**).

5 Tilt the ellipse using the transform tool.

6 Use the transform tool again to reduce the ellipse to a few pixels high, then select it with the rectangular marquee tool. Go to *Edit* > **Define Brush**.

7 When the dialog box appears, just hit OK.

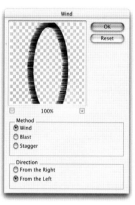

8 Select the brush tool in the toolbox and the new sampled brush in the toolbar. Increase the spacing to around 25%, and name the brush "coil." In Photoshop 7, toggle the Brushes palette (click on the icon in the options bar); click on Brush Tip Shape and adjust the spacing to 25%. Rename the brush "coil."

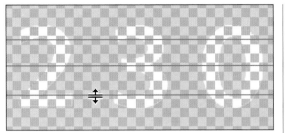

9 Select *Show Rulers* and *Snap to Guides* in the View menu. Make the "type" channel visible and drag guides out from the ruler in order to position the "coil" brush.

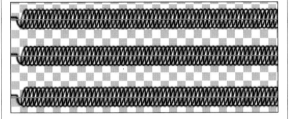

10 Click at the left side of the document with the paintbrush, hold down the Shift key and click again at the right side. Erase the extremities of the coils and paint a connecting wire. Duplicate twice.

11 Colorize the coils of wire (*Image* > *Adjustments* > *Hue/Saturation* > **Colorize**) and duplicate the layer. Colorize the lower layer and blur it to create a glow. A white background layer has been added to make these effects more distinct.

12 Create a new layer, load the "type blur" selection, and fill it with color.

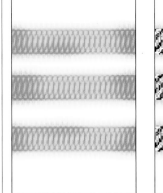

13 This is the effect of setting the new layer to **Color Dodge** mode relative to the lower layer.

14 Create a second new layer, load the "type" selection, and fill it with a contrasting color. Make a new selection from the "wire" layer.

15 Use the selection to re-color parts of the letterforms. Set the layer mode to **Color Burn**.

16 With all layers visible, it is possible to treat the top layer with *Image* > *Adjustments* > **Hue/Saturation** to achieve the required color combination.

Alternative styles

This technique lends itself to several variations. A strong background helps define the heated wires, which in their turn can be modified to appear dead, twisted, or ready to melt completely. Try applying the Wave filter to the wires for a totally frantic effect.

LIGHT
INFORMATION

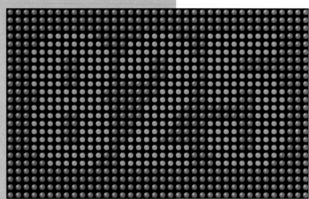

THIS EXAMPLE AND the one on the following spread take different routes to imitate the familiar stadium-style display board, though they both rely on the Pattern function to ensure precise register of the component layers. Keen operators could adapt these techniques to produce ranks of lights in diagonal rows as well as multicolored displays. Very keen operators might attempt to imitate the tiny red/green/blue phosphors of the monitor screen itself. The possibilities are endless for those of an iron constitution.

Lightbulb panel

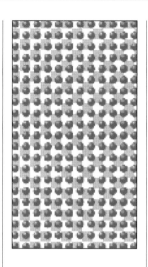

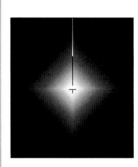

1 To create the underlying pattern, make a square canvas, invert foreground and background colors, select *View > Show Rulers*, and use the diamond gradient tool from the precise center of the image to the edge. Hold Shift down to keep the axis perpendicular.

2 Make a new layer and draw a circular marquee centered exactly on the gradient below. To produce a circle centered on a point, hold down Shift-Option (Mac)/Shift-Alt (Windows) while dragging. Fill the selection with a white-to-black gradient as before, but this time using the radial gradient. To get this kind of highlight, click and drag only a short gradient line as shown.

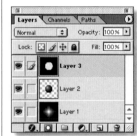

3 Make a third layer, invert the selection (*Select > Inverse*), and fill it with black. Deselect, and hide Layer 3.

4 Reduce the canvas size: this will have the eventual effect of bringing the points in the matrix closer together. Then reduce the image size to a few pixels square–in this case 25 x 25. Enlarge the screen image to around 500% so you can see what you're doing.

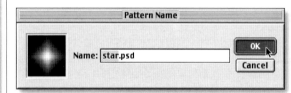

5 Hide Layer 2, leaving only Layer 1 visible and selected. Go to *Edit > Define Pattern* and name it "star." Do the same for Layers 2 and 3, naming them "bulb" and "mask" respectively.

6 Make a new document, and fill it with the "bulb" pattern, which is now stored and named in the patterns palette (*Edit > Fill > Pattern*). Colorize this layer using *Image > Adjustments > Hue/Saturation* with **Colorize** selected.

Alternative styles

Use the "star" instead of the "bulb" pattern for a different effect. Use *Image > Adjustments > Hue/Saturation* to obtain a variety of colors.

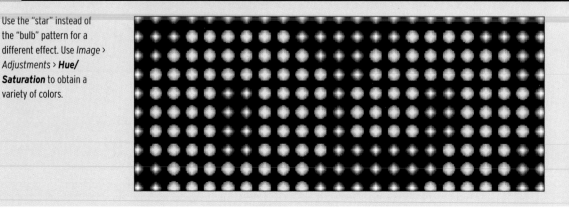

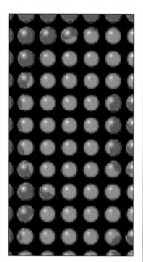

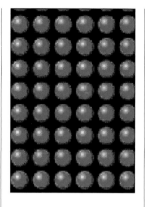

7 Make a new layer, fill it with the "mask" pattern, and blur it very slightly. The two patterns will register perfectly since they are based on the same original document. Set the "overlay" layer to Hard Light mode and reduce its opacity slightly.

9 Nudge the type layer to get the best position over the "bulb" pattern, and then rasterize the type.

10 In the type layer, use the paintbrush with the same color as the type to "switch on" incomplete lamps, and the eraser to tidy up those that are only marginally illuminated. The "overlay" layer allows this retouching to be done without much need for accuracy, since it masks all but the "bulbs."

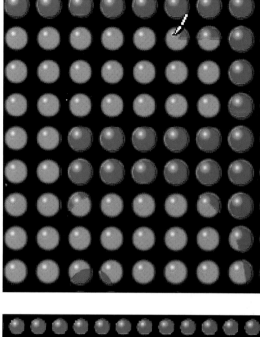

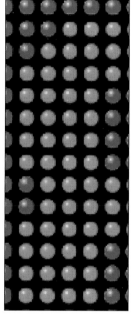

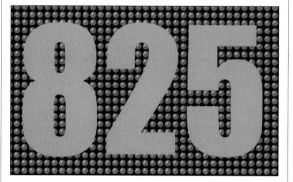

8 Select a contrasting color, and use the type tool with a simple font to form the basis of the matrix. Position this layer under the top layer, and set it to blend mode **Overlay**.

11 You can get a different, brighter appearance by setting the type layer to **Hard Light**.

12 Above: This is the result with the type layer duplicated twice.

13 Below: Here is the result as before but with the "mask" layer inverted to read "white."

Insert a white layer at the foot of the stack and turn off the "bulbs" layer for a simple graphic effect.

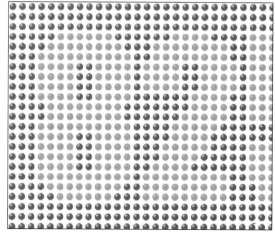

TERMINAL SIGNBOARDS

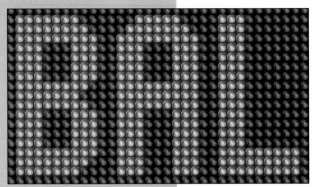

CLATTERING ROWS of electromechanical relays were behind the early versions of these signs. Input was by punched paper tape, which then passed between the jaws of two rows of electrical contacts. A hole in the paper allowed a fleeting circuit to be made, and the bulb was lit momentarily—the tape's passage through further sets of contacts could achieve the illusion of movement. Much more complex displays are now powered by a microscopic chip.

Dot matrix display

1 Begin by creating a pattern. Make a small, square document with a transparent background–this one is 36 pixels wide. An even number of pixels will help in the creation of symmetrical shapes. Create guides halfway along each axis.

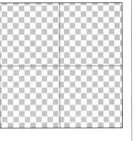

2 Place the cursor at the intersection of the guides, and use the elliptical marquee tool with the Option/Alt and Shift keys pressed to make a centered circle. Be sure to leave at least two pixels clear all around.

3 Choose the gradient tool, set to **Radial gradient** and **Reverse** in the options bar. Select the default "black, white" and fill in the gradients palette. Place the cursor in the top left part of the circular selection, and drag toward that corner.

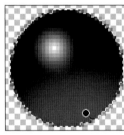

4 With the circle filled, select a largish, soft-edged dodge tool (set to operate on shadow areas) and lighten the lower part of the disk.

5 You can also use *Filter > Render >* **Lens Flare** to enhance the glassy appearance.

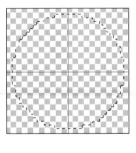

Lens Flare

Brightness: 150 %   OK   Cancel

Flare Center:

Lens Type:
● 50–300mm Zoom
○ 35mm Prime
○ 105mm Prime

6 Now select the whole square and go to *Edit >* **Define Pattern.**

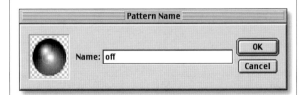

Pattern Name

Name: off   OK   Cancel

7 Name the pattern "off."

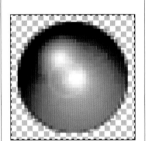

8 With the selection still active, go to *Image > Adjustments >* **Hue/Saturation** and colorize the disk. Define this state also as a pattern, naming it "on."

9 Make a new document and fill it with the new pattern "off." Ideally, the dimensions of the new document should be a multiple of the pattern size. In this case, with a pattern of 36 x 36 pixels, there is a requirement for 33 columns and 19 rows of lights. The canvas size is therefore 33 x 36 = 1188 pixels wide, and 19 x 36 = 684 pixels high.

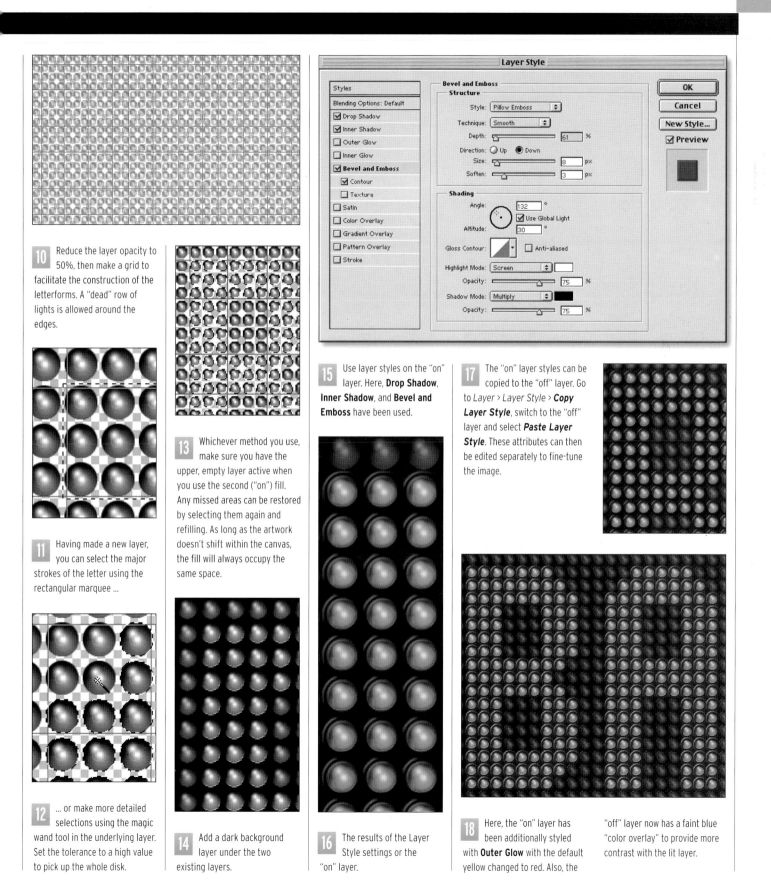

10 Reduce the layer opacity to 50%, then make a grid to facilitate the construction of the letterforms. A "dead" row of lights is allowed around the edges.

11 Having made a new layer, you can select the major strokes of the letter using the rectangular marquee ...

12 ... or make more detailed selections using the magic wand tool in the underlying layer. Set the tolerance to a high value to pick up the whole disk.

13 Whichever method you use, make sure you have the upper, empty layer active when you use the second ("on") fill. Any missed areas can be restored by selecting them again and refilling. As long as the artwork doesn't shift within the canvas, the fill will always occupy the same space.

14 Add a dark background layer under the two existing layers.

15 Use layer styles on the "on" layer. Here, **Drop Shadow**, **Inner Shadow**, and **Bevel and Emboss** have been used.

16 The results of the Layer Style settings or the "on" layer.

17 The "on" layer styles can be copied to the "off" layer. Go to *Layer > Layer Style > Copy Layer Style*, switch to the "off" layer and select **Paste Layer Style**. These attributes can then be edited separately to fine-tune the image.

18 Here, the "on" layer has been additionally styled with **Outer Glow** with the default yellow changed to red. Also, the "off" layer now has a faint blue "color overlay" to provide more contrast with the lit layer.

CRYSTAL GAZING

THE 7-PART MATRIX used in this example recalls the beginnings of LCD technology in the 1970s. The liquid crystals in question change properties in response to an electrical input. Better, quicker-responding, crystals now allow more complex displays. A 35-part matrix is the minimum for showing realistic lower-case letters, symbols, and punctuation. See www.casilrd.com.hk for samples of this more complex matrix in use. One such desk-mounted device offers the facility to "leave business information, personal messages, thoughts, even humorous wordings for office staff."

LCD display

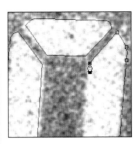

2 Having scanned and pasted a suitable guide image into the document, it's straightforward to use the pen tool to outline the structure. Inverting the guide image and reducing its opacity may make it easier to see what you're doing.

3 In the Paths palette, choose *Save Path*, and call your new path "lcd."

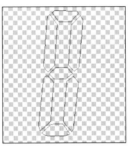

4 Still in the Paths palette, hide the path by clicking anywhere in the palette except on the path icon. Then return to the Layers palette, go to *Select > All* and delete the guide image. Deselect, return the layer to full opacity, and then go back to the Paths palette and click on your saved path.

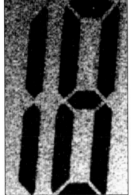

1 Across a crowded room, with the wrong lens and inadequate lighting, this fuzzy image is just clear enough to form the basis of the drawn letterform ...

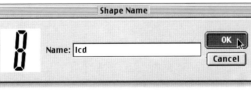

5 With the path visible in the Layers palette, go to *Edit > Define Custom Shape*, and name the new shape "lcd." Hit OK.

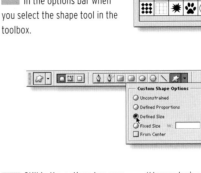

6 The new shape will appear in the options bar when you select the shape tool in the toolbox.

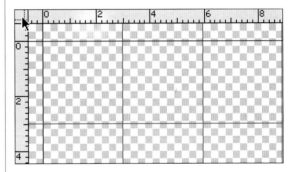

7 Still in the options bar, you can control the way the shape tool operates. Click on *Defined Size*, for example, to make it reproduce at the original path size. Other options allow you to draw in freeform

(*Unconstrained*), proportional, or at a fixed size of your choice. Since the tool is vector-based, these options have no effect on image definition whatever size you choose.

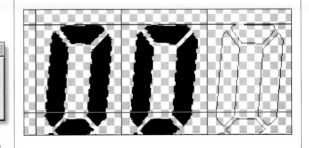

8 Start a new file large enough for the numbers you want to create. To help with spacing (equal letter spacing, by definition) set up a suitable grid in *Edit > Preferences > Guides &* *Grid*. Click and drag in the tiny box at the junction of the page rulers (top left) to displace the finished grid to a more useful position.

9 With *View > Snap To > Grid* selected, the shape tool will produce exactly spaced identical characters when you click near the relevant grid point.

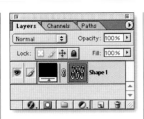

10 The shape tool actually produces a group of masks over a layer of the foreground color.

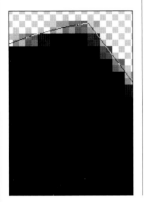

11 Proof positive that these are vector rather than bitmap shapes. Even at an enlargement of 1600%, the edges are still well defined.

12 Make a duplicate of the layer as a backup (but don't leave it visible!), then choose *Layer > Rasterize > **Layer***. Erase the unwanted letter sections.

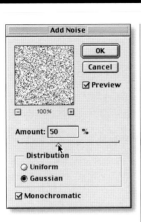

13 Insert a new layer under the letters, fill it with very pale green, go *to Filter > Noise > **Add Noise***, choosing Gaussian and monochromatic, and then soften the result with *Filter > Blur > **Gaussian Blur*** at a low setting.

14 Working in the lettering layer, go to *Layer > Layer Style* and apply **Drop Shadow**. Increase the **Distance** and reduce the **Opacity** settings.

15 Return to the underlying green layer to add a frame. In the Layer Style dialog, click on the **Styles** box (top left) to display the Styles presets. Choose **Fat Chrome**; if this is not available you may need to load the Text Effects presets from the pop-up menu.

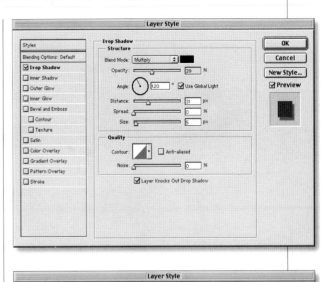

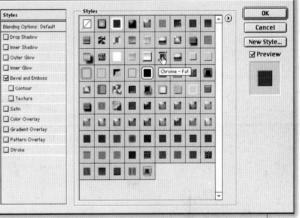

16 In the (nearly) finished version, *Filter > Render > **Lighting Effects*** has been used to enliven the background, while the lettering layer blend mode has been changed to *Multiply* at a reduced opacity. You could reduce the opacity still further to simulate flat batteries

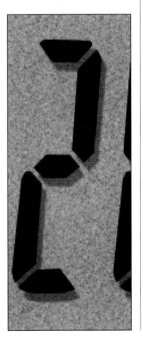

Alternative styles

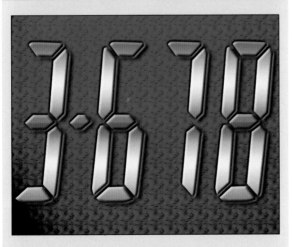

Equipped with the infinitely repeatable LCD shape, the scope for crass type creation is unlimited. Over a pattern background of spotlit lighting effects, float numerals treated in the Layer Style dialog with *Drop Shadow*, *Gradient Overlay* (the preset **Chrome** at reduced opacity), and *Bevel and Emboss*. Unscientific research suggests that 3.6% of all typographers are responsible for 78% of all vulgar typography.

ARTIFICIAL FIRE

IN THE FIREWORKS
gunpowder mixture, steel
filings and charcoal make
sparks of orange and yellow,
strontium gives red, copper
makes blue-green, and copper
chloride is for blue and
purple. After the show has
ended it's hard to describe
what you saw. The dynamics
of the explosions and the
pulsating brilliance of the
colors lack a decent
vocabulary. Moving pictures
(with a soundtrack) come
close; still images on the page
struggle for an approximation.
This example pumps up the
protesting RGB electrons as
far as they will go in an
attempt to cover all the noise
and fury in one image.

Fireworks

3 Still in the options
bar, click the
"Geometry Options"
down-arrow to open
the Custom Shape Options
panel. Select "Defined
Proportions" to keep the shape
circular.

4 First ensuring that "Create
new shape layer" is
selected (at the left of the
options bar), use a selection
of shapes to produce a cluster
of stars.

9 Zoom in on the reduced
image, and select it with
the rectangular marquee tool,
ensuring that there is no
feathering and holding down the
Shift key to ensure a square
selection. Go to *Edit* › **Define
Brush**.

10 Name the new brush "star."

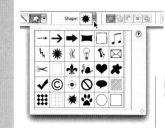

1 Select the custom shape
tool in the toolbox, then
click on the down-arrow to the
right of its icon near the center
of the options bar. Having thus
revealed the default shapes set,
use the pop-up to load the
"Shapes" set.

5 When you have drawn a
sizeable cluster, change the
action of the shape tool by
selecting "Exclude overlapping
shape areas" in the options bar.

7 The last tool application
unifies the cluster and
produces some interesting
subsidiary shapes.

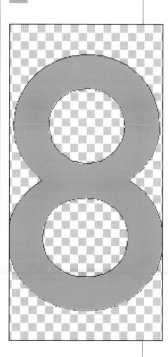

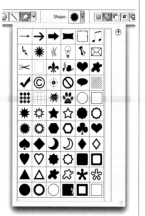

2 Choose "Append" as the
loading option.

6 Choose a solid star, and
hold down the Alt key as
you click and drag out from the
center of the cluster.

8 Go to *Layer* › *Rasterize* ›
Layer to allow the image
to be edited. Use a small amount
of blur, then reduce the star
image to around 10% of its
original size (use Cmd/Ctrl-T, then
click and drag with the Shift key
depressed).

11 Hide the existing layer,
select a bright foreground
color (we used RGB settings R231,
G115, B0) and set the type in a
plain bold face. Choose *Layer* ›
Type › **Create Work Path**, then
Layer › *Rasterize* › **Type**.

12 Blur the type, then select the paintbrush tool, using a contrasting color and setting the blend mode to **Overlay**. Choose the newly created brush on the Brushes palette, click on Brush Tip Shape, and increase the spacing. Decrease the opacity to 50%.

13 Insert a new black layer at the base of the Layers palette, return to the type layer and make sure the work path is active. If it's not, click on the Work Path icon in the Paths palette. Choose **Stroke Path** from the Paths pop-up menu, and select Paintbrush. The path will be stroked at the last settings chosen for the paintbrush.

14 Reset the paintbrush characteristics and repeat **Stroke Path** to obtain a mixture of effects. In this case, the color is changed to yellow, the blend mode to **Screen**, and the spacing increased to 170%.

15 Two more applications with change of spacing–green set to **Hard Light**, and purple set to **Color Burn**. The purple brush was set to a much reduced spacing to produce the tight fringe around the letterform. The path has been hidden to show the effects more clearly. Apply a little blur.

16 Zoom in on the image, make a circular selection of one of the more defined stars, feather it by a few pixels, and apply *Filter > Distort > **Twirl***.

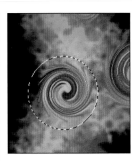

17 Re-use the feathered selection by dragging it across the image with the marquee tool and repeating the filter (Cmd/Ctrl-F). Return to the Twirl filter dialog to reverse the direction of rotation. Try different size selections to add variety.

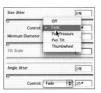

18 Make new, softly feathered selections of the "twirled" areas, and go to *Image > Adjustments > **Curves***.

19 Draw a new curve in the window. With Preview checked, you will be able to follow the changes in the image window.

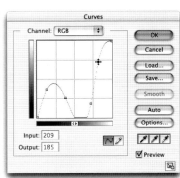

20 Drag the feathered selection over the image, using a different redrawn curve at each new location.

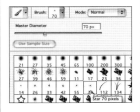

21 To create an active background, make a new layer under the type, and select the default brush "Star 70 pixels." Click on Brush Tip Shape on the Brushes palette.

22 Still in the Brushes palette, enter values for Fade in each category. These numbers are identical, but you can choose any combination, or leave some values untouched.

23 Choose the freeform pen tool (press on the default pen icon to reveal it). Draw some sweeping curves.

24 Go to the Paths palette and select **Stroke Path** from the Paths pop-up menu. Here, the path has been hidden to show the effect more clearly. Continue in this way with different brushes, paths, and fade settings. You can repeat the **Stroke Path** command several times to increase its intensity.

25 The use of individual brushes, not attached to paths, allows random elements to be introduced.

LINE UP

Inline type

WHEN THE CREATIVE impulse fails, it's time to doodle. Maybe constant selection and reselection of the *Select > Modify > Contract* command will stir some dormant thought process. If not, you've made some nice numbers that would look good on anyone's birthday cake.

3 Reduce the selection again by the same number of pixels, and fill it with black.

4 Continue in this way until the letterforms have been reduced to lines with intervening transparent channels. Make a copy of this layer.

1 Choose a fat-faced font and set the type. Rasterize the type layer.

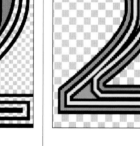

5 Select the lower layer and use the paint bucket tool to fill the transparent areas with color.

6 Continue until all the transparent channels have been filled with different colors.

2 Select the letterforms by Cmd-clicking (Mac)/Ctrl-clicking (Windows) in the Layers palette, and reduce the selection by a few pixels (*Select > Modify > Contract*). Delete the selection.

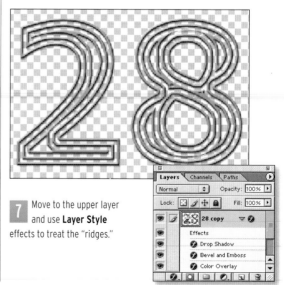

7 Move to the upper layer and use **Layer Style** effects to treat the "ridges."

Outline type

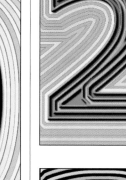

3 Hide all layers except the lowest, and fill the channels with color as before.

4 Show all the layers. Select the top layer and use *Image > Adjustments > Hue/Saturation* to colorize the black lines.

5 Apply *Filter > Render > Lighting Effects*, using the layer's own transparency as the texture map. Fade the resulting effect to around 50% (*Edit > Fade Lighting Effects*).

2 Continue contracting and alternately filling and deleting the selection until the whole image is covered. Deselect finally and hide the original type layer. Move the new layer to the bottom of the stack, duplicate it, and move the copy to the top of the stack.

1 To continue the process beyond the letterforms, hide the upper type layer and Cmd/Ctrl-click in the Layers palette on the lower type layer icon. Invert the selection, then go to *Select > Modify > Contract* and reduce it by the previously-used number of pixels. Make a new layer and fill the reduced selection with black.

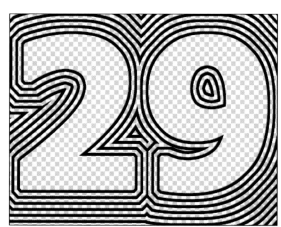

WARPED TYPE

DURING THE Prohibition, a Sacramento winery sold bricks of compressed grapes. The package was labeled: "DO NOT place this brick in a one gallon crock, add sugar and water, cover and let stand for seven days, or an illegal alcoholic beverage will result." Though old conservative typographic bores may suck their remaining teeth, there will inevitably be those who fall for the sinuous temptation of the warp tool. With luck and persistence, they may be redeemed, to rejoin the straight and shining path.

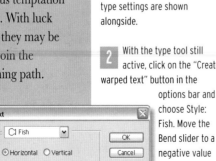

1 Set the type into a layer. Ideally, the type should form a solid block. The actual type settings are shown alongside.

2 With the type tool still active, click on the "Create warped text" button in the options bar and choose Style: Fish. Move the Bend slider to a negative value and hit OK.

Fish

3 The result of applying the warp.

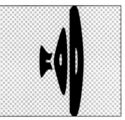

4 Other kinds of fish are not so malleable.

5 To see the range of possible distortions, click again on the "Create warped text" button, and adjust the Vertical and Horizontal Distortion sliders as well.

6 Using the techniques shown in the example opposite, you can change the degree of distortion and edit the actual words.

Flag

1 Discard the warp settings from the previous example (click on the button and choose Style: None), discard the Layer Styles, and set a new word: "PATRIE." Use a similar degree of horizontal type scaling to obtain a solid block of type.

2 Choose Style: Flag from the Warp Text dialog.

3 Go to *Layer > Layer Style*, click on **Gradient Overlay**, click on the down-arrow alongside the gradient image to reveal the pop-up, then select "New Gradient" by clicking on the pop-up button and accept the default name for the new gradient. Click on the gradient image to open it in the Gradient Editor dialog.

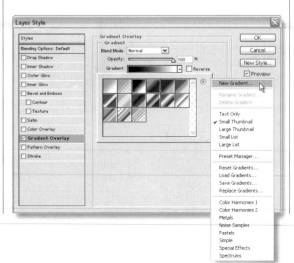

Gradient Editor

Presets

OK
Cancel
Load...
Save...

Name: tricolore   New

Gradient Type: Solid

Smoothness: 100 ▸ %

Stops

Opacity: ▸ %   Location: %   Delete
Color: ▸   Location: 5 %   Delete

Float

4 Rename the gradient "tricolore." and change the default version. First, click below the gradient bar to create new Color Stop tabs. Select a new color when the picker appears. To get a sharp division between colors, drag the small Color Midpoint tabs to sit close to the Color Stop tabs. Hit OK.

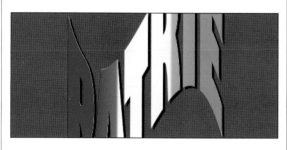

5 In this example, the flag has also been given a drop shadow in the Layer Style dialog. The spread value has been set at zero to give a hard shadow, and a gray layer inserted below to make the effect clearer.

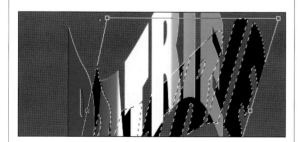

6 For a more dramatic shadow, Cmd-/Ctrl-click on the type layer icon to make a selection from the type. Create a new layer under the type, fill the selection with black, go to *Edit > Transform > Distort*, and move the handles to throw the shadow into perspective. Blur and reduce the opacity of this new layer. Return to the Layer Style effects of the type layer, and add a very small amount of **Bevel and Emboss**.

1 Set some small type in a layer at the foot of the window. Duplicate the layer by pressing Cmd-J (Mac)/Ctrl-J (Windows).

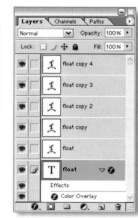

2 Reselect the type tool and click on the Create warped **text button** in the options bar. Choose Arc from the Style list and change the settings as shown. Use the same increments for each new layer.

3 Use the move tool to push the warped type upward.

4 Continue duplicating layers, distorting the type and moving it in this way until the Bend setting reaches 100%.

5 Select the lowest layer and go to *Layer > Layer Style > Color Overlay*; accept the default red color, and hit OK. Link the layers (click in the empty box next to the eye icon on each layer). Choose *Layer > Layer Style > Copy Layer Style* and return to the same menu and choose *Paste Layer Style to Linked*. All the layers now have the same color overlay.

6 Go through the layers one by one, changing the color overlay value and adding an inner bevel and a drop shadow in each case. Unlink the layers by clicking on the chain icons. With the layers unlinked, you can move the words around and change the Layer Style settings. To increase the apparent "height" above the background, increase the Distance setting in Drop Shadow. In the same dialog, increase the Size setting as well to get a softer result.

7 The lower layers need progressively less modification of the shadow values, and the initial type layer needs none at all.

8 Because warped type remains editable until rasterized, you can change the typeface, size, color (though only if you disable Color Overlay), and the words themselves.

Perspective type

MOUNTAIN
HIGH

HOW BIG should type be? Small enough to fit on one side of the paper? Big enough to read? Big enough to make you say out loud, "I say, that's unusually large lettering for its intended purpose!"? The fascination of monumental type is in its rarity. Very few local administrations have the finance, or nerve, to celebrate their township with 50-foot plywood caps on a mountainside (visit hollywoodsigntrust.org to find out that the letters are only a real-estate advertising relic). Go to Estonia and you'll find, on the road between Tallinn and Tartu, the same nine letters on a much smaller hill and only five feet high. Or visit virtualtourist.com.

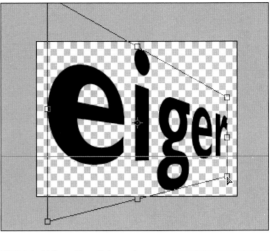

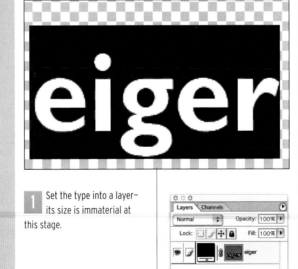

1 Set the type into a layer—its size is immaterial at this stage.

2 Select *Layer* > *Type* > **Convert to Shape**. A filled black panel linked to a clipping path is produced.

3 Select *View* > *Show Rulers* and drag out a horizontal guide to use as the baseline. To make a larger working area, drag out the window view. Go to *Edit* > *Transform* > **Distort** and manipulate the letters to achieve a perspective effect. Though care needs to be taken to ensure that the vertical axes remain so (hold down the Shift key while dragging vertically), this tool is more useful than the **Perspective** manipulation in the same menu.

4 Duplicate the layer and change the color fill (Option-click/Alt-click on the black panel in the **Layers** palette).

5 Distort the new layer in the same way. Move the left edge of the selection more than the right to preserve the perspective illusion.

6 The result of the previous transformation.

7 It's always possible to change the content of a layer. Here, the color fill has been changed to a gradient fill, aligned to the apparent perspective axis. Go to *Layer > Change Layer Content* and choose **Gradient Map**, for example.

8 Since the gradient fill cannot be edited directly while the clipping path is still active, duplicate the previous layer and change its content. Go to *Layer > Change Layer Content* and select **Color Balance**. The dialog box opens and changes can be made. Note that this duplication method preserves the clipping path, so allowing changes to the clipped area only. The dialog box can be reopened at any time by clicking on the layer icon.

9 Using the *Color Balance* dialog, shift the mid-tones toward cyan and blue.

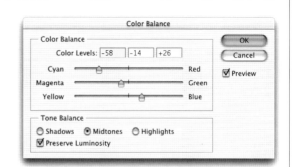

10 To work directly on the individual layers with the usual tools and filters, choose *Layer > Rasterize > **Fill Content***. In this case, the gradient layer has been rasterized and treated with *Liquify* and then the *Glass* filter. The clipping path is still available in the other layers and can be accessed for trimming the artwork if necessary.

11 Finishing touches are made with *Filter > Render > **Lighting Effects***, with the texture channel set to the layer's own transparency, and a large airbrush set to **Soft Light**.

FILLED IN

A Rabelaisian main course demanded a lark stuffed in a blackbird, the combination stuffed in a partridge, and so on via pheasant, chicken, duck, goose, and eventually, a turkey. Other versions added other larger animals, and only considered the dish ready for carving when all was safely enclosed in an average-size horse. Choose a fat character and a folder of ready- or home-made textures, *Select > Modify > Contract*, and get stuffing.

1 Set suitably fat type into a new alpha channel. Commit the type. Do not deselect. Name the channel "plain."

2 With the "plain" channel visible, create another alpha channel, name it "inside 1" and choose *Select > Modify > Contract* to reduce the selection. You may have to repeat the process, since the maximum single reduction is only 16 pixels. The exact number of pixels is not important, just the spacing between the new selection and the original type. When the selection looks right, hit Delete to leave a white area against a black background. Don't deselect.

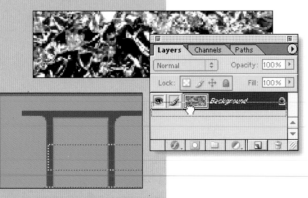

Infilled letters: textured

3 Using the same procedure, make a third channel "inside 2" with a further reduced selection knocked out of the background. Deselect.

4 Return to the Layers palette, fill layer 1 with a color for the background, make a new layer, load the selection of the "plain" channel (use *Select > Load Selection*, or Cmd/Ctrl-click on the channel icon in the Channels palette). Fill this selection with color. Deselect.

5 Load the "inside 1" selection in the same way and hit Delete. Deselect. Name this layer "top."

6 Open a document containing a suitable image or texture. It must be the same pixel size as, or larger than, the type document. This example is a scan of crumpled aluminum foil. Drag the texture document's layer icon into the center of the type document window—a thick line will appear around the window when the transfer is successful.

7 The imported image will create a new layer. Use *Image > Trim* with Based On: Transparent Pixels selected to delete the unseen pixels which Photoshop otherwise preserves outside the image area.

8 Working in the new layer, load the selection of the "inside 1" channel, go to *Select > Inverse,* and hit Delete to remove the surplus background. Deselect.

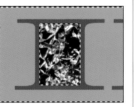

9 Colorize the trimmed layer in *Image > Adjustments > Hue/Saturation*.

10 Apply *Filter > Sketch > Stamp* at a high value of Light/Dark Balance, then use *Edit > Fade Stamp* to change the blend mode to Color Burn. You may also need to reduce the opacity.

Vita

1 Some faces (this is Griffon) obligingly supply a ready-made outline. All that's then necessary is the magic wand tool to start the infilling process. Make a new layer on which to manipulate the selection. A colored background layer has been added here to make the effects clearer.

11 Further changes can be made by loading the selection of the "inside 2" channel. Here the selection has been feathered a few pixels, then color-shifted using *Image* > *Adjustments* > **Color Balance**.

12 Hide the "top" layer and use *Layer* > *Layer Style* > **Bevel and Emboss** to emboss the infill area; use the Pillow Emboss style. As usual, the position of the global light is crucial. Use an alternative gloss contour—this one is "Ring-Double"—to get a well-defined edge.

13 This is the result of applying the **Layer Style**.

14 Make the "top" layer active and use **Layer Style** again, this time with the basic Emboss style, the default gloss contour, and a small drop shadow.

3 Go to *Image* > *Adjustments* > **Curves**, and draw a switchback curve to achieve a faux marble effect.

4 The use of Curves disturbs the contrast levels and produces edge effects; *Image* > *Adjustments* > **Color Balance** has been used as well (highlights 100% cyan, midtones 100% magenta, and shadows 100% yellow) to modify the texture.

2 Fill the selection with **50% Gray**, then use *Filter* > *Render* > **Clouds** to vary the surface. Deselect.

Sunset strip

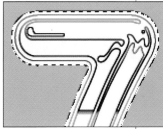

1 Create a new document with a pink background, and set the type. This face, Chromatic, is ideal for dissection. There is no need to rasterize the type.

2 Select elements of the letterforms with the magic wand tool, make a new layer, and fill the selection with a gradient (this is Photoshop's Chrome gradient). The type layer has been reduced in opacity to make the effect clearer. Deselect.

3 Use the magic wand to select other parts of the characters, and fill the selection with a different gradient in the same way. Continue until you have filled the characters, with the remaining highlights filled with white. Deselect.

4 To define the edges of the colored areas, duplicate the filled layer and use *Filter* > *Stylize* > **Find Edges**.

5 The new type layer is set to Color Burn mode and merged with the layer below. A small drop shadow is applied (*Layer* > *Layer Style* > **Drop Shadow**). The original type layer can be discarded.

BY HAND

WHO NEEDS calligraphy when there are swathes of readymade fonts that reproduce the scribe's flowing hand? Nobody. But there is a mesmeric satisfaction to be gained in devising your own style, incorporating fantastic curlicues and eccentric letterforms. No need to worry about running out of ink or vellum, your goose-quill ever sharp, the miracle potion *Undo* at your side. Monastic bliss.

1 Set up a document with a plain (no checkerboard) background and drag out two guides to represent the height of the lower-case characters. (Deselect *View > Snap to > Guides* if necessary).

2 Select the paintbrush in the toolbox, and click to the right of the brush-shape icon in the options palette. Bring up the pop-up menu and select **Calligraphic Brushes**. Select **Append** in the next dialog box.

3 There are 16 preset calligraphic brushes in the set—all can be modified if necessary. For now, choose the largest-angled oval brush.

4 This technique is almost impossible with a mouse or trackball—use a stylus and tablet if possible. To get familiar with the calligraphic brush, disable the pressure-sensitive feature in the **Brush Dynamics** panel in the Brushes palette (PS7).

5 If you are used to calligraphic pen work, this will be second nature; the rest of us have to struggle as best we can. Try to resist the temptation to duplicate the odd successful letter—the effect is diminished by characters that are too similar and perfect.

6 Having decreased the opacity of the first attempt, make a new layer and draw again over the template. Repeat until you are satisfied with the result.

Dot-to-Dot

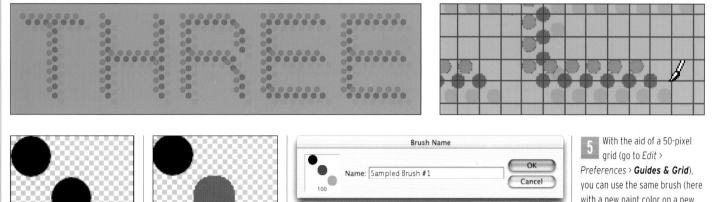

1 Make a new document 100 pixels square. Use the elliptical marquee tool to draw a circle 33 pixels in diameter. Fill it with black and duplicate it twice. (Alternatively use the elliptical shape tool, using the "Fixed Size" option set to 33 px by 33 px, then rasterize the layer.) Arrange the disks as shown (flatten the document if necessary to make one layer).

2 Select the center and lower right disks (use the magic wand tool) and fill them with medium and light gray. Deselect, then click on the layer thumbnail to select all the disks. Confirm in the Info palette that the selection is 100 pixels square (if not, you will have to maneuver the corner disks), deselect, then choose *Select* > **All**.

3 Go to *Edit* > **Define Brush**, and this dialog will appear. Check that the brush width has recorded correctly as 100 pixels. There's no need to name the brush at this stage. Hit OK.

4 Select the paintbrush tool and choose the newly created brush in the drop-down Brushes palette. Click on the Toggle Brushes palette icon in the options bar to open this dialog panel and increase the spacing value in the Brush Tip Shape section. The idea is to provide a space between the individual disks. You can name the brush here if you wish.

5 With the aid of a 50-pixel grid (go to *Edit* > *Preferences* > **Guides & Grid**), you can use the same brush (here with a new paint color on a new background) to produce modular letters made of spots.

Alternative styles

Make a new, large, document. Fill it with a bright color, make a new layer, select a contrasting color for the brush, and draw freehand with the mouse, as above, or with the Shift key held down to produce straight lines, center. More possibilities come with the pressure-sensitive stylus, right, set to increase stroke width and opacity in line with the pressure exerted.

Change the paint color and background again and use *Layer* > *Layer Style* > **Bevel and Emboss** to change the character of the spots. In this example, the "Pillow Emboss" style (with increased depth) has been used with the "Ring–Double" contour. Move the Shading light source around until you get the right result.

The same brush has been used to draw in an alpha channel (with paint color white) and blurred slightly for use as the texture channel in *Filter* > *Render* > **Lighting Effects**

WEATHERED

Peeling paint

A SCOTTISH distillery door shows signs of chromatic indecision—but it is not so. Barrelmakers were thrifty folk, and, over the years, unused paint from the stenciling and painting of barrel-ends was applied to keep out the Lowland weather. Now modern accounting practices mean that there is no surplus paint.

1 Set the type into a new alpha channel.

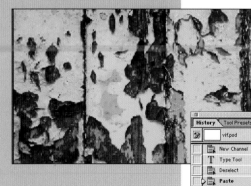

2 Deselect the type outline, return to the **Layers** palette, and paste in a suitable background image. Open the **History** palette and select **Create new Snapshot**.

3 Confirm the name "Snapshot 1" and click in the box alongside the new icon. This establishes the image as the source for the history brush.

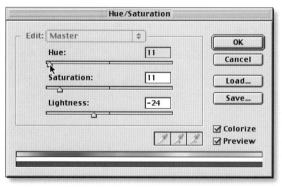

4 Modify the pasted image with, for example, *Image > Adjustments >* **Hue/Saturation**.

5 "Distress" the image with a small amount of monochromatic noise (*Filter > Noise >* **Add Noise**).

6 Continue the distressing process by adding a little blur (*Filter > Blur >* **Gaussian Blur**).

7 Load the selection from the alpha channel and feather it slightly (*Select >* **Feather**).

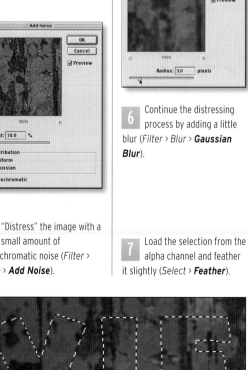

Dock to Palette Well

New Path...
Duplicate Path...
Delete Path

Make Work Path...

Make Selection...
Fill Path...
Stroke Path...

Clipping Path...

Palette Options...

13 To begin to soften the boundary between the "old" and "new" areas, make the feathered selection into a path.

8 Select the history brush from the toolbox.

11 Scrub the history brush diagonally across the selected area.

9 Select an irregular brush style in the options bar, and choose 50% opacity.

12 When the crosshatching is almost complete, change the brush mode to **Dissolve** to achieve an abraded effect. You may find it easier to work with the selection marquee hidden, as here.

14 Choose the blur tool from the toolbox and select a large, soft brush style. Choose **Stroke Path** in the **Paths** pop-up, and click on the blur tool.

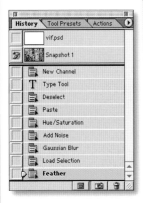

10 Check the **History** palette to see the progress of the successive states in the document.

Alternative styles

To make type disappear (almost) due to the ravages of weather and time, start with a face that's already on its way out. The characters (except the first) are treated incrementally with the listed effects. So, the O is moved to a new layer set to 60% Multiply mode; the N is duplicated as a layer and then treated with *Filter > Pixelate > Mezzotint > **Coarse Dots*** with the mode changed in Edit/Fade to Exclusion; and so on, with the E filtered with *Stylize >*

Diffuse (Lighten Only). "Away" suffers similarly: the A with *Sketch > **Conté Crayon*** with sliders central and Canvas texture, then the mode changed to Hard Light; the W filtered with *Artistic > **Paint Daubs*** (sliders central again); A has *Artistic > **Sponge*** (sliders central), mode changed to Overlay; and finally the Y is reduced to obscurity, after six treatments, through *Stylize > **Find Edges***, with the mode changed to Color Dodge.

IMPRESSIONS

THERE IS NO FIRMER print impression than that left by letterpress. A few tons of pressure is exerted momentarily on a solid piece of ink-coated metal type, into a more or less yielding sheet of paper, itself supported on an immovable base. The actual depth of the impression is microscopic, but that tiny edge effect is paramount in distinguishing letterpress from every other sort of direct contact printing. In the private press world, thick, handmade paper and the inconsistencies of hand-operated presses sometimes lead to impression depths on which you could trip and break a leg. Poetry, mostly, or large chunks of Chaucer.

Rubber stamp

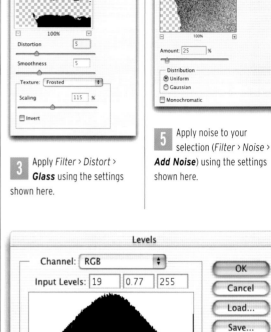

2 Apply *Filter* > *Distort* > **Ripple** using the settings shown here.

3 Apply *Filter* > *Distort* > **Glass** using the settings shown here.

5 Apply noise to your selection (*Filter* > *Noise* > **Add Noise**) using the settings shown here.

1 Create a new document. Select white as the background layer color. Type the word in black. Sans serif fonts work best with this effect. Go to *Layer* > *Type* > **Convert to Shape**; then apply *Edit* > *Transform* > **Perspective**, followed by **Scale** and **Rotate**. Rasterize the layer (*Layer* > *Rasterize* > **Layer**) once you are happy with your distorted text.

6 Adjust levels (*Image* > *Adjustments* > **Levels**) as shown here to "flatten" the effect somewhat.

4 The lettering should look like this now. Load a selection from the type layer (*Select* > **Load Selection**), with the type layer transparency as the selection channel and save

the selection as a channel for later use (*Select* > **Save Selection**)–name the new channel "outline." Next, apply *Filter* > *Render* > **Clouds** to the type layer.

7 Apply *Filter* > *Blur* > **Gaussian Blur** with a radius of about 1.5 pixels.

8 Expand the selection by 2 pixels (*Select* > *Modify* > **Expand**). Create a new layer underneath the type layer and fill the selection with black.

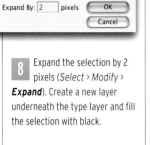

9 Deselect and apply *Filter* > *Blur* > **Gaussian Blur**, then merge the new layer with the white background (*Layer* > **Merge Down**). Deselect.

10 Apply *Filter* > *Noise* > **Add Noise** to the whole of the background layer.

11 The background layer should now look like this. (For clarity the original type layer has been hidden in this screen shot.)

12 Apply *Filter* > *Blur* > **Gaussian Blur** to the background layer with a radius of about 1.7 pixels.

13 Use *Image* > *Adjustments* > **Curves** to lighten the background a little to achieve an appearance like this–you may need to experiment here. (This view shows the original type layer visible on top of the background layer that is being worked on.)

14 In the Channels palette, make a copy of the "outline" channel. Cmd/Ctrl-click on the new channel to select the type, then invert the selection to select the black background. Apply *Filter* > *Noise* > **Add Noise**, then *Filter* > *Blur* > **Gaussian Blur**. Invert the selection again and apply *Filter* > *Render* > **Clouds** followed by *Filter* > *Noise* > **Add Noise**. Finally use *Image* > *Adjustments* > **Curves** to lighten the type so that it looks as shown here. Deselect.

15 Return to the Layers palette and flatten the image (*Layer* > **Flatten Image**), then apply *Filter* > *Render* > **Lighting Effects** using the settings shown here. Select the "outline copy" channel as the texture channel.

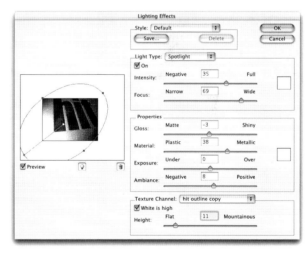

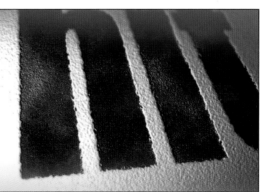

16 To add more drama to the image, make a horizontal selection of the center of the window, invert the selection and feather by around 100 pixelspply *Filter* > *Blur* > **Gaussian Blur** to throw the foreground and background out of focus.

ALL SEWN UP

No ANIMALS SUFFERED during the production of Photoshop leather, nor during its typographic embellishment. This smoothly finished faux antelope glacé obligingly crimps under the pressure of nothing more painful than Bevel and Emboss. Move on from here via Wild Boar (add Noise, KPT FiberOptix, and Smudge) to the more recalcitrant texture of Flayed Reindeer (fill pink, Clouds, then Chalk & Charcoal). Add Beads (page 144), Gold (page 39), or a ceramic plaque (page 80) for a high-fashion look.

Leather stitch

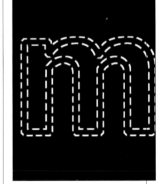

3 Make a selection from the type layer and create a new channel—name it "Moo." Stroke the selection with 7 pixels white, location: center (*Edit* > **Stroke**).

1 Create a leather effect background either by scanning some leather or import one from a picture library. The effect shown was created in Photoshop using *Render* > **Clouds**.

4 Now create the outer stitching for the type. With the selection still active, create a new channel—name it "stitching," expand your selction by 6 pixels, and stroke the selection with 3 pixels white. Save your selection as a path. Deselect. Go to the brushes palette and create a new brush as screen shot–selecting your new brush. Make sure your foreground color is set to black. Then Select "Stoke path" from the Paths palette–with the tool as a painbrush. It should now look the way the picture does!

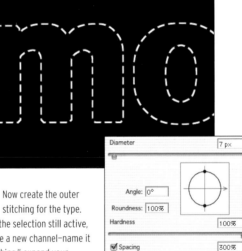

5 Create the inner stitching next. Make a selection of your type layer again, but this time contract the selection by 6 pixels and follow the steps as Step 4 again.

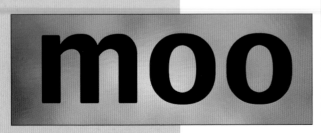

2 Type some text onto a new layer. We picked a nice bold sans serif face since it works particularly well for this fx.

6 Make a selection fron the channel named "Moo." Expand your selection by 8 pixels. Enter Quick mask mode and apply a Gaussian Blur of about 7.8 pixels. Create a new layer (this will be called layer 1) and fill the selection with R130, G130, B125.

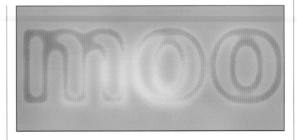

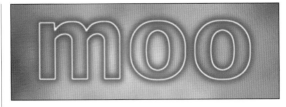

7 Create a new layer (this will call itself layer 2) and make a new selection from channel named "Moo." Contract selection by 2 pixels, Feather by 1 pixel (*Select* > **Feather**), and fill with white.

11 With the selection active, Select the background layer (the leather image) and create a new layer from the background layer. Name the layer "effect" (*Layer* > *New* > **Layer via copy**).

12 With the layer named "effect" as your active layer use the lighting effects filter to give it the embossed effect. *Filter* > *Render* > **Lighting effects**. Don't forget to load the channel named "type" as the texture channel.

8 Make a new selection from the channel named stitching and create a new layer (layer 3). Feather your selelction by a 1-pixel radius. Fill with R60, G60, and B60. Nudge the layer 1 pixel up and to the right to slightly offset it.

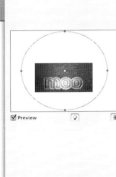

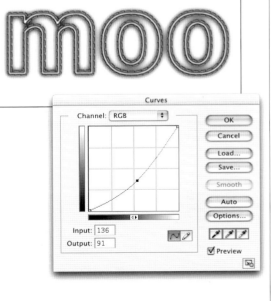

9 Make a new selection from the channel named "Stitching" and create a new layer (layer 4), this time filling your selection with R194, G194, B194.

10 Merge all four layers created since step 6–and Load the layer as a new selection. Then *Edit* > **Copy**. Create a new channel–call it "type." (Make sure the channel is initially filled with white instead of black.) With the selection still active, *Edit* > **Paste** into your new channel. Now use Curves to darken the channel slightly.

13 All that's left to do now is add the color for the stitching. Load the channel named "Stitching" and on a new layer fill it with R247, G240, and B211. Finally, set the layer to 70% opacity.

GRAVEL RASH

Highway

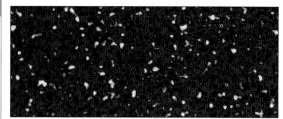

EQUIPPED WITH A JUG of steaming thermoplastic paint, the brave highway typographer does an athletic tango in the traffic with a six-inch applicator on a stick. Imagine the difficulty of applying an even coating while concentrating on the niceties of representing a riderless bicycle. It's hard to love someone who paints "No-parking" lines for a living; simple admiration is probably the correct sentiment.

1 Fill a layer with 50% Gray, and use *Filter* › *Noise* › **Add** **Noise** at around 50% strength to add monochromatic noise.

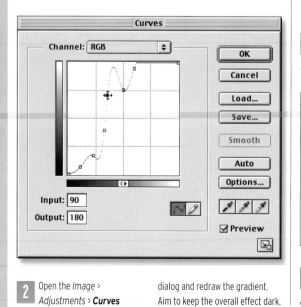

2 Open the *Image* › *Adjustments* › **Curves** dialog and redraw the gradient. Aim to keep the overall effect dark.

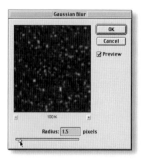

3 The result of applying the Curves command.

4 Copy the layer, make a new alpha channel, and paste in the copy. Blur the channel slightly (*Filter* › *Blur* › **Gaussian Blur**). Hit OK.

5 Remaining in the Channels palette, create another new alpha channel, select foreground color white, set the type, and commit it. Deselect.

6 Having slightly blurred the type, *Filter* › *Noise* › **Median** will round off the edges.

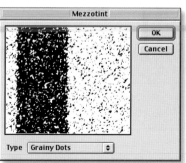

7 Cmd/Ctrl-click in the channel thumbnail to make a selection, then apply *Filter* › *Pixelate* › **Mezzotint** with Type: Grainy dots. Hit OK.

Fade

Opacity: 50 %   OK

Cancel

Mode: Hard Light ⬦

☑ Preview

11 Use the *Edit* › **Fade Lighting Effects** function to reduce the strength of the filter.

8 Cmd/Ctrl -click again in the channel thumbnail to activate the new speckled selection. Return to the Layers palette, make a new layer, select yellow as the foreground color, and fill the selection. Deselect.

10 Merge layers, go to *Filter* › *Render* › **Lighting Effects** and use the preset style "Five Lights Up" as a starting point. Delete three of the lamps by clicking on the white spot and hitting Backspace (Mac)/Delete (Windows); drag the beams of the remaining two lamps to cover the letterforms. Use the alpha 1 channel (the original road surface) as the texture channel.

Lighting Effects

Style: Five Lights Up ⬦   OK

Save...   Delete   Cancel

Light Type: Spotlight ⬦
☑ On

Intensity: Negative   100   Full

Focus: Narrow   60   Wide

Properties

Gloss: Matte   0   Shiny

Material: Plastic   0   Metallic

Exposure: Under   50   Over

Ambiance: Negative   10   Positive

Texture Channel: Alpha 1 ⬦
☑ White is high

Height: Flat   50   Mountainous

☑ Preview

9 Use the eraser tool to break up the lettering edges and the burn tool (with Range: Highlights selected in the options bar) to vary the color intensity. Change the layer's blending mode to Hard Light and reduce its opacity to around 90%.

Alternative styles

When you see this on the road it's time to pull over. Start with a vast canvas and relatively small type to allow for the eventual perspective effect, otherwise the technique is similar to the main example. Try Craquelure in the *Filter* › **Texture** menu as an alternative method of breaking up the characters. Apply the Lighting Effects controls when your image is still "in the flat," and when you're done, select the whole canvas and apply Perspective from the *Edit* › **Transform** menu. You'll have to use Scale as well in the same menu to reduce the vertical size. Drive on.

WRIT LARGE

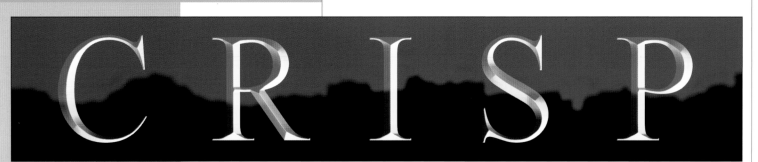

SECURE THE PAPER with your drawn letters to a sheet of glass, and cover the background only with black paint on the reverse of the glass. Set aside to dry. Square up a timber plank and plane it absolutely flat. Use the drawing to lay out and carve the required letters into the wood. Apply gold leaf to the carved characters, and make sure that it continues a little way over their edges. Lay the glass over the wood, paint side down, and fix to your shopfront.

4 The gradient layer letters should resemble these.

1 Choose a suitable face, such as Times New Roman, set the type color to deep yellow, set, and commit the type.

2 Duplicate the type layer and name the copy "gradient."

3 Working on the "gradient" layer, click on the Layer Style icon at the foot of the Layer palette, and choose Stroke. Ensure you can still see at least some part of your image. Four changes are necessary from the default settings: change the Fill type to Gradient; change the accompanying Style to Shape Burst; in the Structure panel, change Position to Inside, and increase the size of the stroke. Note the effect of these changes in your image window, especially the size setting.

5 Insert a solid black layer under the filled characters and merge these two layers. Select all, copy, and go to the Channels palette. Make a new alpha channel, name it "gradient," and select Paste. Return to the Layers palette, delete the merged layer, and make the original yellow type layer active.

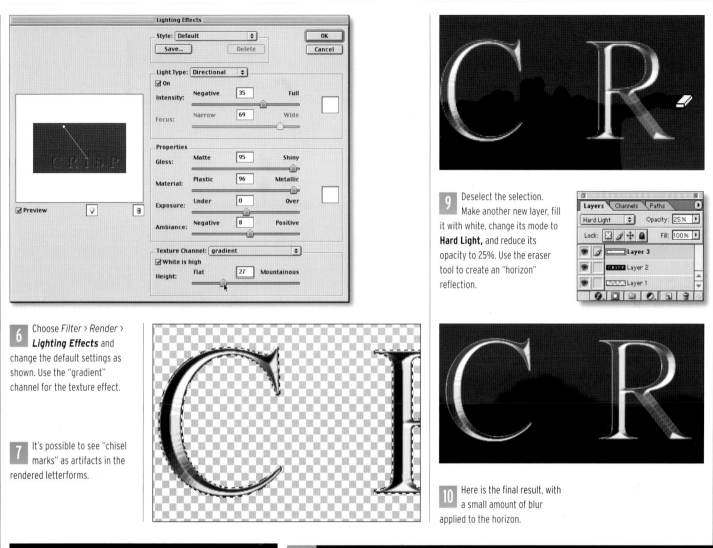

6 Choose *Filter* > *Render* > **Lighting Effects** and change the default settings as shown. Use the "gradient" channel for the texture effect.

7 It's possible to see "chisel marks" as artifacts in the rendered letterforms.

9 Deselect the selection. Make another new layer, fill it with white, change its mode to **Hard Light,** and reduce its opacity to 25%. Use the eraser tool to create an "horizon" reflection.

10 Here is the final result, with a small amount of blur applied to the horizon.

8 Make a new layer, select **Inverse**, then *Select* > *Modify* > **Expand**. Increase the selection by one pixel to ensure it covers the lettering edges and fill it with black.

Alternative styles

With one small amendment, a completely different effect can be achieved. In the Stroke dialog (see step 3 opposite) the selection is changed to Outside. The width of this fill can be extended, even to the extent of encircling adjacent letters. In this case, the fill is enlarged only slightly, and the resulting texture map is used in Lighting Effects to treat a plain pink area rather than the letterforms themselves.

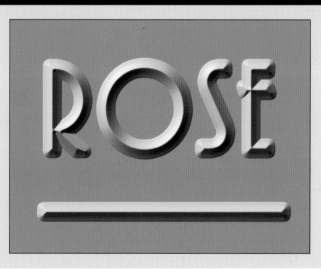

COOK IT UP

WHO REMEMBERS the apocryphal "Please don't throw rocks at this sign" sign? A panel called "Fire" is just asking to get charred. Luckily, Photoshop fire is both harmless and reversible. The key here is to work progressively with soft-edged selections and low filter values, using Edit > Fade to tone down successive results. The intention is to toast rather than to vaporize.

1 Create a new file (10 x 10 cm at 300 dpi), make a new layer called "board," and draw a signboard shape using the selection tools. If necessary, use *Edit* > **Free Transform** to create the angled board shown here. Fill this shape with gray, setting all three RGB values to 100.

Alternative styles

This alternative has the letters spaced out individually. The same effects are applied to the letters as to the board in the main effect (see steps 5-15). Anyone for freshly chargrilled burgers?

Charred wood

2 Create a second new layer, called "post," draw the posts using your selection tools, and fill them with the same gray color. Duplicate both layers and fill the duplicates with black. Move the black layers below the gray layers, and adjust them as shown. Merge the two "board" layers and the two "post" layers.

3 Set the foreground color to black, and use a 5-pixel hard round paintbrush to "join" the black and gray layers on both "board" and "post."

4 Apply *Filter* > *Artistic* > **Sponge** with brush size set at 2, definition at 12, and smoothness at 5 on both layers.

5 On both layers, apply *Image* > **Liquify** (PS6)   *Filter* > **Liquify** (PS7) and create a grain effect using the warp tool.

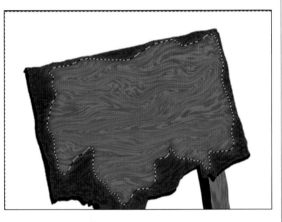

6 On the "board" layer create a mask using the lasso tool. Go to *Select* > **Inverse** and then *Select* > **Feather**, set to 12 pixels. Apply *Filter* > *Stylize* > **Diffuse** *set to* "Normal" to roughen up the edges, then apply *Image* > *Adjustments* > **Brightness/**   **Contrast** with both contrast and brightness set to -45. Repeat the last three steps on the post layer.

7 Go to *Edit* > **Copy Merged** (to merge the "board" and "post" layers), and paste them into a new layer called "sign." On another new layer create the text in white (we have used Franklin Gothic Extra Condensed at 90 pt),   then rasterize the layer and set its blend mode to "overlay." Use *Edit* > **Free Transform** to rotate the text, and apply *Filter* > *Stylize* > **Diffuse** set to "Normal" three times to roughen the edges.

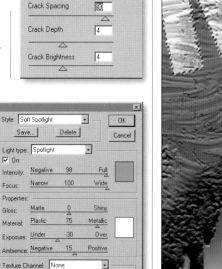

12 Select the "sign" layer and apply *Filter > Texture > Craquelure* with Spacing set to 90, Depth to 4, and Brightness also at 4, then choose *Edit > Fade Craquelure* and fade to 50%.

13 Select the "smoke back" layer and apply lighting effects as shown here. The values for the orange color are R248, G82, and B0.

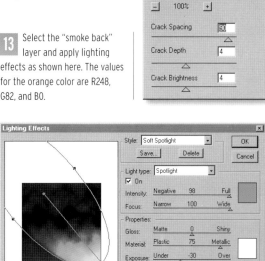

8 On the sign layer, define a shape using the lasso tool, choose *Select > Inverse*, then go to *Select > Feather* set to 12 pixels.

10 Create a new layer called "smoke back," and fill it with a linear gradient from black to white. (If necessary reset the colors by pressing D.) Apply *Filter > Render > Difference Clouds*.

14 Create a selection using the lasso tool, set the feathering to 64, and delete the bottom right area of the layer. Deselect.

15 Select the "text" layer, Cmd/Ctrl-click on it to select the word "fire" and use the 58-pixel spatter airbrush at 10% pressure to dirty the lettering. Deselect.

16 Finally select the "sign" layer and apply *Filter > Render > Lighting effects* as shown here.

11 Duplicate the "smoke back" layer, name it "smoke fore," drag it to the top of the layer stack, and set its blend mode to "screen."

9 Apply *Filter > Texture > Craquelure* with Spacing set to 15, Depth to 6, and Brightness to 9. Deselect.

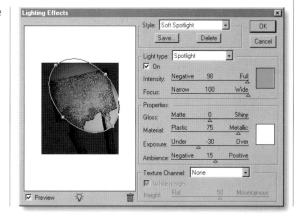

GENUINE ANTIQUE

In a mere 18 moves, William's old wooden grave-marker takes on the gravitas of years in the relentless desert sun, attacked by termites, and eroded by sudden sandstorms and the attentions of thoughtless tourists. Faced with this memorial, all humanity must ponder the fragility of life, but there is a yet more important message contained on these pages. It is addressed to a select group—their names appear when the "About Photoshop" message is accessed. And the message is: "Why can't there be proper preview screens in the Layer Style dialog? If we can do it, why won't you?"

1 Create a new document 6in x 3½in (15 cm x 9 cm) with a white background. Make a new layer, use the lasso tool to create the wooden shape, and name it "wood."

2 Either create a wood pattern from scratch or re-use the wood pattern created for Marquetry (see page 138), and use the paint bucket tool to fill your selection with this pattern.

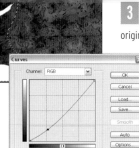

3 Use the lasso tool to select a new shape within the original one. Invert the selection with *Selection > **Inverse***, then choose *Selection > **Feather*** with a radius of 32 pixels. Finally use *Image > Adjustments > **Curves*** to darken the edges. We used an Input value of 70% and an Output value of 49%.

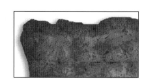

4 Reduce the layer opacity to 84% and apply *Layer > Layer Style > **Drop Shadow*** with the values shown here.

5 Use *Layer > Layer Style > **Inner Glow*** with the values shown here and color values set at R95, G56, B19 to complete the piece of wood.

6 Set the text on a new text layer (here we have used Poster Bodoni, 48/60 pt, with track set to 50, and color settings of R166, G124, B82), and center it within the wooden shape.

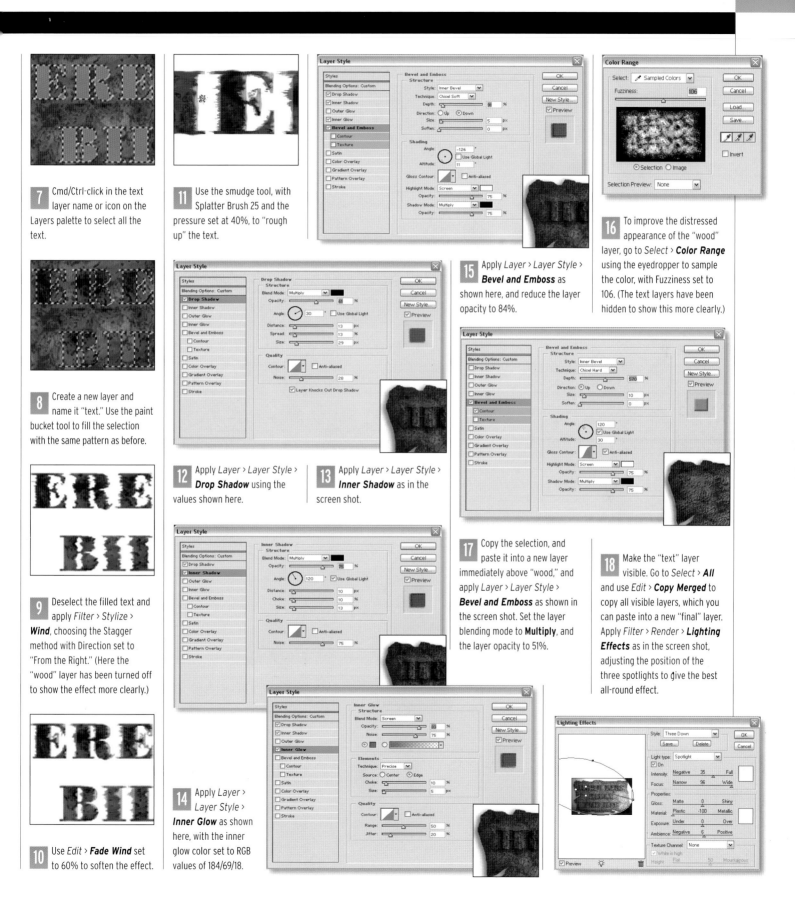

7 Cmd/Ctrl-click in the text layer name or icon on the Layers palette to select all the text.

8 Create a new layer and name it "text." Use the paint bucket tool to fill the selection with the same pattern as before.

9 Deselect the filled text and apply *Filter* > *Stylize* > **Wind**, choosing the Stagger method with Direction set to "From the Right." (Here the "wood" layer has been turned off to show the effect more clearly.)

10 Use *Edit* > **Fade Wind** set to 60% to soften the effect.

11 Use the smudge tool, with Splatter Brush 25 and the pressure set at 40%, to "rough up" the text.

12 Apply *Layer* > *Layer Style* > **Drop Shadow** using the values shown here.

13 Apply *Layer* > *Layer Style* > **Inner Shadow** as in the screen shot.

14 Apply *Layer* > *Layer Style* > **Inner Glow** as shown here, with the inner glow color set to RGB values of 184/69/18.

15 Apply *Layer* > *Layer Style* > **Bevel and Emboss** as shown here, and reduce the layer opacity to 84%.

16 To improve the distressed appearance of the "wood" layer, go to *Select* > **Color Range** using the eyedropper to sample the color, with Fuzziness set to 106. (The text layers have been hidden to show this more clearly.)

17 Copy the selection, and paste it into a new layer immediately above "wood," and apply *Layer* > *Layer Style* > **Bevel and Emboss** as shown in the screen shot. Set the layer blending mode to **Multiply**, and the layer opacity to 51%.

18 Make the "text" layer visible. Go to *Select* > **All** and use *Edit* > **Copy Merged** to copy all visible layers, which you can paste into a new "final" layer. Apply *Filter* > *Render* > **Lighting Effects** as in the screen shot, adjusting the position of the three spotlights to give the best all-round effect.

SNAKE EYES

If SERPENTS, even fake ones, make you nervous, skip this page. There are other, harmless, references to creating your own patterns, and the use of the Liquify tool, throughout this book. Otherwise, take this example as a starting point; selective application of Lighten and Desaturate will give you anything from shedding of the skin to a full moult; Extrude (select Pyramids) could make a hide for Tyrannosaurus Rex; 3D transform might, in time, offer you a complete pocketbook.

3 Use the rectangular marquee tool (with feathering set to 0) to create a selection that exactly bisects the outer diamonds, and use this to create the pattern using *Edit* > **Define Pattern**. Name it "reptile skin."

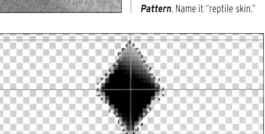

1 Create a new document 4in x 2in (10 cm x 5 cm), with a white background, and start by making the skin pattern. On a new layer, use the custom shape tool set to the diamond shape to make a diamond 0.05 in x 0.07 in (0.12 cm x 0.18 cm). In the options bar, choose "Create filled region," and click the "Geometry options" down-arrow (to the right of the "Custom Shape Tool" button) to open the Custom Shape Options pop-up window, choosing Fixed Size and From Center. Set the foreground color to black and the background color values set at R184, G184, B184. Select and fill the diamond shape with a linear blend (foreground to background), and angle the blend from bottom left to top right.

4 Create a new layer, select the fill tool, and choose the "reptile skin" pattern from the option bar. The new layer will now be filled with the repeated (tiled) pattern—name it "skin."

5 Use the text tool to create text on a new layer. (We used Enya 100 pt, colored with values R184, G184, B184.)

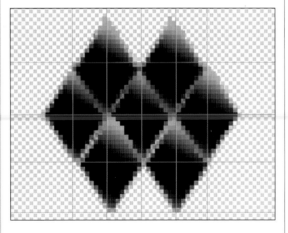

2 Use the move tool with the Option/Alt key held down to drag-copy this diamond six times, creating the arrangement shown here. Add guides to frame your diamond, and use *View* > *Snap To* > **Guides** to help position the new diamonds. Add extra guides as required.

6 Rasterize the text layer, use the magic wand tool to select each letter, and reposition it with the move tool as required. Name this layer "text."

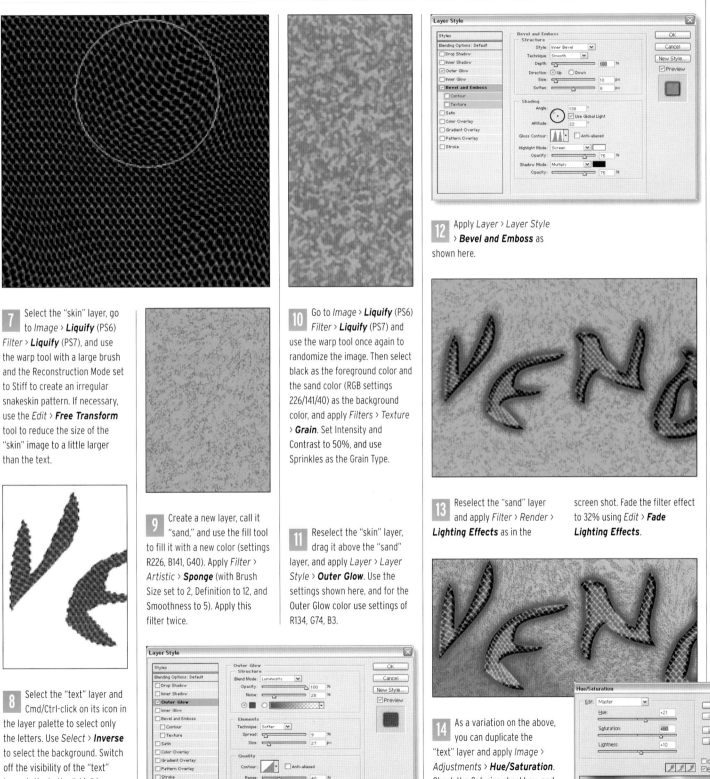

7 Select the "skin" layer, go to *Image* > **Liquify** (PS6) *Filter* > **Liquify** (PS7), and use the warp tool with a large brush and the Reconstruction Mode set to Stiff to create an irregular snakeskin pattern. If necessary, use the *Edit* > **Free Transform** tool to reduce the size of the "skin" image to a little larger than the text.

8 Select the "text" layer and Cmd/Ctrl-click on its icon in the layer palette to select only the letters. Use *Select* > **Inverse** to select the background. Switch off the visibility of the "text" layer. Activate the "skin" layer, and use your selection to delete the background, leaving the skin pattern within the letterforms.

9 Create a new layer, call it "sand," and use the fill tool to fill it with a new color (settings R226, B141, G40). Apply *Filter* > *Artistic* > **Sponge** (with Brush Size set to 2, Definition to 12, and Smoothness to 5). Apply this filter twice.

10 Go to *Image* > **Liquify** (PS6) *Filter* > **Liquify** (PS7) and use the warp tool once again to randomize the image. Then select black as the foreground color and the sand color (RGB settings 226/141/40) as the background color, and apply *Filters* > *Texture* > **Grain**. Set Intensity and Contrast to 50%, and use Sprinkles as the Grain Type.

11 Reselect the "skin" layer, drag it above the "sand" layer, and apply *Layer* > *Layer Style* > **Outer Glow**. Use the settings shown here, and for the Outer Glow color use settings of R134, G74, B3.

12 Apply *Layer* > *Layer Style* > **Bevel and Emboss** as shown here.

13 Reselect the "sand" layer and apply *Filter* > *Render* > **Lighting Effects** as in the screen shot. Fade the filter effect to 32% using *Edit* > **Fade Lighting Effects**.

14 As a variation on the above, you can duplicate the "text" layer and apply *Image* > *Adjustments* > **Hue/Saturation**. Check the Colorize checkbox, and set Hue to +21, Saturation to +60, and Lightness to +10 for an alternative colorway.

MUMMIFIED

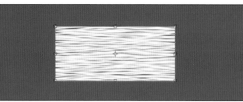

NERVOUS OR FRIGHTENED children can have their cuts and grazes bound up with adhesive bandages printed with comforting little furry animals. From now on, diffident typographers, unsure of which type effect to employ, can put off the evil day of decision by swathing the words in bandages. Imagine your domestic electrical goods client, looking forward at presentation to the unveiling of a shiny new logo. What a piece of theater when it appears first mummified, then coyly revealed through artful dissolves in all its chromium glory. And there are hardly any sticky residues.

1 Create a new file (this one was 4½ x 2in (12 x 5 cm). Change the RGB settings for your foreground and background colors to 137/12/12 and 100/100/100 respectively. Then create a new layer called "red" and fill it with the foreground color. Change the foreground color to white, create a second new layer called "bandage," and fill it with this color. Cmd/Ctrl-click on the "bandage" layer, go to *Filter > Artistic > Sponge* and set Brush Size to 2, Definition to 15, and Smoothness to 13. Click OK to apply the filter.

2 Apply *Filter > Blur > Motion Blur*, then *Filter > Sharpen > Unsharp Mask* with the settings shown here.

3 Repeat *Motion Blur*, *Unsharp Mask*, and *Motion Blur* again, with the same settings, then apply *Image > Adjustments > Invert* to create a white image with black detail.

4 Using *Edit > Free Transform*, reduce the size of the image to approximately that shown on the screen shot, holding down the Shift key to keep the original proportions.

5 Duplicate the "bandage" layer and move the duplicate to the right so it abuts on your original image. Apply *Edit > Transform > Flip Horizontal* to create a seamless join between the two layers. Hide all other layers, click on the flyout arrow at the top right of the Layers palette, select **Merge Visible**, and rename the merged layer as "bandage."

6 Show the other layers, then change the blending mode for the bandage layer to **Screen** and its opacity to 54%. Using the rectangular marquee tool, select a thin strip of the image. Invert the selection, delete, and then deselect. This leaves a thin strip of bandage. Invert the selection again, and then, using *Edit > Free Transform*, rotate the image to a diagonal position–about -45 degrees.

7 Duplicate the "bandage" layer (the duplicate is auto-named "bandage copy") and on this new layer move the image so that it just overlaps the original layer, then apply *Edit > Free Transform* to rotate the image a couple of degrees. Repeat until most of the document is covered. Vary the amount of overlap, the angle, and the north-south position of each layer so that they are not too uniform. Although the text has not yet been created, these bandage strips must cover it.

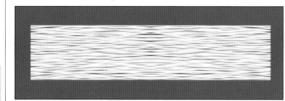

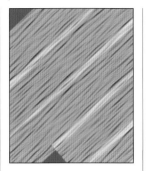

8 Hide all layers except the "bandage" layers, click the flyout arrow on the Layers palette, and select **Merge Visible**. Set the layer blending mode to **Screen** and rename this layer "bandage."

9 Select *Image* > **Liquify** (PS6) *Filter* > **Liquify** (PS7), and, using the twirl and pucker tools (at their default settings), distort the image so it looks more like bandages.

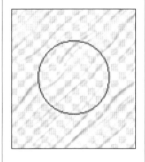

10 Select *Image* > *Adjustments* > **Brightness/Contrast** and apply contrast only at -15.

11 Set the foreground color to white. Create a new layer and name it "text." Using the type tool, add the text–in this instance PHARAOH. (We have used the font Blur Bold at 60 pt: any other rounded bold sans serif font would do.) Move the text to a central position and then move the "text" layer below the "bandage" layer.

12 On the "text" layer use the magic wand tool (and *Select* > **Similar**) to select the background. Contract the selection (*Select* > *Modify* > **Contract**) by 16 pixels, then *Select* > *Modify* > **Feather** by 6 pixels. Now click on the "bandage" layer and delete the background.

13 Select the "text" layer and go to *Layer* > **Layer Style** to apply the Drop Shadow, Outer Glow, and Bevel and Emboss effects, as shown in the screen shots.

14 Hide the "text" layer and deselect. Select the "bandage" layer and apply *Image* > *Adjustments* > **Hue/ Saturation**, with Lightness set to 70 and the other settings at 0. Change the layer opacity to 85%. Show the "text" layer and choose *Select* > **All**. Go to *Edit* > **Copy Merged**, and then *Edit* > **Paste**, which will create a new layer. Rename this layer "final."

15 Apply *Filter* > *Render* > **Lighting Effects** as shown below, then go to *Edit* > **Fade Lighting Effects** and set the fade to 50%.

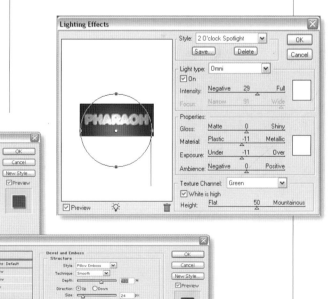

LEAD AND LIGHT

Stained glass

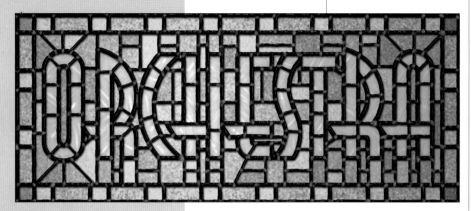

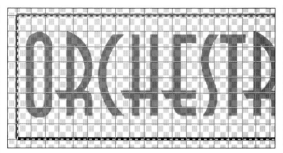

THERE ARE THREE methods of producing stained-glass panels. Traditionally, an H-section (on its side) lead bar (a "cane") is formed around the cut-glass pieces, and the adjoining parts soldered together. Crucial equipment: a small piece of wood (a "fid") for opening out the "arms" of the lead section to accept the glass. Handy tip: brush special cement under the cane edges when finished to stop the glass from rattling. The second method employs self-adhesive copper foil to bind the glass edges. Solder is again used to secure the panel. Crucial equipment: a small piece of plastic (known as a "lathekin") to burnish the foil. Handy tip: when soldering, don't spill the acid flux on your shoes. The third method is outlined here. Crucial equipment: coffee. Handy tip: take a break every two hours.

1 Create a document with a round number of pixels (or whatever unit you prefer) in each dimension. Set the type into a layer and rasterize it (*Layer > Rasterize > Type*). Leave sufficient surrounding space to allow for a supporting framework.

Stroke

Stroke
Width: 15 px
Color: ▮

OK
Cancel

Location
● Inside ○ Center ○ Outside

Blending
Mode: Normal
Opacity: 100 %
☐ Preserve Transparency

2 Make a new layer, *Select > All* and go to *Edit > **Stroke*** to make a frame at the edge of the document; choose Location: Inside, and deselect the "Preserve Transparency" checkbox. Deselect.

3 Set up a grid (using *Edit > Preferences > **Guides, Grid & Slices**, Preferences* is under the "Photoshop" menu in Mac OS X), which divides the image into whole squares, select *View > Snap To > **Grid*** and draw a rectangular marquee one square from the edge. Stroke this selection with the same settings as before, but with Location: Center selected. Hit OK. Deselect. The type layer has been reduced in opacity to make these moves clearer.

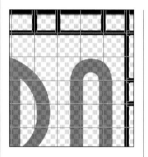

4 Select the line tool from the shapes palette in the toolbox. In the options bar, choose the line width to match the existing strokes, and draw a short line between the two rectangles. You'll see a new, automatically created, "Shape 1" layer appear in the Layers palette. Make sure that "Add to shape area" is selected, and continue to develop the framework.

5 Turn off the grid (*View > Show > Grid*). Cmd/Ctrl-click on the type layer to select the shape of the type, then return to the layer with the frames. Stroke the selection as before, but this time choose Location: Outside. Deselect.

6 Make sure *View > Snap* is turned off, return to the "Shape 1" layer and choose a narrower line tool to fill in the detail of the framework. Be careful not to leave gaps between the elements of the frame.

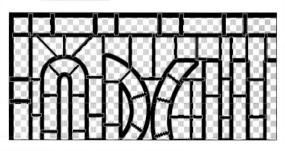

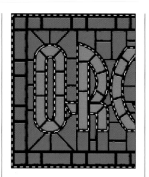

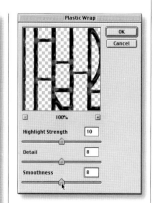

7 Create a new layer under the framework layer, make a selection of the type, increase it by a few pixels (*Select* > *Modify* > **Expand**) and fill it with the main lettering color. Go to *Select* > **Inverse** and fill with a contrasting color–the actual hue is not important. Deselect.

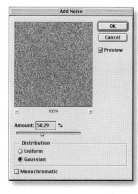

8 Make the top layer invisible, and apply *Filter* > *Noise* > **Add Noise** to the colored layer. Blur the result using *Filter* > *Blur* > **Gaussian Blur** at a low radius setting.

9 Reactivate the top layer (which contains the frames) and rasterize it. Choose the magic wand tool set to a large tolerance, check the "Contiguous" and "Use All Layers" boxes, and use the tool, with Shift held down to add to the existing selection, to select about a quarter of the cells that make up the lettering. For the best results, don't choose adjoining cells.

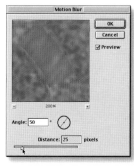

10 Move to the colored layer and apply motion blur (*Filter* > *Blur* > **Motion Blur**) to the selected cells. Deselect.

11 Continue in the same way, but using different motion blur settings, until all the lettering cells have been treated. Additionally, you can use the dodge and burn tools to introduce the striations that often appear in handmade glass.

12 To increase the glowing effect, make a selection of the original type, contract and feather it, then choose *Image* > *Adjustments* > **Hue/Saturation** to shift the hue and lightness. Deselect.

13 Continue in the same way with the background elements, again using *Image* > *Adjustments* > **Hue/Saturation**. Use related colors for the background elements to retain contrast with the letters.

14 Select the entire colored layer and use *Filter* > *Render* > **Lighting Effects** to simulate a light source. Deselect.

15 Return to the framework layer. Use the dodge tool (with Range: Shadows selected in the options bar) at the joins to simulate the effect of the solder that holds the whole structure together. Then use *Filter* > *Artistic* > **Plastic Wrap** to give some form to the "lead" work.

16 Go to *Edit* > *Fade* > **Plastic Wrap** if necessary to reduce excessive gloss. Finally, apply a small drop shadow to the lead framework (*Layer* > *Layer Style* > **Drop Shadow**).

WOOD WORKS

Marquetry

TOP-CLASS MARQUETRY demands devoted skills, ultra-sharp instruments, and a truly artistic eye. The colors are limited to naturally occurring wood tones, though some deviation is allowed by heating veneers in hot sand to vary the color. Photoshop marquetry is an easier discipline. Lack of artistic vision is easily compensated for with a photographic underlay. Scan in a photograph, apply *Filter > Artistic > Cutout* set to 8 levels, and you have a handy ready colored template. Images of wood abound, but why confine yourself to tree products? Any texture than can be scanned, photographed or found on a clip-art CD—grass, water, rock, metal, or fabric—will serve to be sliced and butted up to its neighbor. Typographic marquetry, however, is a serious business.

1 Create a new file, 5in x 1in in size. You need to start by creating a wood pattern (this technique is also used for Distressed Wood on page 128). Begin by setting your foreground color to values of R96, G57, B19, and your background color to values of R166, G124, B82. Create a new layer, name it "wood1," and apply *Filter > Render > **Clouds***.

2 Apply *Image > Adjustments > **Posterize*** with Levels set to 20, then duplicate "wood1" and name it "wood2."

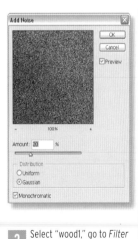

3 Select "wood1," go to *Filter > Noise > **Add Noise***, set the amount to 20, choose "Gaussian" and check the Monochromatic option.

4 Apply *Filter > Blur > **Motion Blur*** with Angle set to 45˚ and Distance to 40 pixels.

5 Apply *Image > Adjustments > **Brightness /Contrast*** with Contrast is set to +25.

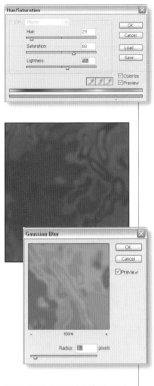

6 Apply *Filter > Blur > **Gaussian Blur*** set to 1.5 pixels.

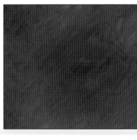

7 Select "wood2" and apply *Filter > Sketch > **Chrome*** with Detail set to 5 and Smoothness to 6. The layer will turn gray.

8 Apply *Image > Adjustments > **Hue/Saturation*** with Hue set to 29, Saturation set to 68, and Lightness set to 17. Be sure to check the "Colorize" checkbox. Apply *Filter > Blur > **Gaussian Blur*** set, once again, to 1.5 pixels.

9 Change the layer blending mode to **Multiply**. Go to *Select > **All*** and then to *Edit > **Copy Merged*** to copy these two layers, and paste them as a new layer called "wood combined." This layer can also be used for Distressed Wood on page 128, so it's worth saving as a pattern (simply go to *Edit > **Define Pattern*** and save as "walnut"). It has not been prepared for tiling, but, because it is dark, the joins will not show much if it is tiled, and can easily be retouched.

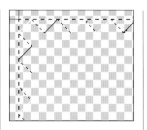

10 On a new layer, named "sawtooth," create a 2in x 1in triangle (we used the shape tool). If you choose the "Create filled region" (PS6) or "Fill Pixels" (PS7) option on the option bar you can fill it with any color you like– we reversed the foreground and background colors so we could use the original background color. Move or paste the triangle to place it at the top left. Drag guides out and they will snap to the triangle.

11 Use the magic wand tool to select the triangle, and the move tool (with the Option/Alt key held down) to drag and copy the selection to the right–it will snap to the guide. Continue doing this until you have created a complete row of triangles.

12 To create the sides, we used the marquee tool to select four triangles plus an additional half-triangle at either end. Copy the selection, paste it, and then use *Edit* > *Transform* > *Rotate 90° CW* to turn it into the correct position. Paste again and use *Edit* > *Transform* > *Rotate 90° CCW* for the other end. Finally copy and paste the top row of triangles to create the lower border, use *Edit* > *Transform* > *Flip Vertical*, and drag the row into position, lining up with the two side edges. If this process has created multiple layers, link them together and select *Layer* > *Merge Linked*, renaming the new layer as "sawtooth."

13 Create a new layer called "wood" and fill it with the original background color (RGB settings 166/124/82). Apply *Filter* > *Noise* > *Add Noise* with Amount set to 20%, Gaussian distribution and the Monochrome checkbox selected.

14 Apply *Filter* > *Blur* > *Motion Blur* with the angle set to 0° and Distance to 14 pixels.

15 Apply *Filter* > *Sharpen* > *Unsharp Mask* with Amount at 500%, Radius at 1.7 pixels, and Threshold at 27 levels.

16 Go to *Image* > *Liquify* (PS6) or *Image* > *Liquify* (PS7, shown above) and use the warp tool to simulate the grain in the wood, with the brush size at 89 and the pressure at 50. Use fluid strokes that originate from within the image for the best results.

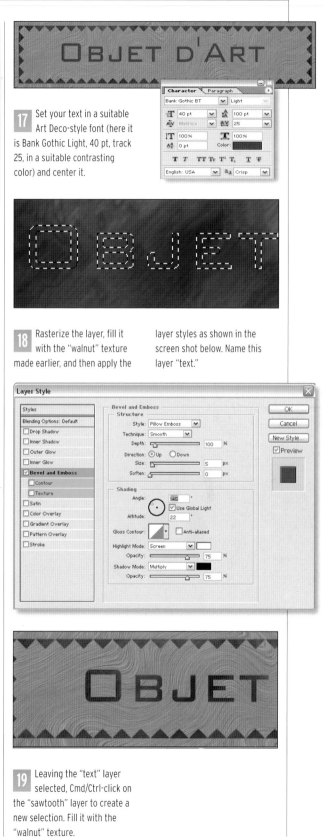

17 Set your text in a suitable Art Deco-style font (here it is Bank Gothic Light, 40 pt, track 25, in a suitable contrasting color) and center it.

18 Rasterize the layer, fill it with the "walnut" texture made earlier, and then apply the layer styles as shown in the screen shot below. Name this layer "text."

19 Leaving the "text" layer selected, Cmd/Ctrl-click on the "sawtooth" layer to create a new selection. Fill it with the "walnut" texture.

ALL KEYED UP

THE WORLD RECORD for typing speed hovers around 150 words per minute. The average for the rest of us is probably around 20. Designers faced with inputting large amounts of copy, say five words or more, would rather struggle with optical-character-recognition scanners or get a passerby to do it. This leaves the theoretically attractive alternative of voice-recognition software, though embarrassment in a crowded studio may follow. Clattering keys are the vehicle for the foreseeable future. This example portrays part of the US/British layout—with apologies to those more familiar with other styles.

1 Make a small, square document in which to produce a template for one key. This one is 0.155 in. (1 cm) square at 300 ppi printing size. Choose the rounded rectangle tool from the shapes pop-up, and increase its corner radius as necessary in the options bar (30 px was used in this example). Place the cursor in one corner of the canvas and, holding down the Shift key, drag to fill the frame.

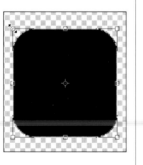

2 Select all and hit Cmd-t (Mac)/Ctrl-t (Windows) to transform the shape. Click and drag on a corner handle while holding down the Shift and Option (Mac)/Alt (Windows) keys. When the shape has been scaled, confirm the transformation, and go to *Layer > Rasterize > Shape* to render it as a normal layer.

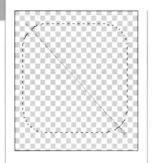

3 Make a selection from the contents of the layer by Cmd-clicking (Mac)/Ctrl-clicking (Windows) in the layer palette. Create a new layer, and use the default (black, white, linear gradient) gradient tool to fill the selection diagonally.

4 This should be the result of the last move.

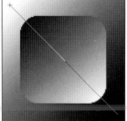

5 Deselect and return to the original layer. Use the gradient tool again in the opposite direction to fill the layer.

6 Use the dodge tool as necessary on the upper layer to lighten it.

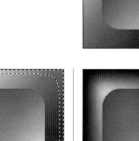

7 Merge the layers, select all, and go to *Select > Modify > Border*. Specify a low value (e.g. 8 pixels) and hit OK; then feather the selection (*Select > Feather*) by a similar amount.

8 Fill the feathered selection with black (*Edit > Fill*). Fill again to ensure a completely black edge, then deselect.

9 Treble the canvas width (*Image > Canvas Size*), with the imaged anchored at the midleft.

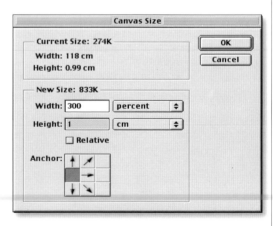

10 Duplicate the layer, and use the move tool to move the copied image to the right of the original. Repeat this, so that you now have three "key" images side by side. Merge the layers.

11 Double the depth of the canvas with the image anchored at the top.

12 Duplicate the layer and drag this copied image to the foot of the canvas while holding down the Shift key. Select it and hit Cmd-t (Mac)/Ctrl-t (Windows) to move it using the numerical input in the options bar. Select the small midleft anchor box on the Reference point location control on the options bar. The image needs to move sideways by half the width of a key. So in this example 118 pixels divided by 2 = 59 pixels. Key this into the x-axis box in the options bar, and hit Enter to confirm.

13 Go to *Image* > **Canvas Size** and reduce the width to the same value as the height (in this case 236 pixels) to make it square, with the image anchored at the right side. Hit OK and, at the warning, confirm you wish to proceed. Then merge the layers.

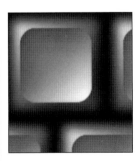

14 Use a small amount of Gaussian blur (*Filter* > *Blur* > **Gaussian Blur**) to soften the edges, and apply a subtle tint at low saturation in *Image* > *Adjustments* > *Hue/Saturation* > **Colorize**. Finally go to *Edit* > **Define Pattern**, and name the pattern "keyboard."

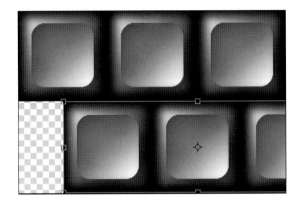

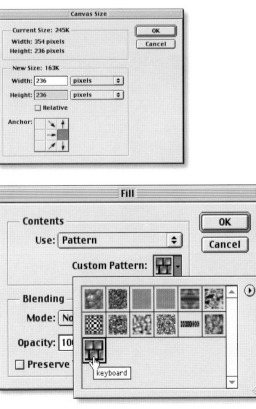

15 Make a new document at a multiple of the key size and fill it with the new pattern (*Edit* > **Fill**).

16 Set some suitable type, positioning each character on a key, and rasterize the type (*Layer* > *Rasterize* > **Type**). Merge the rasterized type layers, and Cmd-click (Mac)/Ctrl-click (Windows) in the layers palette to select the contents of the merged layer. With the selection still active, go to the channels palette and create a new alpha channel.

17 In the new alpha channel, fill the selection with white, deselect and blur the lettering slightly (*Filter* > *Blur* > **Gaussian Blur**).

18 Return to the layers palette, lighten the type slightly (*Image* > *Adjustments* > **Hue/Saturation**, and merge the layers. Go to *Filter* > *Render* > **Lighting Effects** and use the new alpha channel as the texture channel, but set it at a relatively low value.

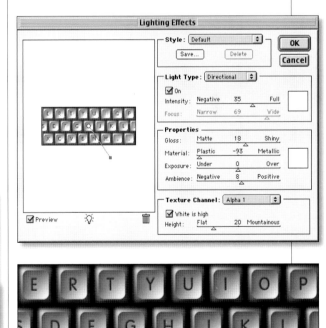

19 The lighting effects treatment will probably be too emphatic. Go to *Edit* > **Fade** **Lighting Effects** and choose **Overlay** for the mode at around 50% for a subtler result.

STUCK FOR A NAME

UGLY LETTERFORMS, erratic strike, fixed letter spacing, garish colors, an air of cheap and tawdry expediency. Just what is it that makes the embossing tapegun so attractive?

1 Create a new document. Select a suitable monospaced font (one in which each character occupies the same width) and increase the letter spacing. Set the type and commit it.

Alternative styles

Even cheaper tape. Set the type as big as possible on your screen, with extra letterspaces at the beginning and end of each line. Select all the text and make a screen grab (Mac: Cmd-Shift -3 and drag across the required area, Windows: Ctrl-Alt-Print Screen then paste into a new Photoshop document). Open the resulting grab and copy and paste it into a new alpha channel in a larger document. Duplicate the channel and blur it slightly. Use the blurred channel as in the main example for a texture map in Lighting effects. Using the unblurred channel, make a selection of the letters and fill the characters with white (you'll have to deselect the unwanted bits of the selection). Select alternate strips, skew and scale them, and repeat in the opposite direction for the remaining strips. Colorize, arrange in a layer stack (six deep in this case), and apply a little shadow at the folds. Put all tools away neatly when you're done.

Embossed tape strip

2 Rasterize the type layer (*Layer* > *Rasterize* > **Type**) and shift the individual characters a few pixels up or down to simulate the inconsistent strike of the tape gun.

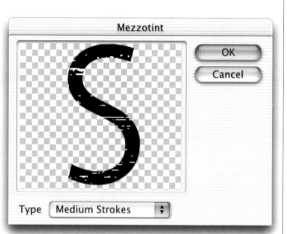

3 Choose *Filter* > *Pixelate* > **Mezzotint** and apply **Medium Strokes** to the letters.

4 Return to the *Pixelate* menu and choose **Fragment**.

5 Zoom in and randomly break up the edges of the lettering with a small soft-edged paintbrush, painting white at 50% opacity. Make a duplicate of the lettering layer before adding these painted "defects" in case you need to start again. When you have the required result, merge the layers, blur the new layer slightly, select the type by Cmd/Ctrl-clicking in the layer in the Layers palette, and paste it into a new alpha channel. The result is shown here. Name the channel "map." Deselect.

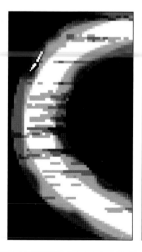

6 Return to the Layers palette, hide the lettering layer, and fill a new layer with the chosen tape color. Go to *Filter > Render > **Lighting Effects*** and use the "map" channel for the texture.

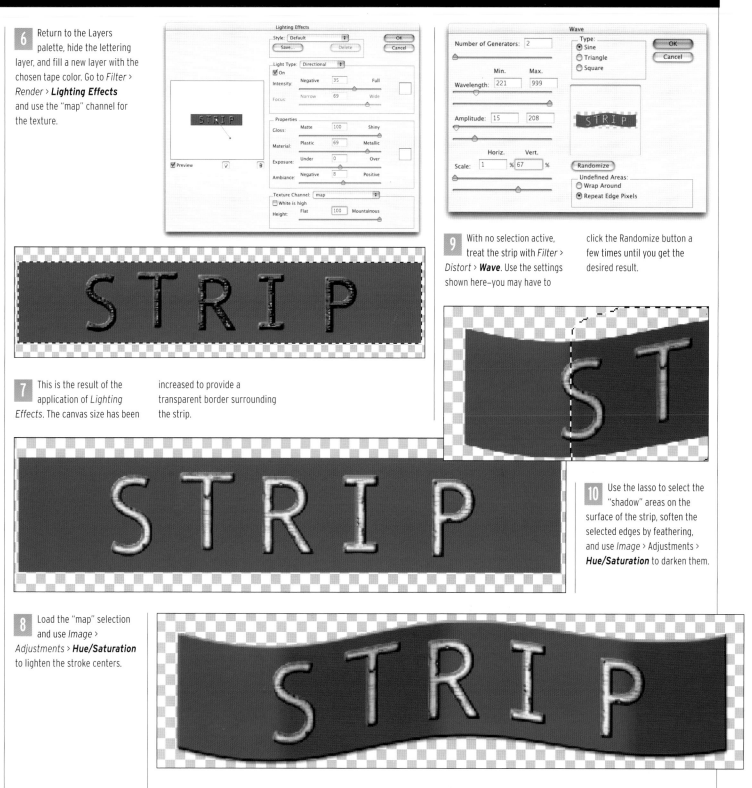

9 With no selection active, treat the strip with *Filter > Distort > **Wave***. Use the settings shown here—you may have to

increased to provide a transparent border surrounding the strip.

click the Randomize button a few times until you get the desired result.

7 This is the result of the application of *Lighting Effects*. The canvas size has been

10 Use the lasso to select the "shadow" areas on the surface of the strip, soften the selected edges by feathering, and use *Image > Adjustments > **Hue/Saturation*** to darken them.

8 Load the "map" selection and use *Image > Adjustments > **Hue/Saturation*** to lighten the stroke centers.

11 Finally, use *Layer > Layer Style > **Bevel and Emboss*** to give the strip a degree of thickness.

STITCH UP

Beads

When (and if) old graphic designers get rich and vain enough to afford heraldic devices on their wheelchair cushions, the shiny highlighted pinhead with its loyal drop shadow will be as common a device in their coats of arms as castles were for knights of old. No graph or battlefield analysis seemed complete without a flock of thumbtacks, almost always red. These beads pay sentimental tribute to a bygone age. Try green ones for a more up-to-date effect, square ones for a post-modern look, or rhinestones for country chic.

1 Create a new document (1200 x 1000 pixels), set the foreground color to black, and set the type in 96 pt.

2 Go to *Layer > Type >* **Create Work Path**.

3 Deselect the path by clicking in the blank area of the Paths palette. Make a new layer, create a circular selection almost the full height of the document, fill it with black (*Edit > Fill >* **Black**), and add a white highlight with a soft brush.

4 Reduce the size of the bead to 2% using *Edit > Transform >* **Scale** and commit the transformation.

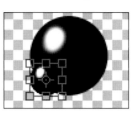

5 Zoom in on the reduced bead, select it with the rectangular marquee tool (hold Shift down to get a square selection) and go to *Edit >* **Define Brush**. The brush size should be about 18.

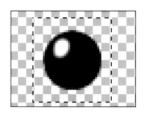

Brush Name

● Name: Sampled Brush #1   [OK] [Cancel]

18

6 Click OK to save the new brush. Don't bother to change the default name.

7 Deselect the bead. Zoom out to a normal view, and select the paintbrush tool, Click on the "Toggle the Brushes palette" in the Options Bar. On the Brushes palette, click on "Brush Presets" and choose the brush you just defined. Then click on "Brush Tip Shape" and increase the brush spacing to 125%. Then click on the "Create New Brush" icon at the bottom of the palette and name the brush "Bead."

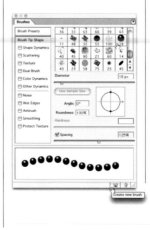

8 Make sure the "Bead" brush is still selected, make a new layer, and choose a new foreground color. Reactivate the work path by clicking on it in the Paths palette. Select *Stroke Path* in the Paths pop-up, followed by **Paintbrush**.

9 Since the brush can only paint with one color, a close-up of the screen shows that the highlights are transparent. To fill the highlights, first select the background with the magic wand tool using the highest tolerance setting (255) with the "Contiguous" box checked.

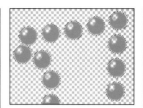

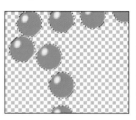

10 Go to *Select >* **Inverse**, then reduce the selection by one pixel (*Select > Modify >* **Contract**). Make a new layer under the existing one, and–with the selection still active–fill it with a new highlight color (*Edit > Fill >* **Foreground Color**) or white. Deselect.

11 Finishing touches could include the addition of a drop shadow to the beads (*Layer > Layer Style >* **Drop Shadow**), a thin "string" made by stroking the original path in black with a small hard paintbrush, and a color infill using the same path (select *Fill Path* in the Paths pop-up). Deselect the work path for the best view of the final result.

Cross Stitch

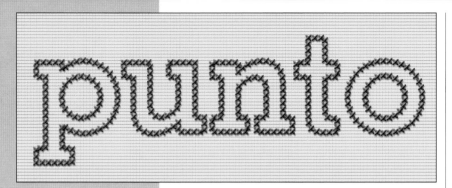

IN THE 19TH-CENTURY schoolroom, top marks were awarded to the child who could best reproduce The Lord's Prayer in cross-stitch. Spelling errors might lead to long periods in a dark corner, or worse. The currently insoluble problem is that the chosen brush pattern will not rotate to follow the path orientation, limiting the technique to horizontal, vertical, or as in this example, 45° strokes. Energetic operators might invent a set of progressively angled brushes in an attempt to side step the issue, but lack of control over the stroke spacing when using a series of separate paths will inevitably lead to tears at bedtime.

1 Create a small square document—say 20 pixels across—and use a small brush to join opposite corners. Use the eraser to break up the regularity of the line. Go to *Edit* > **Define Brush**.

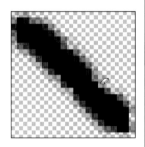

2 The dialog box should look like this. Don't rename the brush at this stage.

3 Deselect the bead. Zoom out to a normal view, and select the paintbrush tool, Click on the "Toggle the Brushes palette" in the Options Bar. On the Brushes palette, click on "Brush Presets" and choose the brush you just defined. Then click on "Brush Tip Shape" and increase the brush spacing to 125%. Then click on the "Create New Brush" icon at the bottom of the palette and name the brush "Bead."

4 Go to *Edit* > *Transform* > **Flip Horizontal**. Follow the previous sequence to define this brush, being careful to choose the same spacing (100%). Name the brush "right stitch."

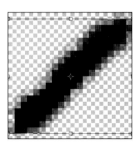

5 Create a new document and set the type.

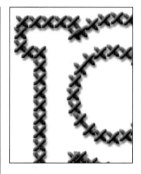

6 Choose *Layer* > *Type* > **Create Work Path**.

7 Create a new layer. Make sure that the paintbrush tool and the "left stitch" brush are selected. Choose Stroke Path and Paintbrush from the paths palette pop-up.

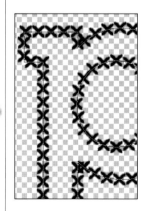

8 Make another new layer and proceed as before, but with "left stitch" selected.

9 Use *Image* > *Adjustments* > **Hue/Saturation** to colorize the "stitched" layers, Apply layer styles—in this case Bevel and Emboss and Drop Shadow—to one layer, copy the style and paste it to the other. The relevant paste and copy commands are in the *Layer* > **Layer Style** menu.

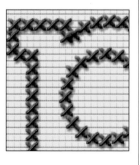

10 Insert a new layer under the stitched layers, fill it with a light color, and apply *Filter* > *Texture* > **Patchwork**. After application, use *Edit* > **Fade Patchwork** to soften the effect.

FAT AND FIBER

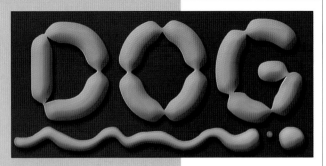

Sausage-writing has yet to achieve the same status as ice-sculpture, but this harmless technique can be applied to all kinds of foodstuffs. Pasta is the obvious target, with special reference to rigatoni (start with lightly-striped lettering); fusilli (the Twirl filter might be helpful); regular spaghetti (any light face will do). Cheese on top comes from a faint yellow airbrush set to Spatter in Dissolve mode. Black pepper on that?

Sausage

1 Choose a bold face with an even stroke width (this is VAG Roundel), set the type into a layer, commit it, and rasterize (*Layer > Rasterize > **Type***).

2 Use *Image > Adjustments > **Hue/Saturation*** to colorize the type. You may need to repeat this operation to achieve the right color. Insert a new layer under the type and fill it with a neutral dark color to make the type manipulations easier to see.

3 Zoom in on one letter, go to *Image > **Liquify*** and choose the pucker tool (fourth from the top in PS6, fifth from the top in PS7). Place the tool in the middle of the stroke and wave it from side to side on the axis of the crease. Experiment with the Brush Size and Pressure settings– it may also help to "click and hold" on the area you want to affect. Hit OK. You will probably be left with a small amount of retouching. Repeat with each letter.

4 Use layer *styles–Layer > Layer Style > **Drop Shadow, Inner Shadow***, and ***Bevel and Emboss**–*on the type layer. In each effect, uncheck Global Light and set a separate value for the light direction. In Bevel and Emboss, the best reflections are obtained when the shading source is at a high altitude setting. Hit OK.

5 You will have to return to the Layer Style dialog to fine-tune the Inner Shadow values. Select a low Distance value (a pixel or two) and a higher Size value (around 15 pixels in this case).

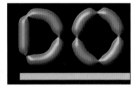

6 You want mustard on that? Make a new layer, fill a rectangular marquee with yellow (PANTONE™ 130 for American or 118 for French), deselect, and return to *Image > **Liquify***.

7 Use a combination of tools in Liquify to produce a trail. Hit OK. Copy the layer styles (*Layer > Layer Style > **Copy Layer Style***) from the type layer to this layer, then go to each effect in turn in the Layer Style dialog and recheck Global Light. Hit OK.

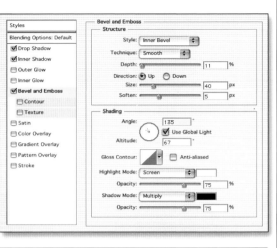

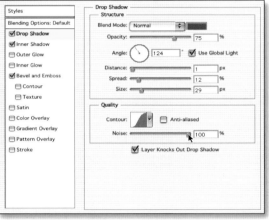

8 For a variation, add Inner Shadow (above) to the sausage image. A high noise value introduces a texture based on a new color selection–click on the color box alongside the Blend Mode drop-down list box to open the Color Picker dialog. You can also add a green Inner Glow. Hit OK.

9 The result: lightly herbed sausage–with accompanying ketchup through refilling the trail image with PANTONE™ 189.

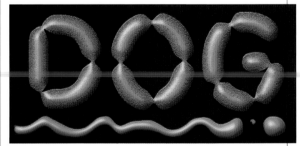

Toast

 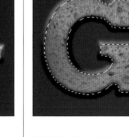 

1 Scan a slice of bread on a dark background. Use *Image* > **Extract** (PS6) or *Filter* > **Extract** (PS7) to cut the bread from its background.

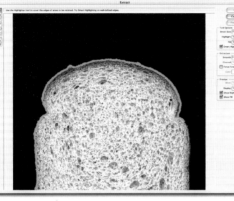

7 Applying the default **Bevel and Emboss** in the Layer Style dialog (*Layer* > *Layer Style* > **Bevel and Emboss**) gives an edge to the initial cut-out letters. A dark background has been added to make the effect clearer.

10 Cmd/Ctrl-click to select the cutout letters again, and set a soft brush to **Multiply** at a low pressure. Spray patches of different hues of brown, then go to *Select* > *Modify* > **Contract** to reduce the selection area. Feather this selection by a few pixels, then choose *Select* > **Inverse**. Use *Image* > *Adjustments* > **Hue/Saturation** to "burn" the edges. Deselect.

2 Go to *Image* > **Canvas Size** and quadruple the width of the canvas. Click in the left side of the Anchor Point box and hit OK. Use the Move tool with Option/Alt and Shift pressed to duplicate the image three times. Merge the resulting layers.

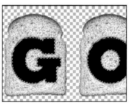

5 Use *Filter* > *Distort* > **Ripple** to disturb the edges of the type. Then apply a small amount of blur to soften the edges.

8 Nothing is wasted–return to the bread layer, get the type selection again, *Select* > **Inverse**, and copy and paste. Apply the same layer styles as the previous layer.

11 Treat the "crust" image in the same way.

3 Set the type into a new layer and space the lettering until it aligns with the images of the bread.

4 Commit the type, then open the type palettes to add tracking to separate the letters. Rasterize the type (*Layer* > *Type* > **Rasterize**).

6 With the "bread" layer active, Cmd/Ctrl-click on the type layer icon to select the softened type outline. Next copy and paste in order to generate a new layer of type made of the bread texture.

9 Viewing the two layers together offers an alternative "stamped" effect.

12 Merge both bread layers and go to *Image* > *Adjustments* > **Curves**. Draw a sinuous curve in the Curves dialog to enhance the toasted appearance.

THE SCRAPBOX

THE MORE RETENTIVE you are, the less you need these examples. You will already have several (used) envelopes filled with interesting textures and surfaces. Family members already rely on you for the elusive scrap to finish a home-made greeting card. Stick it all in the scanner and see what comes out. Some surfaces respond in different ways dependent on their orientation in the scanner; the light source will cast shadows on deeply textured subjects and maybe produce colored reflections of the scanner's RGB tubes on shiny items.

1 Set the type into a new alpha channel, commit it, and deselect.

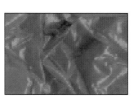

2 Scan an object of your choice. This happens to be a garbage bag, but any substance with a texture and/or reflective qualities will suffice. Copy the image and return to the Channels palette in the main document.

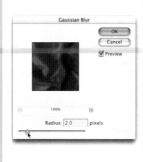

3 Paste the texture image into a new alpha channel, deselect, and blur the image slightly (Filter > Blur > **Gaussian Blur**).

4 Return to the Layers palette and paste the image again into a layer. At this point, use Image > **Trim** to delete the surplus pixels outside the image area. Load the selection of the type channel.

5 Select > **Inverse** and hit Delete, but don't deselect. Select > **Inverse** again, and duplicate the layer as a backup.

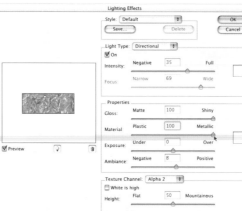

6 Use Filter > Render > **Lighting Effects** with maximum values for the "shiny" and "metallic" properties. Select the blurred image channel as the texture channel. As usual, the preview window is no help at all.

7 The initial result of applying the filter. A white background has been inserted to make the effect clearer.

8 Using Edit > **Fade Lighting Effects** with a reduction to 50% opacity and a change of blend mode to **Color Burn** gives a softer effect.

9 Deselect. Use Image > **Liquify** (PS6) or Filter > **Liquify** (PS7) to disturb the letter shapes. The Pucker tool, fourth from the top in the tool palette at the left of the Liquify dialog, is useful for accentuating creases. The tools are progressive –the longer you press on the mouse button or stylus, the more pronounced the effect will be.

Voyage

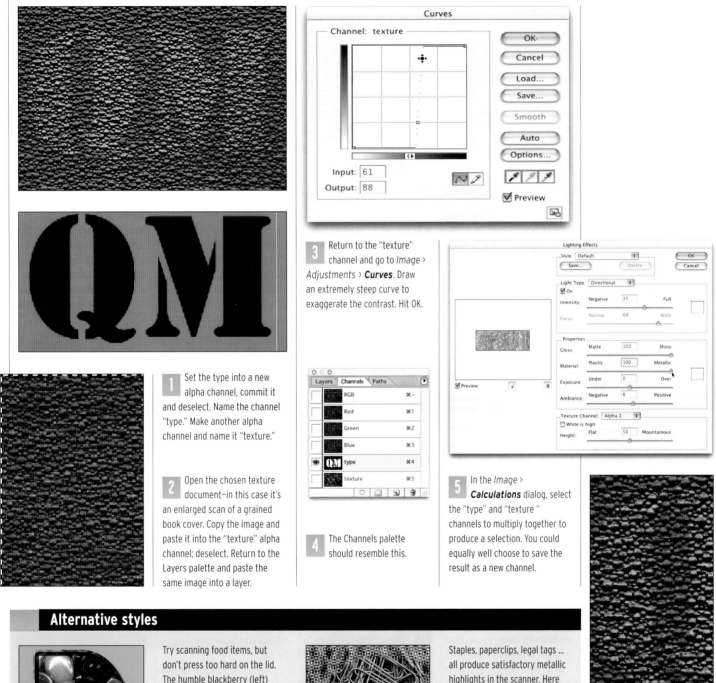

3 Return to the "texture" channel and go to *Image > Adjustments > **Curves***. Draw an extremely steep curve to exaggerate the contrast. Hit OK.

1 Set the type into a new alpha channel, commit it and deselect. Name the channel "type." Make another alpha channel and name it "texture."

2 Open the chosen texture document–in this case it's an enlarged scan of a grained book cover. Copy the image and paste it into the "texture" alpha channel; deselect. Return to the Layers palette and paste the same image into a layer.

4 The Channels palette should resemble this.

5 In the *Image > **Calculations*** dialog, select the "type" and "texture " channels to multiply together to produce a selection. You could equally well choose to save the result as a new channel.

6 Make a new layer and fill the selection with a bright color. Deselect and change the blend mode to **Overlay**. Duplicate this layer if necessary to make the lettering more intense.

Alternative styles

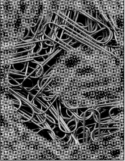

Try scanning food items, but don't press too hard on the lid. The humble blackberry (left) takes on a new and dignified aura when cut out, beveled and embossed.

Staples, paperclips, legal tags ... all produce satisfactory metallic highlights in the scanner. Here the tangled background has been tamed with a shot of the Color Halftone filter (*Filter > Pixelate > **Color Halftone***).

WHAT A MESH

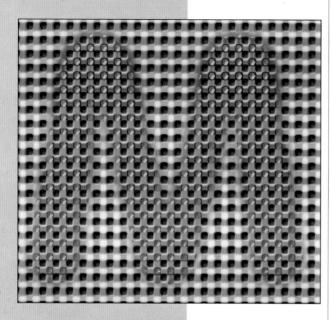

THE FIRST EXAMPLE in this Mood Effects section stands for the reversal of most of what has gone before. Though there may be passing resemblances to familiar surfaces and textures, the intention has been to use Photoshop's capabilities to generate type effects that don't refer to real life. This relatively restrained example also ignores color harmony, the demands of legibility, and good typographic form. Everyone needs a vacation.

1 Make a new document (square format) and fill the background layer with a dark brown. Create a new layer, fill it with dark gray, and apply *Filter > Sketch > Halftone Pattern* to produce horizontal lines.

Matrix

2 Click the eyedropper tool in the white area between the lines and go to *Select > Color Range*. Delete the white areas to leave only the black lines. Name this layer "horizontal."

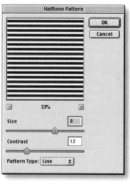

3 Duplicate the horizontal-lined layer, and rotate it through 90 degrees (*Edit > Transform > Rotate 90° CW*). Name the transformed layer "vertical."

4 Return to the horizontal-lined layer and color the lines (*Image > Adjustments > Hue/Saturation > Colorize*).

5 Colorize the vertical-lined layer in a contrasting color.

6 Duplicate both layers and move the copies to the top; set one copy to **Multiply** over the other and merge them.

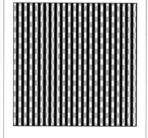

7 The merged layer should look like this. Duplicate it and leave the original visible in the background.

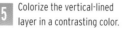

8 Use the eyedropper tool on a black disk, and go to *Select > Color Range* to select all such disks. Go to *Select > Inverse* and delete all but the disks.

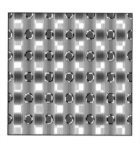

9 Select the black disks once more and colorize them with a third contrasting color.

10 Set the type into a new layer, hit *Enter,* and use the selection, inverted and feathered, to treat the layers below.

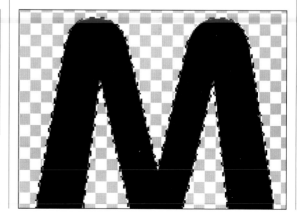

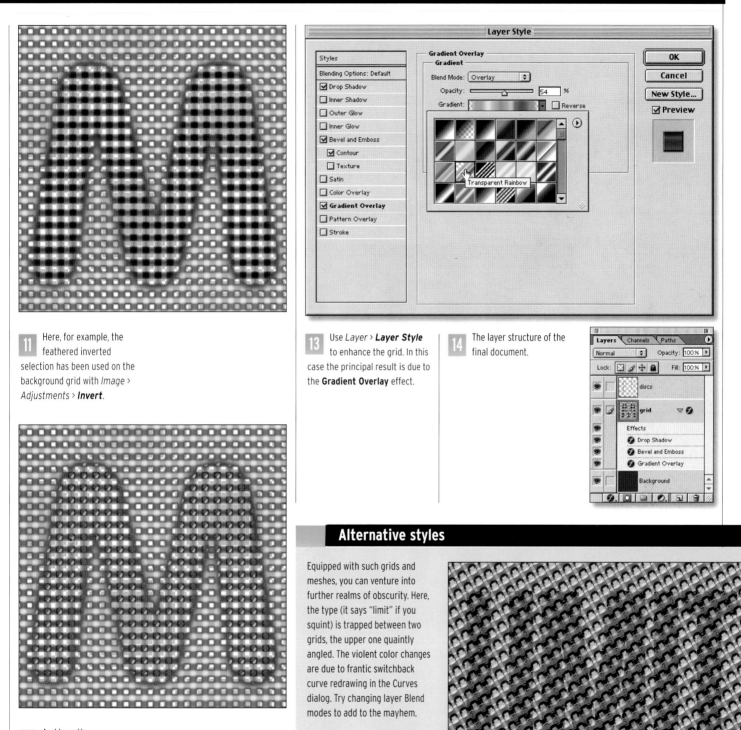

11 Here, for example, the feathered inverted selection has been used on the background grid with *Image* > *Adjustments* > **Invert**.

12 And here the same selection, inverted, has been used on the disks layer, with *Filter* > *Stylize* > **Emboss**. The background disks have been deleted.

13 Use *Layer* > **Layer Style** to enhance the grid. In this case the principal result is due to the **Gradient Overlay** effect.

14 The layer structure of the final document.

Alternative styles

Equipped with such grids and meshes, you can venture into further realms of obscurity. Here, the type (it says "limit" if you squint) is trapped between two grids, the upper one quaintly angled. The violent color changes are due to frantic switchback curve redrawing in the Curves dialog. Try changing layer Blend modes to add to the mayhem.

TEENY DOTS

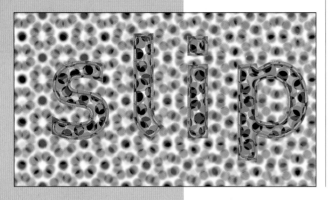

THE FOUR-COLOR process rosette of cyan, magenta, yellow, and black normally slides by unnoticed. The "Color Halftone" filter allows you to play with the size and orientation of the dots, either applied to an existing image or to a flat color. The maximum allowable dot is 127 pixels—an enlargement of around 1000% compared with the dots that make up this page.

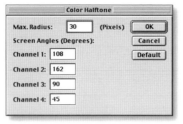

4 With the selection still active, go to *Filter* > *Pixelate* > **Color Halftone**, and change only the pixel radius setting.

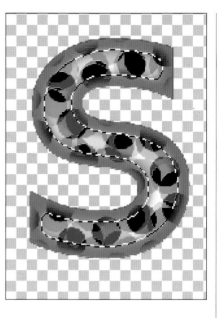

5 This is the result of applying the **Color Halftone** filter to the selection.

1 Set the type into a new alpha channel.

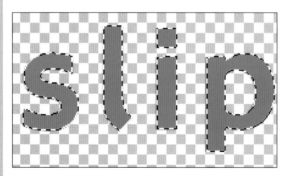

2 With type selection still active, return to the **Layers** palette and fill the selection with a midtone color.

3 Reduce the size of the active selection (*Select* > *Modify* > **Contract**) and feather it slightly. Change the color of the reduced selection using *Image* > *Adjustments* > **Hue/Saturation**.

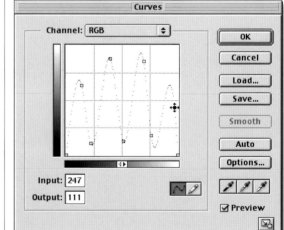

6 Invert the selection and use *Image* > *Adjustments* > **Curves** to treat the edge of the letterforms. The shape of the curves is not critical–you just need distinct peaks and troughs.

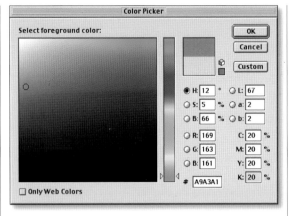

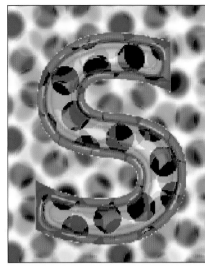

7 The result of adjusting the curves in the inverse selection.

10 Open the **Color Picker** and set each of the CMYK values to 20%.

13 Finally, apply blur to the lower layer to simulate a lenticular effect.

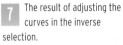

8 Duplicate the layer and change its mode to **Color Burn**. Merge the layers. Deselect.

9 Layers 1 and 2 merged.

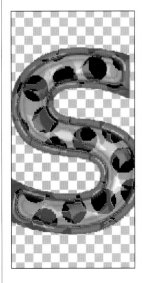

11 Make a new layer under the type and fill it with the new foreground color.

12 Apply the **Color Halftone** filter to the gray layer at the same settings as before. You can move the upper layer around until the pitch of the two sets of dots coincides.

Alternative styles

Alongside Color Halftone in the Pixelate menu sits the Mosaic filter. The fat jagged pixels it produces are a generally a Bad Thing in artwork terms, but its staggered terraces have their uses. Start with Color Halftone as above, then apply Mosaic. Experiment with the Cell Size slider–this example started with a setting of 80, then was treated again at 40. Type set into an alpha channel was selected, and the selected area copied to a new layer and inverted (Cmd-I). The new layer was treated with the Displace filter in the Distort menu, using Random Strokes as the Displacement map, and given a shot of Bevel & Emboss with the Ring-Double contour selected. The background was blurred and darkened for contrast.

SWING

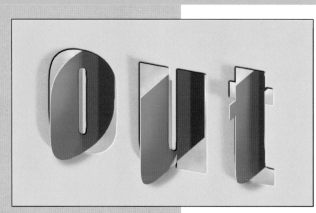

SIMPLE MANIPULATION of the Paths palette can result in intriguing "false perspective" effects. This example attempts to recall the dangerous days of the 80s when it seemed that every second book was a paper-engineering production. Sharp cardboard mountains concealed rubber-band-powered snapping dragons. Riveted planets spun in orbit. Virgins fled in terror. All discarded now.

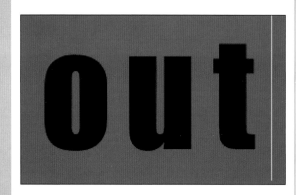

1 Set the type into a new alpha layer. Use the type palette to add extra space between the letters.

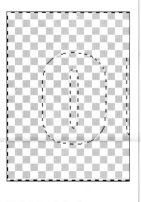

2 Return to the **Layers** palette, and with the type selection still active, go to Select > *Inverse*.

Cardboard cutout

3 Go to the **Paths** palette and save the selection as a work path.

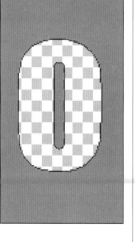

4 With the work path still visible, choose *Layer* > *New Fill Layer* > **Solid Color**. The choice of fill color is unimportant at this stage. Name the new layer "wall." Click in the unused area of the **Paths** palette to deselect the new clipping path.

5 Load the original type selection from the alpha channel by Cmd/Ctrl-clicking on it, go to the **Paths** palette and choose *Make Work Path*. Return to the **Layers** palette, and with the work path visible, select *New Fill Layer* as before. Fill with a different color and name the layer "door."

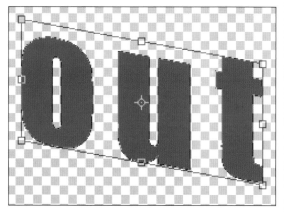

6 Click on the "door" layer. Go to the **Paths** palette and ensure the "door" **Clipping Path** is active. Return to the active layer and transform the contents—Cmd-t (Mac)/Ctrl-t (Windows)—by skewing. Choose, for example, 10 degrees of vertical skew in the options palette.

7 The path components of the "wall" layer have to be selected individually using the direct selection tool with the Shift key held down. Don't forget to include isolated sections like the center of the letter "o," for example. Skew the selected group of paths with the same values as the previous layer.

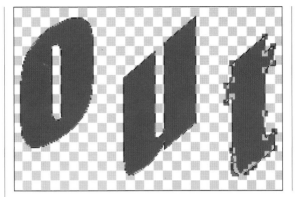

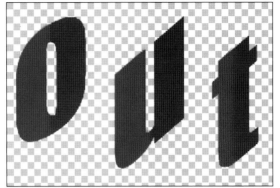

8 Return to the "door" layer and, again using the direct selection tool, skew the characters one by one (hold down Cmd/Ctrl + Alt). Use quite a lot of skew. At the same time, reduce the characters' width slightly to simulate a perspective effect.

9 With the "wall" layer uppermost, the image should look like this. Duplicate both layers as a fallback and rasterize one of each (*Layer > Rasterize > **Layer***).

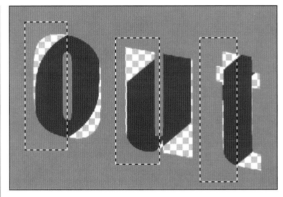

10 Working in the "door" layer, use the rectangular marquee tool to select the parts of the letters that should appear in front of the "wall." Copy these areas and paste them, forming a new layer. Name the new layer "front door." You will need to nudge this new layer to get it in the right position. Duplicate the "front door" layer as before.

Layers | Channels | Paths
Normal | Opacity: 100%
Lock: | Fill: 100%
front door
wall
door

11 Arrange the layers like this, and darken the "door" layer (*Image > Adjustments > **Brightness/Contrast***).

12 Treat the "wall" layer with *Filter > Render > **Lighting Effects***, using the layer's own transparency as the texture channel. Add layer effects in the form of **Bevel and Emboss** to increase the illusion. Cast shadows can be added with the burn tool.

13 As regards the letters, it's possible to disguise the harsh join between the leading and trailing parts by blurring a feathered selection at the edge of the "front door" layer.

14 The letters can be enhanced by duplicating the "front door" layer again, nudging it a few pixels upward and leftward, then coloring it white using *Image > Adjustments > **Hue/Saturation***, and finally sending it behind the original layer. A feathered selection of the original "door" path was used to create a new shadow layer. Individual soft shadows were skewed to follow an imaginary light source, and the layer set to **Multiply** at low opacity.

Alternative styles

To maximize the effect of this technique, choose a face with an irregular outline. The cut-out illusion is enhanced by the elaborately fretted edge. To confuse the eye further, employ a chiselled or open face, even one with a ready-made drop shadow.

NETWORK

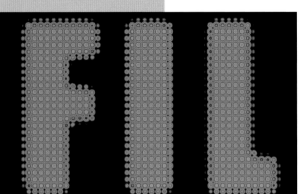

THERE WAS A British rock band called Eyelid Movies, whose efforts in the 1980s never troubled the record charts and whose demise went unreported. One articulate member explained that they had spent childhood time pressing on their closed eyelids. The resulting moving patterns, remembered in relative maturity, gave the band its name. Try it now, but only very lightly, and under medical supervision, to see whether you get square grids like these, or the more rewarding swirling galactic clouds.

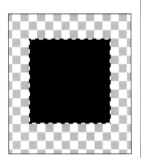

1 Start by making a custom pattern. Using the rectangular marquee tool set to **Fixed Size** style in the options bar, fill a very small square–say 20 pixels wide–with black. You will need to view the document at a high zoom setting, such as 400%.

2 Reduce the marquee area by two pixels (*Select > Modify > **Contract***) and fill with white. Cmd/Ctrl-click in the Layers palette to select the filled square, and go to *Edit > **Define Pattern***.

3 Save the pattern as "square grid."

4 Delete the small square from the canvas, deselect, and go to *Edit > Fill > **Pattern***. Choose the new "square grid."

5 Duplicate the filled layer as a backup.

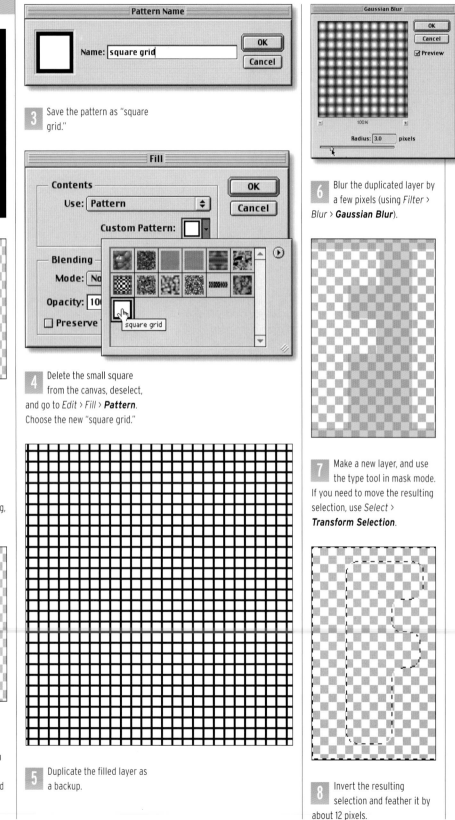

6 Blur the duplicated layer by a few pixels (using *Filter > Blur > **Gaussian Blur***).

7 Make a new layer, and use the type tool in mask mode. If you need to move the resulting selection, use *Select > **Transform Selection***.

8 Invert the resulting selection and feather it by about 12 pixels.

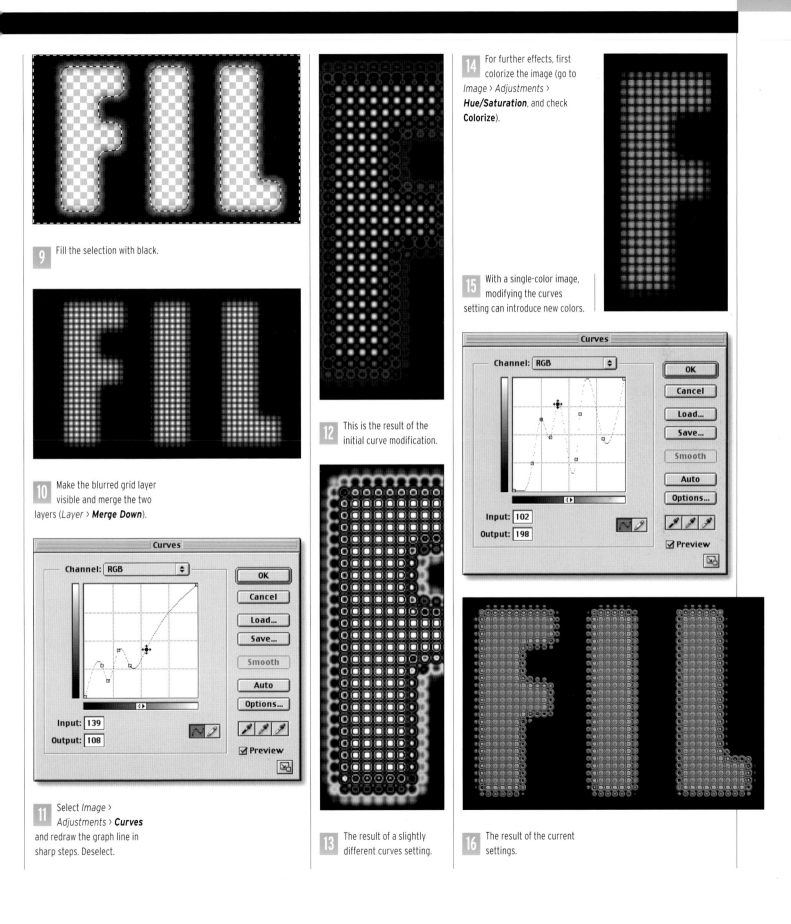

9 Fill the selection with black.

10 Make the blurred grid layer visible and merge the two layers (*Layer* > **Merge Down**).

11 Select *Image* > *Adjustments* > **Curves** and redraw the graph line in sharp steps. Deselect.

12 This is the result of the initial curve modification.

13 The result of a slightly different curves setting.

14 For further effects, first colorize the image (go to *Image* > *Adjustments* > **Hue/Saturation**, and check **Colorize**).

15 With a single-color image, modifying the curves setting can introduce new colors.

16 The result of the current settings.

BASIC FILTERS

THIS COMPENDIUM of 187 basic filter effects is designed to save you time and effort. Each filter is first demonstrated on the group of characters only—see the columns headed "Character"—and then on the whole image, where the characters are flattened into the background image (columns headed "Image." Depending on the filter, the difference between the two examples may be dramatic or negligible. Compare the effect of Colored Pencil, the first filter of all, on the characters alone (alongside), with the effect on the flattened image at the top of the last column on this page. You will also find some experimental combinations scattered through the compendium. Here the "middle of the road" settings have been overridden, often bringing unexpected results.

Artistic
Character

Colored Pencil
settings: 6, 1, 19

Cutout
settings: 4, 10, 1

Dry Brush
settings: 5, 7, 3

Film Grain
settings: 20, 15, 5

Fresco
settings: 10, 10, 2

Neon Glow
settings: -5, 25

Paint Daubs
settings: 8, 7 simple

Palette Knife
settings: 20, 2, 3

Plastic Wrap
settings: 20, 10, 10

Poster Edges
settings: 4, 4, 2

Rough Pastels
settings: 22, 10, defaults

Smudge Stick
settings: 5, 4, 10

Sponge
settings: 3, 10, 10

Underpainting
settings: 10, 10

Watercolor
settings: 7, 5, 2

EXPERIMENTAL

Neon Glow experiment
settings: -15, 25

Artistic
Image

Colored Pencil
settings: 16, 5, 50

Dry Brush
settings: 5, 8, 1

Film Grain
settings: 13, 9, 3

Fresco
settings: 10, 10, 2

Neon Glow
settings: -5, 25

Paint daubs

Pallette knife

Underpainting
settings: 10, 10

Blur
Character

Gaussian Blur
settings: radius: 10

Blur
Image

Gaussian Blur
settings: radius 10

Brushstrokes
Character

Accented Edges
settings: defaults

Plastic Wrap
settings: 20, 10, 10

Watercolor
settings: 5, 1, 2

Motion Blur
settings: angle: 38, distance: 30

Motion Blur
settings: angle: 38, distance: 30

Angled Strokes
settings: 60, 20, 10

Poster Edges
settings: 4, 4, 2

EXPERIMENTAL

Colored Pencil experiment
settings: 6, 3, 20

Radial Blur
settings: spin: 10

Radial Blur
settings: 35, zoom, best

Crosshatch
settings: 45, 5, 2

Rough Pastels
settings: 22, 10, defaults

Cutout experiment
settings: defaults

EXPERIMENTAL

Radial Blur 2
settings: 10, spin, best

Dark Strokes
settings: 8, 6, 2

Sponge
settings: 3, 10, 10

Neon Glow experiment
settings: 13, 30, custom glow color

Gaussian Blur experiment
settings: a: 12, K: 25, s: 5

Radial blur 3

Ink Outlines
settings: 30, 20, 202

Smudge Stick
settings: 2, 12, 8

Spatter
settings: 20, 5

Brushstrokes
Character/Cont.

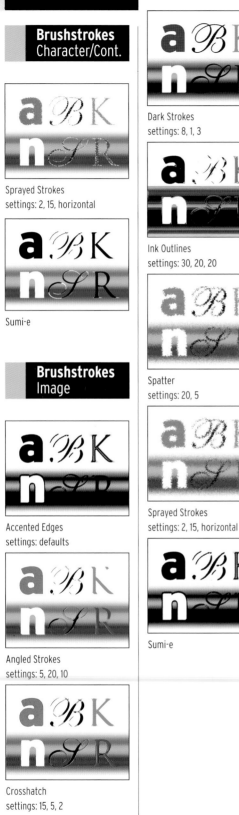

Sprayed Strokes
settings: 2, 15, horizontal

Sumi-e

Brushstrokes
Image

Accented Edges
settings: defaults

Angled Strokes
settings: 5, 20, 10

Crosshatch
settings: 15, 5, 2

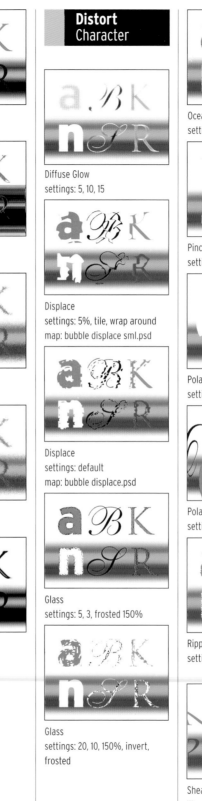

Dark Strokes
settings: 8, 1, 3

Ink Outlines
settings: 30, 20, 20

Spatter
settings: 20, 5

Sprayed Strokes
settings: 2, 15, horizontal

Sumi-e

Distort
Character

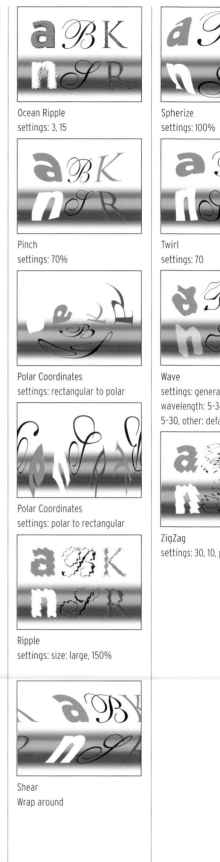

Diffuse Glow
settings: 5, 10, 15

Displace
settings: 5%, tile, wrap around
map: bubble displace sml.psd

Displace
settings: default
map: bubble displace.psd

Glass
settings: 5, 3, frosted 150%

Glass
settings: 20, 10, 150%, invert, frosted

Ocean Ripple
settings: 3, 15

Pinch
settings: 70%

Polar Coordinates
settings: rectangular to polar

Polar Coordinates
settings: polar to rectangular

Ripple
settings: size: large, 150%

Shear
Wrap around

Spherize
settings: 100%

Twirl
settings: 70

Wave
settings: generators: 5,
wavelength: 5-340, amplitude:
5-30, other: defaults

ZigZag
settings: 30, 10, pond ripples

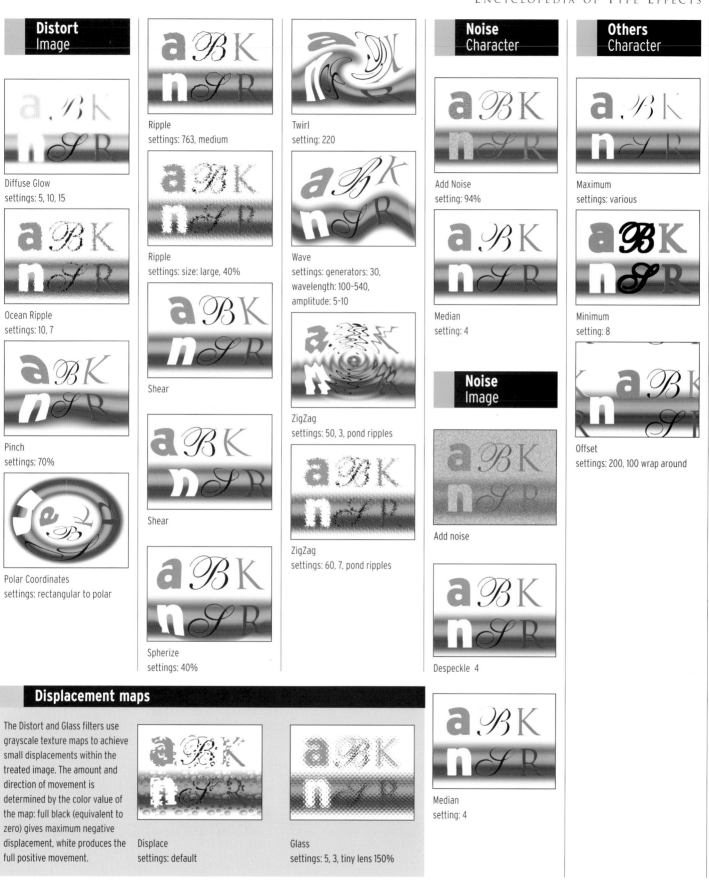

Distort
Image

Diffuse Glow
settings: 5, 10, 15

Ocean Ripple
settings: 10, 7

Pinch
settings: 70%

Polar Coordinates
settings: rectangular to polar

Ripple
settings: 763, medium

Ripple
settings: size: large, 40%

Shear

Shear

Spherize
settings: 40%

Twirl
setting: 220

Wave
settings: generators: 30,
wavelength: 100-540,
amplitude: 5-10

ZigZag
settings: 50, 3, pond ripples

ZigZag
settings: 60, 7, pond ripples

Noise
Character

Add Noise
setting: 94%

Median
setting: 4

Noise
Image

Add noise

Despeckle 4

Median
setting: 4

Others
Character

Maximum
settings: various

Minimum
setting: 8

Offset
settings: 200, 100 wrap around

Displacement maps

The Distort and Glass filters use grayscale texture maps to achieve small displacements within the treated image. The amount and direction of movement is determined by the color value of the map: full black (equivalent to zero) gives maximum negative displacement, white produces the full positive movement.

Displace
settings: default

Glass
settings: 5, 3, tiny lens 150%

Texture maps

Bubble

Stained glass

Ripple

Silk

Texture

Others
Image

Custom
settings: saved custom settings file

Maximum
setting: 3

Minimum
setting: 8

Offset
settings: 300, 100

Pixelate
Character

Color Halftone
settings: default

Facet

Fragment

Mezzotint
settings: coarse dots

Mosaic
cell size: 10

Pointillize
cell size: 40

Pixelate
Images

Color Halftone

Crystallize
cell size: 12

Facet

Fragment

Mezzotint
settings: medium dots

Mosaic
cell size: 12

Pointillize
cell size: 15

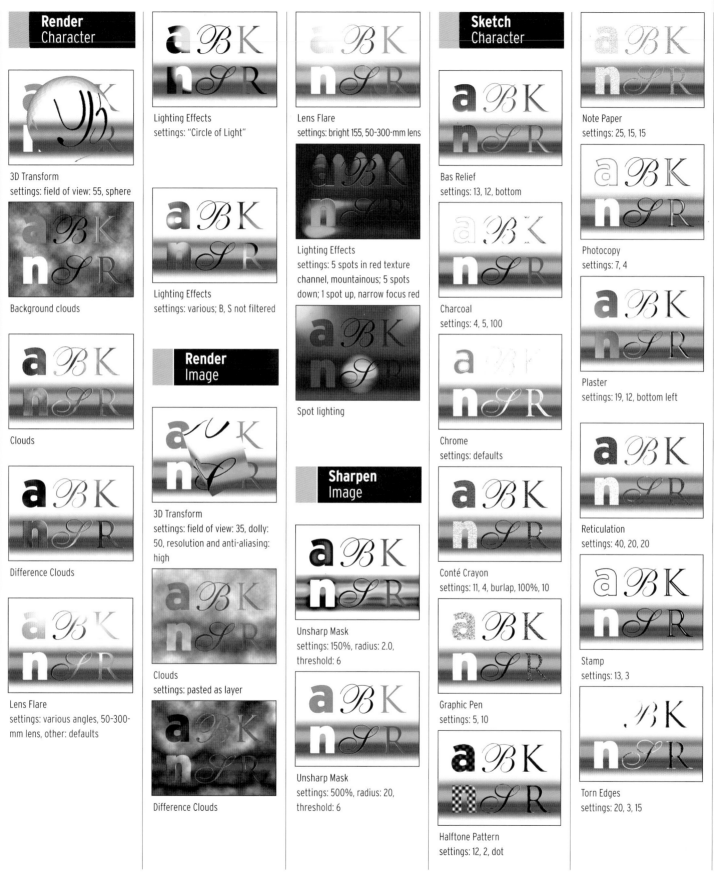

Render
Character

3D Transform
settings: field of view: 55, sphere

Background clouds

Clouds

Difference Clouds

Lens Flare
settings: various angles, 50-300-mm lens, other: defaults

Lighting Effects
settings: "Circle of Light"

Lighting Effects
settings: various; B, S not filtered

Render
Image

3D Transform
settings: field of view: 35, dolly: 50, resolution and anti-aliasing: high

Clouds
settings: pasted as layer

Difference Clouds

Lens Flare
settings: bright 155, 50-300-mm lens

Lighting Effects
settings: 5 spots in red texture channel, mountainous; 5 spots down; 1 spot up, narrow focus red

Spot lighting

Sharpen
Image

Unsharp Mask
settings: 150%, radius: 2.0, threshold: 6

Unsharp Mask
settings: 500%, radius: 20, threshold: 6

Sketch
Character

Bas Relief
settings: 13, 12, bottom

Charcoal
settings: 4, 5, 100

Chrome
settings: defaults

Conté Crayon
settings: 11, 4, burlap, 100%, 10

Graphic Pen
settings: 5, 10

Halftone Pattern
settings: 12, 2, dot

Note Paper
settings: 25, 15, 15

Photocopy
settings: 7, 4

Plaster
settings: 19, 12, bottom left

Reticulation
settings: 40, 20, 20

Stamp
settings: 13, 3

Torn Edges
settings: 20, 3, 15

KPT FILTERS

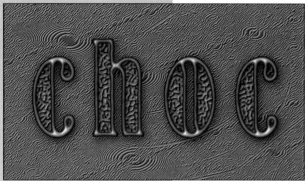

THINGS THAT ARE bad for you have a seductive sheen. Foie gras and the silver Porsche roadster spring to mind. Though KPT's Reaction filter makes complex effects (fairly) easy to achieve, with a bonus of background artifacts, Photoshop's native Layer Style dialog can offer a useful handful of soft lighting effects. Dark chocolate has its apologists—it contains a high concentration of catechins, a chemical group which is believed to offer protection against heart disease and cancer. Icing sugar has no defenders.

1 Fill Layer 1 with a mid-brown color. Set some type in a slightly different shade.

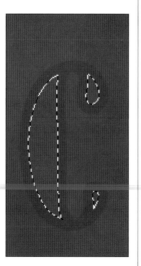

2 Rasterize the type layer, select the letterforms, go to *Select > Modify> **Contract*** to reduce the selection. Delete the contents of the new selection but let it remain active. Merge the two layers.

Chocolate

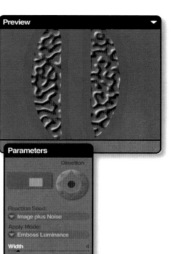

3 Choose *Filter > KPT6 > **Reaction***. Select **Image Plus Noise** as the reaction seed and **Emboss Luminance** as the apply mode. Hit OK.

4 Use the magic wand to select the brown background, and return to the Reaction filter. Change the reaction seed to **Voronoi** and decrease the **Width** setting to zero. Click on the "direction" compass rose to establish a diagonal movement. Leave the other settings untouched and hit OK.

5 Select the letter outline with the magic wand tool and go to *Filter > KPT5 > **Shape Shifter***. Of the seven control panels, select the three shown. Increase the default bevel height, change the environment color to dark brown (choose **Plastic** for the surface finish), and add a few extra lights in the 3D lighting panel. Hit OK.

KPT FILTERS

KAI KRAUSE changed the face of filtration single-handedly. While other software designers were anguishing over this or that drop shadow, and filling tiny boxes with pastel shades, Mr. Krause was carving great intuitive swathes through the interface and filling the screen with granite sliders. His lasting monument is Spheroid Designer in the KPT3 Filter set. Like adherence to a minority sect, the day-to-day use of KPT filters brought a strange sense of calm in a changing world. His KPT filters are now in different, and maybe more restrained, hands. The Turbulence filter is an ornery beast, much more suited to producing short and frantic animations than the refined business of type manipulation. Nevertheless, it can do things that the more ponderous Liquify can't. "Stoormis" is Dutch for disorder.

1 This effect is achieved using Kai Power Tools 6. Fill the opening layer with a light color and set the type in a contrasting color. Rasterize and duplicate the type layer for later use. Merge one of the type layers with the light background. This is the layer where the turbulence will be applied, so keep it visible and hide the other one.

2 Use *Filter* > *KPT6* > **KPT Turbulence**. The window opens with **Blend with Gradient** selected. Deselect it, but leave the other settings untouched.

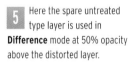

3 To produce a trial distortion, click and drag the pointer in a wavelike motion across the image window. The animation will begin to play (for 10 seconds in the default mode). The "step forward" button on the right allows you to advance frame-by-frame until you find a satisfactory image. If nothing useful appears, press the "stop" button on the left to clear the current distortion, and then drag again.

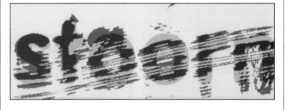

4 One or more re-applications of the filter may be required to break up the image to the desired degree.

5 Here the spare untreated type layer is used in **Difference** mode at 50% opacity above the distorted layer.

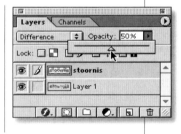

KPT FILTERS

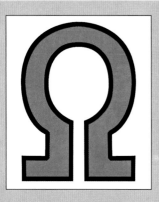

THE PREVIOUS KPT examples come from a more recent collection (version 6.0). This page includes examples from that and previous releases, all applied to the same target, all worth pursuing. On the opposite page are examples from the most recent collection – KPT 7.

KPT 3 Interform: Mother > Cubist Breakfast; Father > Fire Yawn

KPT 3 Interform: Mother > Galactic Nebula Sheets; Father > Bullets in Giraffes

KPT 3 Spheroid Designer: Random Spheres; Make 50 Spheres; Lighting Directions and Colors changed

KPT 3 Spheroid Designer: Random Spheres; Bump Map > Rays; Lighting Directions and Colors changed

KPT 3 Texture Explorer: Medium mutation

KPT 6 Gel: Default

KPT 3 Planar Tiling: Target not selected; Rotate 30; Scale 80

KPT 3 Planar Tiling: Target selected; Rotate 30; Scale 80

KPT 6 Goo: Brush Twirl

KPT 3 VortexTiling: Mode Normal Vortex; Maximum Radius

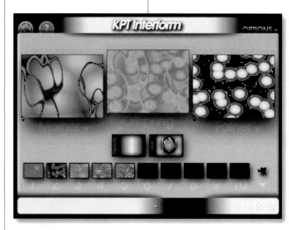

In the Interform dialog, Mother and Father make Child. So far, so uncontroversial. But these parents are leaping around in any one of 16 agitated styles, and can be dressed in any one of 116 textures. No wonder the child is disturbed. You can even make a 10-second movie of the event.

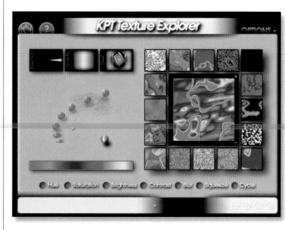

A calmer companion to Interform, Texture Explorer is a more manageable beast. There are only 20 categories of effect, which contain a total of only 348 textures, from Scottsdale on LSD to Sioux Me Bullseye. Take your choice of a mere seven levels of mutation, and as few as nine Blend modes

KPT 6 Projector: Default: Image shifted

KPT 5 Radwarp: Alpha 0.8; Beta -0.4

KPT 6 Lensflare: Default; Reflection Searchlight; Streaks Zoom Lens

KPT 5 FraxFlame: Default; Reflection Searchlight; Streaks Zoom Lens

KPT 5 FraxPlorer: Mandelbrot set; Julia variations; Zoom

KPT 5 FiberOptic: Default

KPT 5 Orb-It: Default: 3D Lighting changed; Average Size increased

KPT 5 ShapeShifter: Default: Bevel Scale increased; 3D Lighting changed

Frax4D operates in two modes: Cogiternion, with three parameters, and Quaternion with an unsurprising four. The default end product is a vitreous chunk like an extraterrestrial telephone pole insulator. Press more buttons to explore further. Block in a working week to get a reasonable grip.

KPT effects (version 7)

Channel Surfing: Default settings

Fluid: Brush Size > 77; Velocity > 58; Blend > 100%

Hyper Tiling: Default; Type > Cylinder; Depth Cue > Lighten; Scale > 32 %

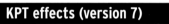

Gradient Lab is KPT version 7. It enables you to create just about any combination of colors and apply them to just about any combination of images.

Ink Dropper: Preset > Bacteria

Lightning: Preset > Tangled Bolt

Scatter: Preset > Inward Hue Spiral

ALIEN SKIN

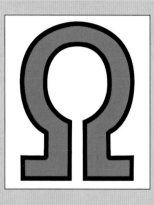

THE MEN (and women) at Alien Skin aver "we will never wear suits." This liberal disposition is also evident in their recommendation that you email your most successful Eye Candy filter settings to colleagues and friends, presumably not in a spirit of boastful arrogance, nor in the expectation of reward, but simply in the hope of enriching their lives. There are 23 filters, from AntiMatter to Wood. Some effects have been supplanted by Photoshop's Bevel & Emboss, but there is still a mountain of material to be explored.

Bevel Boss: Default; Grooved profile selected

Bevel Boss: Default; Bevel Width increased

Chrome: Default; Liquid Metal selected in the Settings menu; Roadside as the reflection map

Fire: Default; Column Length decreased; Flame Width increased; Side Taper increased; Start from FarSide selected.

Corona: Default

Cutout: Default; set to Transparent in a Layer in the Settings menu

Chrome: Default; Outdoor selected as the reflection map

Drip: Default: Maximum Length decreased

Fur: Default; Curl Size increased; Curliness decreased; Draw Only Inside Selection checked; HairColour changed

Cutout 2: as above, but with "Keep original image" selected

Glass: Default; Bevel Width decreased

Glass: Default; Bevel Width decreased

Gradient Glow: Default: Glow Width decreased; Rainbow selected in Color dialog

Xenofex

Star: Default: Number of Sides increased; Overall Opacity decreased; Center Offset Direction set to 90º

Melt: Default; Ripple Width decreased; Stretch Length decreased; Pooling decreased

Motion Trail: Default; Length decreased; Taper decreased; Overall Opacity decreased

Shadowlab: Default; Center Offset decreased; Overall Opacity increased; Over all Blur increased; Perspective Blur increased

Default: Vein Size decreased; Vein Coverage increased; Vein Thickness increased; Vein Roughness increased; Bedrock Color changed; Vein Color changed

Default: Column Length decreased; Eddy Size decreased; Turbulence Roughness increased; Start From Far Side checked

Squint: Radius reduced

Default: Tall Streaks selected in settings menu

Default: Whirlpool Spacing increased; Smear Length decreased; Twist increased; Streak detail increased; Seamless Tile checked

Wood: Default; Number of Knots increased

Water Drops: Drop Size decreased; Coverage increased; Round Drops checked

Weave: Default; Ribbon Width decreased; Gap Width decreased

Wood: Default

Wood: Default; Ring Thickness decreased; Cut Offset increased; Pulp Color changed; Bark Color changed

OTHER 3RD-PARTY FILTERS

Ticket

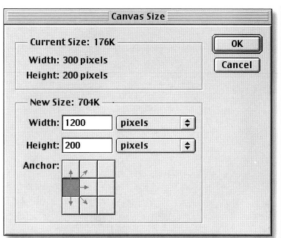

THE PROPELLER PAINT ENGINE lies in wait for the unwary operator. Its unique ribbon-making functions come at a terrible price. The learning curve is frustratingly steep, many of the detailed functions very counter-intuitive and the lack of a proper Undo function will reduce you to tears. However, for those who like to deal with two-and-a -half-dimensional graphics, it's an addictive procedure. The nearest equivalent activity is shooting fish in a barrel with a water-pistol.

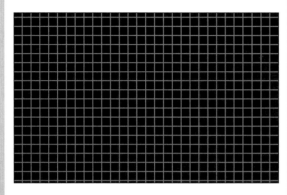

1 Create a new file with dimensions of a round number of pixels (this one is 300 by 200 pixels) and a transparent background. The dimensions of this document will determine the maximum possible size of the finished brush. Choose the rectangle tool from the shapes pop-up in the toolbox. Select

View > *Snap To* > **Grid**, then click and drag the rectangle tool to fill the whole area. (If no grid is visible, select *View* > *Show* > **Grid** first. The grid settings used here are one grid line every 10 pixels, with one subdivision. You can change these settings using *Edit* > *Preferences* > **Guides & Grid**.)

2 Choose the ellipse tool and select **Subtract from shape area** by clicking on the second button in the options bar.

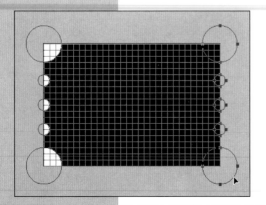

3 Drag out the lower right corner of the window to reveal the surrounding rebate, and use the ellipse tool to delete parts of the rectangle. Hold down Alt + Shift to ensure an accurate circle is drawn on an intersection each time. With the move tool, duplicate a group of "subtracting" shapes by selecting with the Shift key, then hold down the Alt and Cmd keys and drag the group to a new location. To preserve the new shape for future use, open the **Paths** palette and select its path by clicking on the thumbnail. Go to *Edit* > **Define Custom Shape** and name the new shape "ticket."

4 Go to *Image* > **Canvas Size**, and increase the width of the canvas to accommodate the required number of shapes (a total of four in this case). Don't forget to set the anchor point to center left, as shown here.

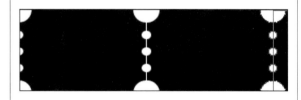

5 Duplicate the layer three times, and slide the shape along in each successive layer by going to *Select* > **All** and using the **Move** tool (top right of the toolbox) with Shift held down.

6 When all the shapes are correctly aligned, create a new blank layer at the foot of the palette and turn off its visibility; then select one of the other layers. To make clear which parts of the image are transparent, you may need to change the transparency setting in Preferences to medium checkerboard using *Edit* > *Preferences* > **Transparency & Gamut**. Go to *Layer* > *Rasterize* > **All Layers**, then *Merge Visible* in the Layers palette pop-up.

7 Select the shapes (by Cmd/Ctrl-clicking on the layer thumbnail), and make a new alpha channel by clicking on the "Save selection as channel" button. This channel will establish the transparent areas when the shapes are used in Propeller.

8 Return to the Layers palette. With the selection still active, go to *Edit > **Fill***, and fill with a pattern (this is "denim" from the Photoshop patterns 2 collection, which you can reach through the pop-up at the side of the Patterns palette).

12 Go to *Filter > Nowhouse > **Propeller***. Click on the **Pattern** tab and select "ticket.tif" in the default folder. Uncheck the two tiny letter "c"s immediately above.

9 Further treatment softens the "paper" background–first, the application of a light violet-to-white gradient at about 40% opacity (using the gradient tool's default **Foreground to Background** option), then a canvas texture from Photoshop's own Texturizer (*Filter > Texture > Texturizer > **Canvas***), and finally *Filter > Texture > **Patchwork***. The effect of both filters was reduced in *Edit > **Fade Filter***.

10 The numerals are set in the normal way, rasterized (*Layer > Rasterize > **Type***), treated individually with *Image > Adjust > **Hue/Saturation*** and then stroked with *Edit > **Stroke***. Change the blend mode of the type layer to **Color Burn**. Set each pair of numerals in turn by choosing the text tool, selecting the option to create a mask on the options bar, moving the selection (if necessary) by using *Select > **Transform Selection***, treating it with *Image > Adjust > **Hue/Saturation***, and then stroking it with *Edit > **Stroke***.

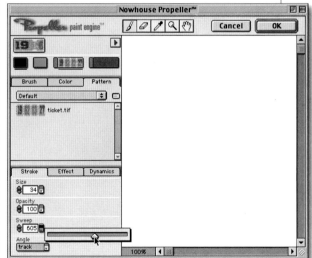

13 The default settings are very unlikely to produce a good result. Start by adjusting *Size* and *Sweep* in the *Stroke* dialog. You can try different settings by painting directly on the canvas area, but the best initial guide is the thumbnail at top left of the window.

11 Make the alpha channel visible; its mask color should appear faintly in the transparent areas of the image. Then save the document as a TIFF file (ticket.tif) in the default folder of Propeller's Pattern Library (not the Brush Library). Make sure that the "Alpha Channels" option is checked.

Ticket continued

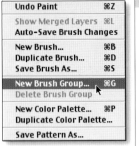

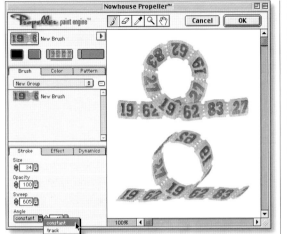

14 When you have the basic pattern settings established, click on the pop-up menu near the top center of the window and choose **New Brush Group**. You could at the same time choose to uncheck **Auto-Save Brush Changes**. If it remains checked, possibly unwanted changes to your chosen brush will be silently saved and may be difficult to reverse. Now choose *Save Brush As* from the same menu. When the dialog box appears, navigate to the "New Group" folder you have just made, and save the brush in it.

15 With new brush selected, you can switch the **Angle** control between **track** (the default setting) as in the upper image, and **constant** as in the

lower one. **Constant** has an angle setting of its own which, like a calligraphic brush, is at 45º by default.

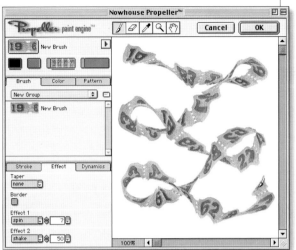

17 It is possible to add a second effect. In this case **shake** has been selected from the **Effect 2** menu.

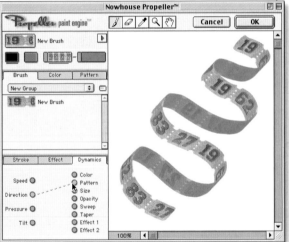

18 In the third tab, movements of the mouse or stylus can be used to vary the stroke settings on the fly. Here, a link has been made between the **Direction** and **Pattern** parameters. Where the movement

is left to right the stroke is normal; when it changes direction the pattern is suppressed in favor of the background color. The **Pressure** and **Tilt** connections are active only with a suitable stylus.

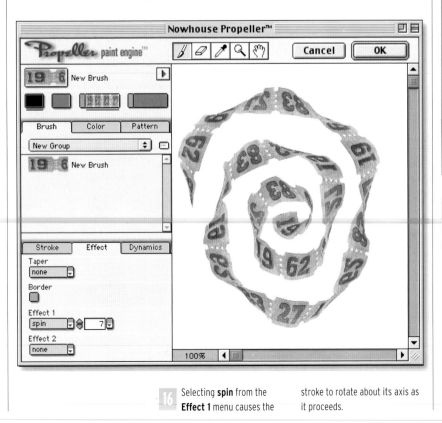

16 Selecting **spin** from the **Effect 1** menu causes the

stroke to rotate about its axis as it proceeds.

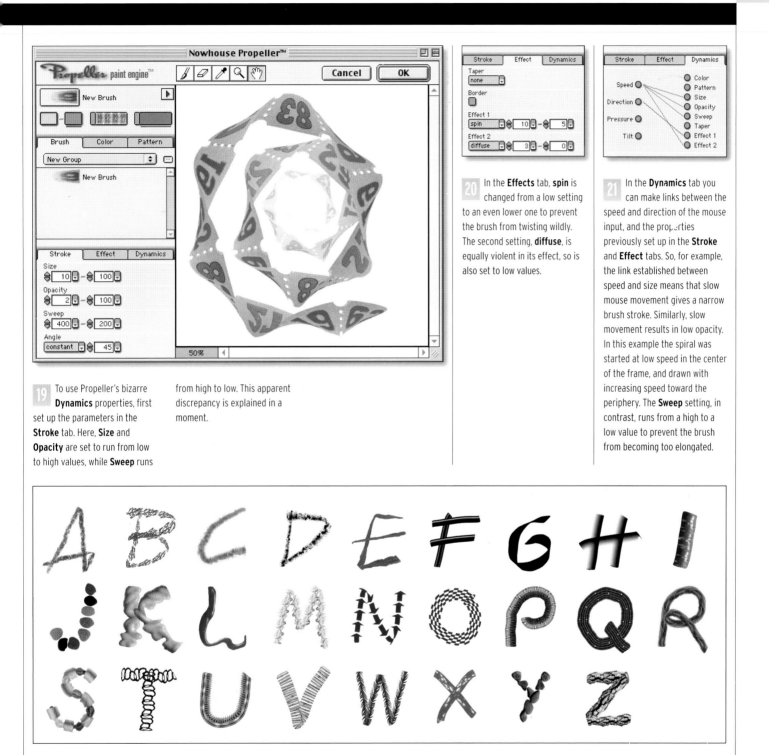

20 In the **Effects** tab, **spin** is changed from a low setting to an even lower one to prevent the brush from twisting wildly. The second setting, **diffuse**, is equally violent in its effect, so is also set to low values.

21 In the **Dynamics** tab you can make links between the speed and direction of the mouse input, and the properties previously set up in the **Stroke** and **Effect** tabs. So, for example, the link established between speed and size means that slow mouse movement gives a narrow brush stroke. Similarly, slow movement results in low opacity. In this example the spiral was started at low speed in the center of the frame, and drawn with increasing speed toward the periphery. The **Sweep** setting, in contrast, runs from a high to a low value to prevent the brush from becoming too elongated.

19 To use Propeller's bizarre **Dynamics** properties, first set up the parameters in the **Stroke** tab. Here, **Size** and **Opacity** are set to run from low to high values, while **Sweep** runs from high to low. This apparent discrepancy is explained in a moment.

22 This alphabet shows a selection of the ready-made brush styles within Propeller as follows:
A: crayon thick; B: pencil scribble; C: spray 1; D: spray clog; E: wet acrylic 1; F: glossy pen thick; G: calligraphic spin; H: pen tapered; I: pretzel; J: gum candy 2; K: frosting; L: plastic 2; M: powder; N: arrow; O: deco 3; P: cord; Q: guitar; R: hair; S: necklace; T: chain 2; U: tube; V: bamboo 4; W: fern; X: sky; Y: rocks; Z: bark 2.

3RD-PARTY EFFECTS

THERE ARE hundreds of other third-party products filters and plug-ins designed to work with Photoshop. This is a necessarily abbreviated roundup. Some, like Andromeda 3D, are commercial products designed to plug a hole in Photoshop's own facilities. Others, mainly low-cost, share- and free-ware items, come close to duplicating effects which are already achievable, with a little industry, to the average user employing only the basic set of native filters. Some vile productions will even crash your machine. Moreover, Photoshop runs less quickly with an increased load of plug-ins—the strategy should be ruthless culling of the lesser offerings.

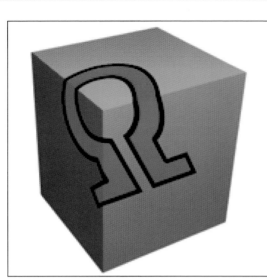

Andromeda 3D, Box; Wrap corner;
Box faces colored

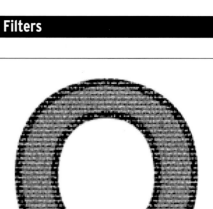

Andromeda Screens
Default: Pattern + Mezzo blend

Flaming Pear: India (sic) Ink:
scaled increased 2x

Right: Flaming Pear: Blade Pro
dialog box, using a random setting
(with the "dice throw" icon)

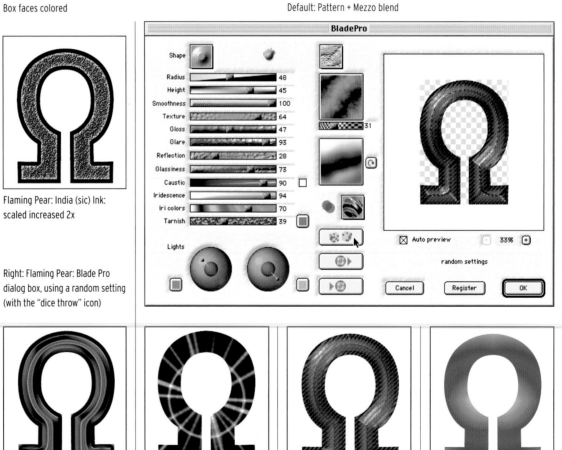

Flaming Pear: Lacquer Random

Flaming Pear: Solar Cell Random;
Master Brightness increased

Flaming Pear: BladePro Random
(dice throw). See dialog box above

Harry's Filters: Double-
SphereGradients; Default

Neology: Checkered Tiling

Neology: Transparent Pizza Slices
increased to 255

Neology: A Different Sin; Default.

Paint Alchemy:
Preset; Teardrop Brush Styles > Hairy Fuzz

Neology: Polar Waves
Cycle Angle 70; Cycle Magnitude 30;
Amplitude a 50; Amplitude B 10.

Paint Alchemy: Vortex Styles >
Vortex Thick, Paint Variation 50

Paint Alchemy: Default; Brush
Color: Hue, Saturation and
Lightness all changed to 25;
Brush Density 2300

Nirvana: RadialSinality
Default

PHOTOSHOP DEFAULT ACTIONS

These can be used with layer styles to produce, say, neon effects, among other things

Thin Outline

Applied to a type layer of any color but the result is always black, the final result can be placed in an alpha channel, loaded as a selection and colored. This example uses a bold font in black, set with negative tracking.

Medium Outline

Applied to a type layer of any color but the result is always black, the final result can be placed in an alpha channel, loaded as a selection and colored. This example uses a bold font in black, set with negative tracking.

Bold Outline

Applied to a type layer of any color but the result is always black, the final result can be placed in an alpha channel, loaded as a selection and colored. This example uses a bold font in black, set with negative tracking.

Brushed metal

Applied to a type layer of any color but the result is always gray. This example uses a bold font in black, set with negative tracking.

Cast shadow

Applied to a type layer of any color. The shadow is always gray. This example uses a bold font in black, set with negative tracking.

Chrome

This requires a photograph layer as the starting point (click "Continue" when the action asks you to select a photograph layer). The action halts part way through with an alert asking you to edit the type (click "Stop")–choose a word, its size, and its position on the background (which forms the fill for the type). Then click the "Play Selection" button on the Actions palette to resume. This example uses a bold font in black, set with negative tracking.

Clear emboss

This simply applies a bevel-and-emboss Layer Style to the type. It doesn't matter what color the type is to start with. It works well on top of a blurred picture.

Frosted glass

This requires a photograph layer as the starting point (click "Continue" when the action asks you to select a photograph layer.) A pale photograph works best with this action and it works even better if you blur the photograph layer slightly either before or after ruunning the action. The action halts part way through with an alert asking you to edit the type (click "Stop"). Choose a word, its size and position on the background (which forms the fill for the type). Color doesn't matter. Then click the "Play Selection" button on the Actions palette to resume. This example uses Cochin bold italic.

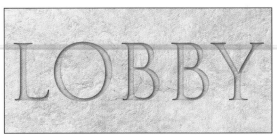

Die cut

Applied to a type layer of any color. The shadow is always grey. This works best against a textured background with a pale color. A paper texture from Artbeats Wood and Paper was used here for the background, otherwise the background would be white. This example uses Trajan.

Sprayed stencil

Applied to a type layer of any color, it puts a glow of the foreground color around the type, leaving the type area transparent against the background. This works best against a textured background. A brick texture from the "Texturizer" filter was used here. The font is Stencil.

Water reflection

Applied to a type layer, this places a rippled "reflection" in front of the type. The color applied to the type is also applied to the reflection. The second example shows what it looks like with a graduated background color ("Render Clouds" then "Glass" then "ZigZag" filters were applied). This example uses a bold font (Interstate), set with negative tracking.

Wavy

Applied to a type layer. This example uses Interstate regular, set with negative tracking.

Confetti

Applied to a type layer, this action simply applies the "Pointillist" filter to the type, using both background and foreground colors. The font used here is Ribbon.

Wood paneling

Applied to a type layer, this action uses both the foreground and background colors rather than the color set for the type, so choose both colors before starting. This example uses Fette Fraktur.

Warp squeeze

Applied to a type layer, this action simply applies the "Warp Text" text style to the type.

Running Water (above and right)

Applied to a type layer, this applies an effect in front of the original type, leaving the original unaltered on a separate layer, which could be switched off if desired (as in the example shown to the right). The font used here is Trajan.

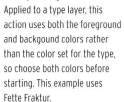

3RD-PARTY ACTIONS

As well as recording on the fly, you can load extra Actions via the popup in the actions palette. There are the native Photoshop sets, both general and type-oriented, and you can also obtain Actions made by others. Searching "photoshop actions" on the internet will find masses. All these Actions are editable, and can be re-saved with your improvements. You can also find the actions shown here on the CD that accompanies this volume.

Amber

This action is applied to a type layer (color doesn't matter; it defines these for you.) The action first duplicates your original document. It works better at fairly small type sizes.

Chrome

This action is applied to a type layer (color doesn't matter; it defines these for you.) The action first duplicates your original document. Thinner fonts work best since this action relies on the "Render > Clouds" filter, which looks too obvious on bolder faces. This duplicates the original document. The effect is random so it's different each time it's run. The font used here is ITC Garamond Condensed (90% horizontal scaling).

Acrylic

This action is applied to a type layer (color doesn't matter; it defines these for you.) The action first duplicates your original document. Use a bold face set with tight tracking so that the characters seep into each other. The font used here is Interstate Ultra Black Condensed.

Aqua

This action creates a document and asks you to edit the type (change the font, weight, etc.) the action continues after you commit the type by clicking the checkmark in the toolbar along the top of the window.

Chrome

This action is applied to a type layer (color doesn't matter; it defines these for you.) The action first duplicates your original document. Thinner fonts work best since this action relies on the "Render > Clouds" filter, which looks too obvious on bolder faces. This duplicates the original document. The effect is random so it's different each time it's run. The font used here is ITC Garamond Condensed (90% horizontal scaling).

Screwed letters

This action is applied to a type layer (color doesn't matter as it defines these for you)–the action first duplicates your original document. The action first creates a screwhead and then prompts you to position these on the text by dragging and dropping–as many as you like. The font used here is Interstate Ultra Black Condensed.

Broken metal

This action requires you to define type as a selection in a newly created document.

Charmed

This action is applied to a type layer (color doesn't matter; it defines these for you.) The action first duplicates your original document. The action offers you a couple of opportunities to edit colors along the way.

Splat

This creates a new document which starts by allowing you to edit the text (default is "splat") (color doesn't matter; it defines these for you.) If you want to change the format of the document you need to stop the action (you can start it again by pressing the "Play" button. This requires that you load the "Crumbles" displacement map and "Bumpy Leather" texture (which only comes with Photoshop versions prior to 6). However, you can use an alternative texture. The font used here is Devotion.

Concrete

This action is applied to a type layer (color doesn't matter; it defines these for you.) The action first duplicates your original document. The font used here is Interstate Ultra Black Compressed.

Western

This is a two part action. The first action defines the pattern which is used when you run the text effect action. The font used here is Interstate Ultra Black Condensed.

Pebble

This action is applied to a type layer (color doesn't matter; it defines these for you.) The action first duplicates your original document. The font used here is Chilada.

Granite

This action is applied to a type layer (color doesn't matter; it defines these for you.) The action first duplicates your original document. The font used here is Interstate Ultra Compressed.

Beach

This action is applied to a type layer (color doesn't matter; it defines these for you.) The action first duplicates your original document. The font used here is Freak Freehand.

Marble

This action is applied to a type layer (color doesn't matter; it defines these for you.) The action first duplicates your original document. This produces random results–no two are the same. The font used here is Interstate Ultra Compressed.

Tray

This action is applied to a type layer (color doesn't matter; it defines these for you.) The action first duplicates your original document. The font used here is Interstate Ultra Compressed.

Metals/Chrome

Metals/Corroded

Metals

These actions are applied to a type layer (color doesn't matter; it defines these for you.) The action first duplicates your original document. The font used here is ITC Garamond Condensed.

Metals/Polished gold

Metals/rusty steel

Oxidized copper

This action is applied to a type layer (color doesn't matter; it defines these for you.) The action first duplicates your original document. The font used here is Chilada.

Rust Stamp

This action is applied to a type layer (color doesn't matter; it defines these for you.) The action first duplicates your original document. The font used here is Chilada.

Rust

These two actions action are applied to a type layer (color doesn't matter; it defines these for you.) The action first duplicates your original document. The font used here is Helvetica Neue Black Compressed.

Photoshop Shortcuts

Mac

Channels

Load Composite as Selection	⌘+⌥+ ~
Load Layer Mask as Selection	⌘+⌥+\
Load Selection Channel 1-9	⌘+⌥+1-9
Select Channel 1-9	⌘+1-9
Select Composite Channel	⌘+ ~
Select Layer Mask (Channel)	⌘+\
Toggle Channel / Rubylith View	~
Toggle Layer Mask as Rubylith	\

Layers

Ascend through Layers	⌥+]
Bring Layer to Front	⌘+⇧+]
Descend though Layers	⌥+[
Group with Previous	⌘+G
Layer Opacity 10% -100%	1-Ø (Zero)
Layer via Copy	⌘+J
Layer via Copy (with Dialog Box)	⌘+⌥+J
Lock Transparent Pixels	/
Merge Down (Linked / Grouped)	⌘+E
Merge Visible	⌘+⇧+E
Merge Visible to Active Layer	⌘+⌥+⇧+E
Move Layer Backward	⌘+[
Move Layer Forward	⌘+]
New Layer	⌘+⇧+N
New Layer (without Dialog Box)	⌘+⌥+⇧+N
Select Bottom Layer	⌥+⇧+[
Select Top Layer	⌥+⇧+]
Send Layer to Back	⌘+⇧+[
Stamp Down	⌘+⌥+E
Stamp Visible	⌘+⌥+⇧+E
Ungroup Layers	⌘+⇧+G

Editing

Copy	⌘+C
Copy Merged	⌘+⇧+C
Cut	⌘+X
Duplicate Free Transform	⌘+⌥+T
Duplicate Transform Again	⌘+⌥+⇧+T
Extract	⌘+⌥+X
(6) Extract	⌘+⌥+⇧+X
Fade Last Filter / Adjustment	⌘+⇧+F
Fill Dialog	⇧+←
Fill from History	⌘+⌥+←
Fill from History & Preserve Trans.	⌘+⌥+⇧+←
Fill w/ Background & Preserve Trans.	⌘+⇧+←
Fill w/ Foreground & Preserve Trans.	⌥+⇧+←
Fill with Background Color	⌘+←
Fill with Foreground Color	⌥+←
Free Transform	⌘+T
Last Filter	⌘+F
Last Filter Dialog Box	⌘+⌥+F
Liquify	⌘+⇧+X
Paste	⌘+V
Paste Into Selection	⌘+⇧+V
Paste Outside	⌘+⌥+⇧+V
(7) Pattern Maker	⌘+⌥+⇧+X
Step Backward in History	⌘+⌥+Z
Step Forward in History	⌘+⇧+Z
Transform Again	⌘+⇧+T
Undo	⌘+Z

Editing Paths

Select Multiple Anchor Points	↖ +⇧+click
Select Entire Path	↖ +⌥+click
Duplicate Path	✒ +⌥+Ctrl+drag

Blending Modes

Cycle Blending Modes Backward	⇧+⊟
Cycle Blending Modes Forward	⇧+⊞
Behind	⌥+⇧+Q
Clear	⌥+⇧+R
Color	⌥+⇧+C
Color Burn	⌥+⇧+B
Color Dodge	⌥+⇧+D
Darken	⌥+⇧+K
Difference	⌥+⇧+E
Dissolve	⌥+⇧+ I
Exclusion	⌥+⇧+X
Hard Light	⌥+⇧+H
Hue	⌥+⇧+U
Lighten	⌥+⇧+G
Luminosity	⌥+⇧+Y
Multiply	⌥+⇧+M
Normal	⌥+⇧+N
Overlay	⌥+⇧+O
Saturation	⌥+⇧+T
Screen	⌥+⇧+S
Soft Light	⌥+⇧+F
6) Pass Through (Layer Sets)	⌥+⇧+P
(6) Desaturate (Sponge Tool)	⌥+⇧+J
(6) Saturate (Sponge Tool)	⌥+⇧+A
(6) Highlights (Dodge & Burn Tools)	⌥+⇧+Z
(6) Midtones (Dodge & Burn Tools)	⌥+⇧+V
(6) Shadows (Dodge & Burn Tools)	⌥+⇧+W
(7) Linear Burn	⌥+⇧+A
(7) Linear Light	⌥+⇧+J
(7) Vivid Light	⌥+⇧+V
(7) Linear Dodge	⌥+⇧+W
(7) Pin Light	⌥+⇧+Z

Type

Align Left	⌘+⇧+L
Align Right	⌘+⇧+R
Center Text	⌘+⇧+C
Change Tracking by 100/1000em	⌘+⌥+←,→
Change Tracking by 20/1000em	⌥+←,→
Decrease / Increase Baseline by 10pt	⌘+⌥+⇧+↑,↓
Decrease / Increase Baseline by 2pt	⌥+⇧+↑,↓
Decrease / Increase Leading by 10pt	⌘+⌥+↑,↓
Decrease / Increase Leading by 2pt	⌥+ ↑, ↓
Justify Paragraph (Force Last Line)	⌘+⇧+F
Move Cursor One Word Left or Right	⌘+ ←, →
Move Cursor to End of Line	↘
Move Cursor to End of Story	⌘+↘
Move Cursor to Start of Line	↖
Move Cursor to Start of Story	⌘+↖
Move to Previous / Next Paragraph	⌘+↑,↓
Select One Character to Left or Right	⇧+←,→
Select One Line (to end) Up or Down	⌘+⇧+↑,↓
Select One Line Up or Down	⇧+↑,↓
Select One Word to Left or Right	⌘+⇧+←,→
Select Type to End of Line	⇧+↘
Select Type to End of Story	⌘+⇧+↘
Select Type to Start of Line	⇧+↖
Select Type to Start of Story	⌘+⇧+↖
Set Horizontal Scale to 100%	⌘+⇧+X
Set Leading to Auto	⌘+⌥+⇧+A
Set Tracking to 0	⌘+⇧+Q
Set Vertical Scale to 100%	⌘+⌥+⇧+X
Toggle Hyphenation On / Off	⌘+⌥+⇧+H
Toggle Single / Every-Line Composer	⌘+⌥+⇧+T
Toggle Small Caps On / Off	⌘+⇧+H
Toggle Strikethrough On / Off	⌘+⇧+ /
Toggle Subscript On / Off	⌘+⌥+⇧+⊞
Toggle Superscript On / Off	⌘+⇧+⊞
Toggle Underlining On / Off	⌘+⇧+U
Toggle Uppercase On / Off	⌘+⇧+K
Cancel Type Changes	Esc

Image Adjustment

Auto Contrast	⌘+⌥+⇧+L
Auto Levels	⌘+⇧+L
Color Balance	⌘+B
Color Balance (with Last Settings)	⌘+⌥+B
Curves	⌘+M
Curves (with Last Settings)	⌘+⌥+M
Desaturate	⌘+⇧+U
Gamut Warning	⌘+⇧+Y
Hue / Saturation	⌘+U
Hue / Saturation (with last settings)	⌘+⌥+U
Invert	⌘+I

PHOTOSHOP SHORTCUTS

Mac

Levels	⌘+L
Levels (with Last Settings)	⌘+⌥+L
Proof Colors (CMYK Preview)	⌘+Y

TOOL BOX

Marquee Tool	M
Move Tool	V
Lasso Tool	L
Magic Wand	W
Crop	C
Slice/Slice Select	K
(6) Air Brush	J
(7) Healing Brush/Patch	J
Paintbrush/Pencil	B
Clone/Pattern Stamp	S
History Brush	Y
Eraser	E
Gradient/Paint Bucket	G
Blur/Sharpen/Smudge	R
Dodge/Burn/Sponge	O
Type Tool	T
Path Component Selection Tool	A
Rectangle/Ellipse/Polygon Tool	U
Pen Tool	P
Eyedrop/Measure	I
Notes/Audio Anno	N
Zoom	Z
Switch Colors	X
Hand	K

note: Holding down shift key in addition to above keys will enable toggling thru tool type, where applicable.

Default Fore/Background Colors	D
Edit Standard/QuickMask	Q (toggle)
Screen Mode	F (toggles thru)
Jump to Image Ready	⌘+⇧+M

DOCUMENT MANAGEMENT

Close	⌘+W
Close All	⌘+⇧+W
Color Settings	⌘+⇧+K
New Document	⌘+N
New Document (Last Settings)	⌘+⌥+N
Next Document	⌘+⇧+Tab
Open	⌘+O
Open As	⌘+⌥+O
Page Setup	⌘+⇧+P
Preferences	⌘+K
Preferences (Last Used)	⌘+⌥+K
Previous Document	⌘+Tab

Print Options	⌘+P
Quit	⌘+Q
Revert	F12
Save	⌘+S
Save As	⌘+⇧+S
Save As (Copy)	⌘+⌥+S
Save For Web	⌘+⌥+⇧+S

DOCUMENT VIEWS

Actual Pixels	⌘+⌥+Ø (Zero)
Extras, Show/Hide	⌘+H
Fit on Screen	⌘+Ø (Zero)
Gamut Warning, Show/Hide	⌘+⌥+Y
Grid, Show/Hide	⌘+⌥+'
Guides, Lock/Unlock	⌘+⌥+;
Guides, Show/Hide	⌘+;
Palettes, Show/Hide	⇧+Tab
Rulers, Show/Hide	⌘+R
Snap, On/Off	⌘+⇧+;
Zoom in	⌘+⊞
Zoom out	⌘+⊟

LIQUIFY TOOLS

Warp Tool	W
(7) Turbulence Tool	A
Twirl Clockwise Tool	R
Twirl Counter Clockwise Tool	L
Pucker Tool	P
Bloat Tool	B
Shift Pixels Tool	S
Reflection Tool	M
Reconstruct Tool	E
Freeze Tool	F
Thaw Tool	T
Zoom Tool	Z
Hand Tool	H

EXTRACT TOOLS

Edge Highlighter Tool	B
Fill Tool	G
Eraser Tool	E
Eyedropper Tool	I
Cleanup Tool	C
Edge Touchup Tool	T
Zoom Tool	Z
Hand Tool	H

SELECTION

Deselect	⌘+D
Delete Selection	←
Feather Selection	⌘+⌥+D
Invert Selection	⌘+⇧+I
Move Selection, 1 pixel increments	⌘+←,↑,→,↓
Move Selection, 10 pixel increments	⌘+⇧+←,↑,→,↓
Move Selection Area, 1 pixel increments	←,↑,→,↓
Move Selection Area, 10 pixel increments	⇧+←,↑,→,↓
Reselect	⌘+⇧+D
Select All	⌘+A

Windows

CHANNELS

Load Composite as Selection	Ctrl+Alt+ ~
Load Layer Mask as Selection	Ctrl+Alt+\
Load Selection Channel 1-9	Ctrl+Alt+1-9
Select Channel 1-9	Ctrl+1-9
Select Composite Channel	Ctrl+ ~
Select Layer Mask (Channel)	Ctrl+\
Toggle Channel / Rubylith View	~
Toggle Layer Mask as Rubylith	\

LAYERS

Ascend through Layers	Alt+]
Bring Layer to Front	Ctrl+⇧+]
Descend though Layers	Alt+[
Group with Previous	Ctrl+G
Layer Opacity 10% -100%	1-Ø (Zero)
Layer via Copy	Ctrl+J
Layer via Copy (with Dialog Box)	Ctrl+Alt+J
Lock Transparent Pixels	/
Merge Down (Linked / Grouped)	Ctrl+E
Merge Visible	Ctrl+⇧+E
Merge Visible to Active Layer	Ctrl+Alt+⇧+E
Move Layer Backward	Ctrl+[
Move Layer Forward	Ctrl+]
New Layer	Ctrl+⇧+N
New Layer (without Dialog Box)	Ctrl+Alt+⇧+N
Select Bottom Layer	Alt+⇧+[
Select Top Layer	Alt+⇧+]
Send Layer to Back	Ctrl+⇧+[
Stamp Down	Ctrl+Alt+E
Stamp Visible	Ctrl+Alt+⇧+E
Ungroup Layers	Ctrl+⇧+G

EDITING

Copy	Ctrl+C
Copy Merged	Ctrl+⇧+C
Cut	Ctrl+X
Duplicate Free Transform	Ctrl+Alt+T
Duplicate Transform Again	Ctrl+Alt+⇧+T
Extract	Ctrl+Alt+X
(6) Extract	Ctrl+Alt+⇧+X
Fade Last Filter / Adjustment	Ctrl+⇧+F
Fill Dialog	⇧+←
Fill from History	Ctrl+Alt+←
Fill from History & Preserve Trans.	Ctrl+Alt+⇧+←
Fill w/ Background & Preserve Trans.	Ctrl+⇧+←
Fill w/ Foreground & Preserve Trans.	Alt+⇧+←
Fill with Background Color	Ctrl+←
Fill with Foreground Color	Alt+←
Free Transform	Ctrl+T
Last Filter	Ctrl+F
Last Filter Dialog Box	Ctrl+Alt+F
Liquify	Ctrl+⇧+X
Paste	Ctrl+V
Paste Into Selection	Ctrl+⇧+V
Paste Outside	Ctrl+Alt+⇧+V
(7) Pattern Maker	Ctrl+Alt+⇧+X
Step Backward in History	Ctrl+Alt+Z
Step Forward in History	Ctrl+⇧+Z
Transform Again	Ctrl+⇧+T
Undo	Ctrl+Z

EDITING PATHS

Select Multiple Anchor Points	↖ +⇧+click
Select Entire Path	↖ +Alt+click
Duplicate Path	✒ +Alt+Ctrl+drag

BLENDING MODES

Cycle Blending Modes Backward	⇧+−
Cycle Blending Modes Forward	⇧+＋
Behind	Alt+⇧+Q
Clear	Alt+⇧+R
Color	Alt+⇧+C
Color Burn	Alt+⇧+B
Color Dodge	Alt+⇧+D
Darken	Alt+⇧+K
Difference	Alt+⇧+E
Dissolve	Alt+⇧+ I
Exclusion	Alt+⇧+X
Hard Light	Alt+⇧+H
Hue	Alt+⇧+U
Lighten	Alt+⇧+G
Luminosity	Alt+⇧+Y
Multiply	Alt+⇧+M
Normal	Alt+⇧+N
Overlay	Alt+⇧+O
Saturation	Alt+⇧+T
Screen	Alt+⇧+S
Soft Light	Alt+⇧+F
(6) Pass Through (Layer Sets)	Alt+⇧+P
(6) Desaturate (Sponge Tool)	Alt+⇧+J
(6) Saturate (Sponge Tool)	Alt+⇧+A
(6) Highlights (Dodge & Burn Tools)	Alt+⇧+Z
(6) Midtones (Dodge & Burn Tools)	Alt+⇧+V
(6) Shadows (Dodge & Burn Tools)	Alt+⇧+W
(7) Linear Burn	Alt+⇧+A
(7) Linear Light	Alt+⇧+J
(7) Vivid Light	Alt+⇧+V
(7) Linear Dodge	Alt+⇧+W
(7) Pin Light	Alt+⇧+Z

TYPE

Align Left	Ctrl+⇧+L
Align Right	Ctrl+⇧+R
Center Text	Ctrl+⇧+C
Change Tracking by 100/1000em	Ctrl+Alt+←,→
Change Tracking by 20/1000em	Alt+←,→
Decrease / Increase Baseline by 10pt	Ctrl+Alt+⇧+↑,↓
Decrease / Increase Baseline by 2pt	Alt+⇧+↑,↓
Decrease / Increase Leading by 10pt	Ctrl+Alt+↑,↓
Decrease / Increase Leading by 2pt	Alt+ ↑, ↓
Justify Paragraph (Force Last Line)	Ctrl+⇧+F
Move Cursor One Word Left or Right	Ctrl+ ←, →
Move Cursor to End of Line	End
Move Cursor to End of Story	Ctrl+End
Move Cursor to Start of Line	Home
Move Cursor to Start of Story	Ctrl+Home
Move to Previous / Next Paragraph	Ctrl+↑,↓
Select One Character to Left or Right	⇧+←,→
Select One Line (to end) Up or Down	Ctrl+⇧+↑,↓
Select One Line Up or Down	⇧+↑,↓
Select One Word to Left or Right	Ctrl+⇧+←,→
Select Type to End of Line	⇧+End
Select Type to End of Story	Ctrl+⇧+End
Select Type to Start of Line	⇧+Home
Select Type to Start of Story	Ctrl+⇧+Home
Set Horizontal Scale to 100%	Ctrl+⇧+X
Set Leading to Auto	Ctrl+Alt+⇧+A
Set Tracking to 0	Ctrl+⇧+Q
Set Vertical Scale to 100%	Ctrl+Alt+⇧+X
Toggle Hyphenation On / Off	Ctrl+Alt+⇧+H
Toggle Single / Every-Line Composer	Ctrl+Alt+⇧+T
Toggle Small Caps On / Off	Ctrl+⇧+H
Toggle Strikethrough On / Off	Ctrl+⇧+ /
Toggle Subscript On / Off	Ctrl+Alt+⇧+＋
Toggle Superscript On / Off	Ctrl+⇧+＋
Toggle Underlining On / Off	Ctrl+⇧+U
Toggle Uppercase On / Off	Ctrl+⇧+K
Cancel Type Changes	Esc

IMAGE ADJUSTMENT

Auto Contrast	Ctrl+Alt+⇧+L
Auto Levels	Ctrl+⇧+L
Color Balance	Ctrl+B
Color Balance (with Last Settings)	Ctrl+Alt+B
Curves	Ctrl+M
Curves (with Last Settings)	Ctrl+Alt+M
Desaturate	Ctrl+⇧+U
Gamut Warning	Ctrl+⇧+Y
Hue / Saturation	Ctrl+U
Hue / Saturation (with last settings)	Ctrl+Alt+U
Invert	Ctrl+I

PHOTOSHOP SHORTCUTS

Windows

Levels	Ctrl+L
Levels (with Last Settings)	Ctrl+Alt+L
Proof Colors (CMYK Preview)	Ctrl+Y

TOOL BOX

Marquee Tool	M
Move Tool	V
Lasso Tool	L
Magic Wand	W
Crop	C
Slice/Slice Select	K
(6) Air Brush	J
(7) Healing Brush/Patch	J
Paintbrush/Pencil	B
Clone/Pattern Stamp	S
History Brush	Y
Eraser	E
Gradient/Paint Bucket	G
Blur/Sharpen/Smudge	R
Dodge/Burn/Sponge	O
Type Tool	T
Path Component Selection Tool	A
Rectangle/Ellipse/Polygon Tool	U
Pen Tool	P
Eyedrop/Measure	I
Notes/Audio Anno	N
Zoom	Z
Switch Colors	X
Hand	K

note: Holding down shift key in addition to above keys will enable toggling thru tool type, where applicable.

Default Fore/Background Colors	D
Edit Standard/QuickMask	Q (toggle)
Screen Mode	F (toggles thru)
Jump to Image Ready	Ctrl+⇧+M

DOCUMENT MANAGEMENT

Close	Ctrl+W
Close All	Ctrl+⇧+W
Color Settings	Ctrl+⇧+K
New Document	Ctrl+N
New Document (Last Settings)	Ctrl+Alt+N
Next Document	Ctrl+⇧+Tab
Open	Ctrl+O
Open As	Ctrl+Alt+O
Page Setup	Ctrl+⇧+P
Preferences	Ctrl+K
Preferences (Last Used)	Ctrl+Alt+K
Previous Document	Ctrl+Tab

Print Options	Ctrl+P
Quit	Ctrl+Q
Revert	F12
Save	Ctrl+S
Save As	Ctrl+⇧+S
Save As (Copy)	Ctrl+Alt+S
Save For Web	Ctrl+Alt+⇧+S

DOCUMENT VIEWS

Actual Pixels	Ctrl+Alt+Ø (Zero)
Extras, Show/Hide	Ctrl+H
Fit on Screen	Ctrl+Ø (Zero)
Gamut Warning, Show/Hide	Ctrl+Alt+Y
Grid, Show/Hide	Ctrl+Alt+'
Guides, Lock/Unlock	Ctrl+Alt+;
Guides, Show/Hide	Ctrl+;
Palettes, Show/Hide	⇧+Tab
Rulers, Show/Hide	Ctrl+R
Snap, On/Off	Ctrl+⇧+;
Zoom in	Ctrl+⊞
Zoom out	Ctrl+⊟

LIQUIFY TOOLS

Warp Tool	W
(7) Turbulence Tool	A
Twirl Clockwise Tool	R
Twirl Counter Clockwise Tool	L
Pucker Tool	P
Bloat Tool	B
Shift Pixels Tool	S
Reflection Tool	M
Reconstruct Tool	E
Freeze Tool	F
Thaw Tool	T
Zoom Tool	Z
Hand Tool	H

EXTRACT TOOLS

Edge Highlighter Tool	B
Fill Tool	G
Eraser Tool	E
Eyedropper Tool	I
Cleanup Tool	C
Edge Touchup Tool	T
Zoom Tool	Z
Hand Tool	H

SELECTION

Deselect	Ctrl+D
Delete Selection	⏎
Feather Selection	Ctrl+Alt+D
Invert Selection	Ctrl+⇧+I
Move Selection, 1 pixel increments	Ctrl+←,↑,→,↓
Move Selection, 10 pixel increments	Ctrl+⇧+←,↑,→,↓
Move Selection Area, 1 pixel increments	←,↑,→,↓
Move Selection Area, 10 pixel increments	⇧+←,↑,→,↓
Reselect	Ctrl+⇧+D
Select All	Ctrl+A

ACKNOWLEDGMENTS

The author and Ilex Press would like to thank the following people and organizations for all their assistance in the creation of this book: Jeremy Cope and Anjali Ariathurai of Adobe Systems, Inc., Armstrong & Cuthbert, Vernon Morris, Desmond Jeffries, Huck Treadwell, Tony Beeman, Skip Barttels, Rick Kelly, Martin Bland, Slaine art, Francisco López, and Jared Pease.

The author would also like to thank the following people for providing additional material: Graham Davis, Lance Cummings, Andrew Milne, Stephen Parr, Nick Rowland, and Allen Zuk.

National Association of Photoshop Professionals

The only tool you need to master Adobe Photoshop

If you use Photoshop, you know that it's never been more important to stay up to date with your Photoshop skills as it is today. That's what the National Association of Photoshop Professionals (NAPP) is all about, as we're the world's leading resource for Photoshop training, education, and news. If you're into Photoshop, you're invited to join our worldwide community of Photoshop users from 106 different countries around the world who share their ideas, solutions, and cutting-edge techniques. Join NAPP today—it's the right tool for the job.

NAPP MEMBER BENEFITS INCLUDE:

- Free subscription to *Photoshop User*, the award-winning Adobe Photoshop "how-to" magazine

- Exclusive access to NAPP's private members-only Web site, loaded with tips, tutorials, downloads, and more

- Discounts on Photoshop training seminars, training videos, and books

- Free Photoshop tech support from our Help Desk and Advice Desk

- Get special member deals on everything from color printers to software upgrades to Zip disks, and everything in between

- Print and Web designers can earn professional certification and recognition through NAPP's new certification program

- Learn from the hottest Photoshop gurus in the industry at PhotoshopWorld, NAPP's annual convention

The National Association of
Photoshop Professionals
The Photoshop Authority

One-year membership is only $99 (U.S. funds)
Call 800-738-8513 (or 727-738-2728)
or enroll online at **www.photoshopuser.com**

Corporate and International memberships available.
Photoshop and Adobe are registered trademarks of Adobe Systems, Inc.

For more info on NAPP, visit www.photoshopuser.com